Advance Pra

The Making of an E.

Wide-ranging historically, culturally, psychologically, and ecologically, this quietly eloquent and original call to arms is directed at a seemingly unlikely cohort of revolutionaries: the aging but increasingly assertive boomers who will transform America and the world — away from imperial militarism toward a society of interdependence and compassionate entitlements. A paradigm-changing book!

—Ernest Callenbach,
author of *ECOTOPIA*

The Making of an Elder Culture not only brings the baby boomers full circle, since Ted Roszak published *The Making of a Counter Culture*, it elevates the boomer generation's potential as change agents to an ascending orbit. With an historian's deft touch, Roszak links forgotten political realities to the possibility that a better, wiser world is within our grasp.

—Paul Kleyman,
Editor, Generations Beat Online
and Ethnic Elders Editor,
New America Media

This is a book about the "longevity" revolution, that powerful riptide surfacing amidst the political crisis of the early 21st century. Theodore Roszak, a gifted cultural historian, sets out to explore and explain this inevitable force for change in America — he thinks for the better. A good strong, clear book bringing into focus a nation that will sooner than later be dominated and governed by older people.

—James Ridgeway,
correspondent, *Mother Jones*;
editor, unsilentgeneration.com

I was entranced and excited by Roszak's vision… Let's come together and talk about *The Making of an Elder Culture*, not only will we transform our views of aging, but we can help complete the revolution of caring that we started in the Sixties.

—Cecile Andrews,
author of *Less Is More*,
Slow Is Beautiful, and *Circle of Simplicity*

THE MAKING OF AN
ELDER CULTURE

THE MAKING OF AN
ELDER CULTURE

**Reflections on the Future of
America's Most Audacious Generation**

THEODORE ROSZAK

NEW SOCIETY PUBLISHERS

Cataloging in Publication Data:
A catalog record for this publication is available
from the National Library of Canada.

Cover design by Diane McIntosh.
Images: Front cove: © iStock/Acerebel; back cover: © Ross Powell

Printed in Canada by Friesens.
First printing August 2009.

Paperback ISBN: 978-0-86571-661-2

Inquiries regarding requests to reprint all or part of
The Making of an Elder Culture should be addressed to
New Society Publishers at the address below.

To order directly from the publishers, please call toll-free (North America)
1-800-567-6772, or order online at www.newsociety.com

Any other inquiries can be directed by mail to:

New Society Publishers
P.O. Box 189, Gabriola Island, BC V0R 1X0, Canada
(250) 247-9737

New Society Publishers' mission is to publish books that contribute in fundamental ways to building an ecologically sustainable and just society, and to do so with the least possible impact on the environment, in a manner that models this vision. We are committed to doing this not just through education, but through action. This book is one step toward ending global deforestation and climate change. It is printed on Forest Stewardship Council-certified acid-free paper that is **100% post-consumer recycled** (100% old growth forest-free), processed chlorine free, and printed with vegetable-based, low-VOC inks, with covers produced using FSC-certified stock. Additionally, New Society purchases carbon offsets based on an annual audit, operating with a carbon-neutral footprint. For further information, or to browse our full list of books and purchase securely, visit our website at: www.newsociety.com

NEW SOCIETY PUBLISHERS
www.newsociety.com

Mixed Sources
Cert no. SW-COC-001271
© 1996 FSC

FSC

"Well…I've had *that* experience," she said, smiling a bit sadly.

"What experience is that?" I asked, having no idea what she meant.

"Death of the second parent. My mother died this year. That's what started me thinking about…well, about everything."

I offered some kind words, noting that my mother died just a while ago. She expressed her sympathy, but then reminded me that, "I was born in 1946," as if I ought to know that made a difference.

1946, the first year of the baby boom. "So, you see," she said, her smile growing more wistful, "there's no way to avoid it any longer. *I've* become the older generation."

～

Contents

Acknowledgments

Without the help of the good people at Second Journey — and especially Bolton and Lisa Anthony — this book would never have been able to climb out of my computer and go walking in the world. If elder culture is going to begin anywhere, it will be with groups like Second Journey.

I am also grateful to the Gray Panthers of Berkeley and their comrades across the country for keeping the heart and soul of Maggie Kuhn alive. They are the best example I can offer of an elder insurgency that serves old and young alike.

CHAPTER 1

Maturity Rules

We are not "senior citizens" or "golden-agers." We are the
elders, the experienced ones; we are maturing, growing
adults responsible for the survival of our society. We are not
wrinkled babies, succumbing to trivial, purposeless waste of
our years and our time. We are a new breed of old people.
— Maggie Kuhn, *A Dialogue on Age*

R eady or not, like it or not — the modern world is tilting
steadily toward gerontocracy. Irresistible trends in family
life, medical science, public health, and fiscal economics all
run in the direction of senior dominance. Those trends, growing stronger with each passing year, begin to appear as permanent a condition as our species has ever known, the long road
into a future nobody anticipated until the latter years of the 20th
century.

Not that elders stand ready to take over the day-to-day
tasks of government or to lord it over the rest of the population. Rather, what we must now expect is that their priorities
will soon have a claim on political power and our economic resources that few elected leaders will care to question or obstruct.
There will always be many issues governments must face — war
and revolution, poverty and terrorism, domestic strife, the ups
and downs of the world economy. But for as far as we can see
into the years ahead, all these affairs of state will have to play
out against a very different, totally unfamiliar background that
makes the needs and values of the old paramount.

1

How can it be otherwise? In another generation most industrial societies will have arrived at an unprecedented condition: Their populations will number more people above the age of 50 than below. Some nations will take a bit longer joining this "quiet revolution," as the United Nations has called it, but the United States, western Europe, and Japan are already within sight of senior dominance. As of the first decade of the 21st century in the United States, 8,000 people who were born between 1946 and 1964 — the baby-boom generation — began turning 60 every day. By 2011 that number rises to 11,000 — which is the number of American babies currently being born each day. Already, there is one person over the age of 60 in the United States for every child below the age of four.

Move ahead 50 years. By 2050, there will be ten people over 60 for every three children below the age of four. Wait another generation or so, and there will be more people above the age of 60 than below. Wait another generation beyond that, and... well, beyond that, things grow somewhat speculative, as life expectancy becomes more dependent on breakthroughs in biotechnology aimed at identifying the exact source of aging. But breakthroughs there will be. Geneticists are already competing to produce a Methuselah Mouse that will live the equivalent of human centuries. If they succeed, they will receive handsome rewards and much acclaim. Can we doubt that people will clamor to have the same blessing? And once this longevous vermin's genes are grafted into the human genome, who can say how many people will survive to age 160, 200, or beyond? Would that be a good thing? I admit to being uncertain. I cannot envision such a world, nor am I sure I would want to live in it. But it is even harder to imagine anyone willing to demand that we call off the effort.

Meanwhile, even without the aid of advanced genetic tinkering, societies that are preponderantly youthful today will not be so in another 20 years. When we hear that 60% of the population in India is below the age of 30, or that 40% of Iranians are below 25, we should bear in mind that all those young people are grist for the senior mill. They are growing older every day and, like our own boomers, will eventually become the largest senior population in their country's history. Such is the fate of baby booms. (Remember: When the Summer of Love was happening in San Francisco in 1967, there were 90 million people below the age of 25 in the United States — nearly half the population. Youth seemed in a permanent ascendancy. And see where we are today.) Unless we can imagine a science-fiction scenario in which the world is devastated by a plague that primarily targets the elderly, the modern world can only grow older. But, by an ironic twist of fate, the only plague we have going in the world today is AIDS, which strikes at the sexually active young and their afflicted offspring, leaving a disproportionate number of the elderly to inherit the ravaged societies of Africa and Asia.

We lose sight of the demographic force behind mass longevity when we view the baby boom in a short-sighted perspective — a transient demographic bulge rather like a pig being swallowed by a python. Seen in that way, we might imagine that at some point in the course of the 21st century the python will have digested the pig and things will return to their normal state of youthfulness, a society of young families, newborn babies, growing children, citizens in their middle years…and here and there some marginal grandparently boomers helping with the kids or retired to a galaxy of their own far, far away. Nothing could be farther from the truth. Since the late 19th century, aging has been the normal state of all industrial societies; it is *a sustained trend*. Societies designed to cater to the needs of aging populations will soon become the accepted political condition of our species. Acknowledging that fact will, at some point, slide so smoothly into the conventional wisdom that future generations may not realize that this is a major new feature of modern life, this is different, this is not what human culture was ever meant to be — and it all started now.

Odd that something so foreseeable has remained unforeseen for generations. The senior dominance has been wholly predictable since at least the beginning of the 20th century. Smaller families, longer life expectancy — one simply had to follow where the demographic numbers were trending. In the late 1930s, when hard times had placed a spotlight on the plight of the indigent old throughout the western world, the American philosopher John Dewey predicted with some foreboding that our society was headed toward unprecedented longevity — which in his time meant 60, 65, 70 years of age. In a prescient 1937 essay written for the first conference ever held on aging in the United States, Dewey observed, "The changes which have brought about a great reduction of infant mortality and the lengthening of the span of life for those who survive the hazards of infancy have had important social effects so that social conditions have been created which confront civilization with issues of the most serious nature." He might have gone on to add that aging was a principal theme of the country's history. Our society has never been younger than it was at the beginning of white colonization. Then, the continent was experiencing an influx of young immigrant families from Europe who were determined to stock the land with all the children they could beget. Since then we have been growing steadily older, by Dewey's day reaching the point at which a third of the population was over the age of 50. "The main purpose of these introductory remarks," Dewey wrote, "is to call attention to the fact that there is a *problem* and one of a scope having no precedent in human history." So start planning for a longevous society now, Dewey advised.[1]

But nobody did. The war intervened, and then — fatefully — the postwar baby boom. After a fashion that now seems little short of delusionary, policy makers and the public generally immersed themselves in the strange belief that the world was getting *younger* — exactly the opposite of what should have been obvious. The baby boom should have been seen as a blip in the steady trend toward aging. But then the misapprehension is easy to understand. In the aftermath of horror, people everywhere craved renewal and vitality. So the reproductive outburst that followed World War II eclipsed the underlying demographic reality of our time. People, wanting to start over again, were swept up in a cult of youth. The market rushed to reinforce their wishfulness. Here were millions of pampered American kids on whom parents with fat paychecks were willing to lavish their postwar affluence. And what prospering, victorious America was, other societies sought to become: young, young, young. Thanks to an advertising industry eager to move the goods, the youth of the nation came to be seen as prime consumers — in fact, the chief customers — for clothes, music, movies, toiletries, magazines, cars, furnishings. At the same time, pundits, inspired by the country's spectacular wartime achievements, were easily carried away by great technological expectations. Novelty and innovation were in the air: faster means of transportation, more rapid communications, more ingenious electronic gadgets, a new generation of household appliances, automated assembly lines, more glitzy merchandise, artificial intelligence, high-rise cities, the colonization of outer space. And because all these grand designs belonged to the future, they belonged to the young, who came to be spoken of as if they were an ageless class, permanently endowed with vitality, daring, and optimism, a deathless Pepsi generation that would always be there. "What happened in the sixties," the marketing analyst Thomas Frank observed, "is that hip became central to the way American capitalism understood itself and explained itself to the public.... Suddenly youth became a consuming position to which all could aspire.... The conceptual position of *youthfulness* became as great an element of the

marketing picture as youth itself." Frank called this "the conquest of the cool."[2] Unfortunately for his industry, it is a beach-
head that cannot be held.

Once the cool had supposedly been conquered, the main
marketing topic of the day — and for the next 30 years — was,
"What are the young up to? What do they like? What are they
reading, buying, wearing, talking about?" A profession of cool-
hunters emerged, grown-ups who dedicated their lives to the
whims of adolescents. And perhaps those who spent so much
time confabulating with the sensibilities of the young came to
feel vicariously young themselves, people who were hot, clued
in, with it, and all the more unwilling to give up on the youthful
market. In any case, this transitory fascination has remained the
great commercial topic of our economy, even as the young demographic became less numerous and less affluent. In such an
intellectual ambience, those above the age of 40 simply dropped
out of sight. Many elders who could not keep up with the pace
were willing to yield to the spirit of the times, ensconcing themselves (if they could afford to do so) in distant retirement communities in self-imposed exile. Thus, society was surrendered to
the young. From the 1940s through the 1980s, who could have
imagined a world ruled by the elderly? And because such a future was unthinkable, nobody spent much time thinking about
it. Instead, as if the task of defining social reality belonged exclusively to entrepreneurs, market analysts, and engineers, those
who specialized in brainstorming world's-fair visions of things
to come focused on an endless succession of scientific amazements, intoxicating visions that simply ignored the most obvious biological realities of our species. Yet all the while, steadily
and without fanfare and as invincibly as all living things blos-
som, ripen, and mature, more people were living longer. And as
they did so, they were creating a possibility not even the most
far-sighted futurists had anticipated.

Return to the beginning of the 20th century. In 1900 most people in the western world could look back upon a family history where one out of every three babies died within a year, where it was commonplace for women to expire in childbirth, where few grandparents lived into their sixties, where most elderly citizens had little more than the county home or the workhouse to look forward to once they could no longer earn their own way. However amazing people then might find the technological wonders of our day to be, there are things far more incredible: a world where the women of Japan and France are leading the way to a life expectancy beyond 85 years — with their husbands not that far behind them. A world where money needed to pay for the elderly ill could begin to outstrip money spent on the tools of war. A world where, like a target in a gun sight, the genetic locus of senescence could be coming ever more steadily into sharp focus.

Now that it is so clearly upon us, senior dominance is viewed with horrified amazement by many politicians and economists. Because it is the very opposite of what they anticipated, they see mass longevity as a fiscal calamity, a prospect wholly at odds with all they hold dear. The country is filling up with the wrong people — *old* people, people who by definition take little interest in innovation, who care more about secure investments, savings accounts and prescription costs than the next hot thing on the market and who will be claiming more and more of our resources, influencing ever more of our political policies. Hardly a week goes by but the evening news or the op-ed page takes up the drum-beat: "Be warned! Old people are coming! Old people are coming!" Gerontocracy, in the judgment of many pundits, threatens bankruptcy, backwardness, and stagnation. They ask: "How can we afford all these people?" And, less audibly, they ask: "How are we going to sell them i-Phones, HDTV, flashy clothes, new movies, the next American icon?"

Their Finest Hour

That bleak outlook is exactly what *The Making of an Elder Culture* rejects. It is not only wrong, it is *exactly wrong* by 180 degrees. The elder culture that is being improvised all around us day by day may not turn out to be an endless vista of fast-paced economic expansion and technological gadgetry, but it promises to be the road toward a saner, more compassionate, more sustainable world — altogether, a more important turning point than ever presented itself in the 1960s when boomers were coming of age. This, at last, is what the dissenting idealism of the 1960s was, in its highest and brightest expression, all about: a transformation of values that may finally reveal the goal of industrialization, the life-enhancing destiny that has lain hidden in the wrenching violence and extravagant physical and spiritual costs. In raising that possibility, I cling to one hope. Boomers, who will usher us into senior dominance, are the best educated, most socially conscientious, most politically savvy older generation the world has ever seen. They grew up entertaining (if not always endorsing) countercultural values, reveling in their willingness to search beyond the limits of convention. Given sufficient awareness and inspiration, I believe that generation will want to do good things with the power that history has unexpectedly thrust upon it in its senior years. What boomers left undone in their youth, they will return to take up in their maturity, if for no other reason than because they will want to make old age *interesting*. Just as the Dutch have won land back from the sea, we have won years back from death. That gives us the grand project of using those extra years to build a culture that is morally remarkable.

The elder culture we will be exploring in these pages is not the outgrowth of a well-defined social philosophy, much less is it a blueprint for the future. Like the counter culture of the 1960s and 1970s on which it draws in spirit and for ideas, it is a surprising proliferation of divergent values that emerge from a new demographic reality. Far from being a detailed agenda ordered up by a political movement or an ideological faction, it is the way in which our lives are being reconfigured by the convergence of numerous unplanned but inexorable developments in medical science, public health, economics, brain physiology, biotechnology, gender roles, generational relations, and social policy. Under the demographic pressure of an aging population, we are seeing radical changes in work and family life, career choices and retirement, man-woman relationships, health care, and city planning.

As people in greater numbers live long enough to suffer late-onset diseases, those same demographic pressures are redirecting medical research toward new genetic therapies that may contribute to an astonishing extension of life expectancy. We are discovering that the best way to treat many diseases of old age is to nip them in the bud by forms of prenatal intervention that will bring benefits throughout a lifetime. That in turn is forcing new budgetary priorities upon us that will make some traditional expenditures and investments — such as military adventures, space exploration, corporate welfare — less urgent and more difficult to afford. And that will force us to revise public policy. At the same time, as research on the aging brain becomes more widespread, we will find ourselves revising our understanding of the mind, its limits and its unexplored potential — a project that has enormous philosophical implications. This, in time, will open new avenues in education that may lead to the reevaluation of expertise and experience. And as new living patterns arise among a growing population of elders, our relations with the natural environment are likely to change as they come to reflect new, more discriminating patterns of consumption, transportation, housing, nutrition, recreation, lifestyle. A grand panorama of change, but behind it a common theme: more people are living longer.

The greatest challenge of mass longevity is the fact that so few have seen it coming except those who would deny it and defeat it — in large measure by condemning boomers as a failed generation. That is an unusual, perhaps a unique, political tactic. Is there any other generation in history that has faced such adversarial hostility — which is perhaps a clear measure of its power? Conservatives, especially the neoconservatives who came to power during the Reagan presidency, see the cost of an aging society as the prime obstacle to their project of building a corporate-dominated, market-based, highly militarized global economy. They have accurately seen the entitlements and the life expectancy now available to the many as the antithesis of a Social-Darwinist ethic that serves the few. Since the 1970s, far-right ideologues have been doing all they can to make the United States incapable of dealing with the demographic facts of life in the 21st century. Nothing clashes more with their hopes for an American imperial order than a society whose future lies in the hands of 75 million aging boomers. Conservatives cannot turn back the clock on longevity; but they can make it so fearful and painful an experience that we will be ever more reluctant to pay the price that good health and long life demand.

More nefariously, neoconservatives can make the old feel guilty for becoming such a supposedly great burden to their long-suffering children — even though these children will themselves soon be moving into their fifties and sixties. Like the stereotypic welfare queen Ronald Reagan liked to bash, the greedy geezer is a figment of political propaganda, an image of other people's detestable parents somewhere out there in Florida or Arizona or aboard *The Love Boat,* living it up at *your* expense. Even so, conservative guilt-tripping has been remarkably successful among boomers themselves, some of whom, in an astonishing display of social masochism, are willing to bear the blame for being so numerous and living so long. That is what one finds in editorials and commentaries — most of them written by boomers — lamenting how the "rise of the wrinklies" will drain the national treasury. In a brutally satirical novel about his avaricious generation titled *Boomsday*, Christopher Buckley rushed to defend his children from the boomers' legacy: "mountainous debt, a deflating economy, and 77 million people retiring." The heroine of his tale proposes a solution, a morbid sort of annuity. Pay boomers in advance to commit suicide at 75. But what do parents like Buckley need to apologize for? That *their* parents produced so many of them? That they kept fit and lived longer? That they followed doctor's orders and lived longer still? That they lived long enough to need a payback on the help they once gave kids who were in many cases dependent on them for 20 years or more? What such *mea culpa* gestures fail to grasp is that the power that boomers inherit is their chance to create a better world for their children and all who follow them.

There is a terrible irony to the anti-elder campaign that conservatives are waging. Why are they not celebrating mass longevity as capitalism's greatest achievement? For is this not the economic system that has delivered the productivity that makes life longer and richer for all of us? But, then, perhaps that has never been the objective of the corporate elite for whom the gap between have and have-not serves as the first line of defense for social privilege. So, by way of upper-class tax cuts and profligate military spending, they have been rushing to cripple our economy so that there will be no way to meet the needs of an aging population gracefully. They have done a supremely clever job of burning money that might have been set aside for compassionate purposes. In the name of free trade, they have run trade deficits that make the nation far too dependent on foreign support for the cost of basic social programs. They have reinforced the economic dogma that only corporate earnings, the Dow Jones index, and the Gross Domestic Product shall be used to measure the wealth of the nation. They have shipped manufacturing jobs and indeed whole industries offshore, leaving the working and middle classes unprepared for unemployment or retirement and less and less able to afford decent health care. Meanwhile, they have devoted themselves assiduously to building what Robert Frank has called "Richistan," land of the $10,000 diamond-studded martini and the million-dollar time share, where the inequality gap between have-lots and have-less has reached proportions as dire as any in the poorest parts of the world. The boomers' first job as they assume direction of the elder culture will be to repair the fiscal damage that has been done by 30 years of conservative budgetary sabotage and wrong-headed economic priorities.

Almost every book on the subject of aging has been written by a doctor, a gerontologist, a fitness trainer, or a financial planner, as if all that mattered in life beyond a certain age was fending off disease and being comfortably retired. I will pay a good deal of attention in these pages to health care and retirement, but I will come at these matters within a very different context. *The Making of an Elder Culture* is neither a demographic study nor a history, though it includes a bit of both. Rather, it is an exercise in *practical nostalgia*. It mines the past to find solutions for the future. In that respect, it stands somewhere between a critique and an appeal. My purpose is to explore the values, ideals, and reforms that the first generation of senior dominance will bring into the later years of life. I seek to remind and to re-mind and, above all, to create a new paradigm for aging that will enable the baby-boom generation to live out its history with moral courage and high expectation. As boomers reach the age of 60, they will, on average, have 20 to 25 years of life ahead of them. That is more time than they spent being young and more than enough time to become a political and cultural force. My hope is that people who grew up on J. D. Salinger's *Catcher in the Rye*, the poetry of Allen Ginsberg, the folk music of Pete Seeger, the protest ballads of Country Joe, the anarchic insolence of the Beatles and the Rolling Stones, the biting satire of Mort Sahl and Lenny Bruce, the acid rock of Bob Dylan, the sociology of Paul Goodman and Herbert Marcuse, the Summer of Love and the Days of Rage, will not be content to spend their retirement years on cruise ships or feeding their Social Security income into slot machines at the nearest casino.

How might these elders put those extra years to better use? The chapters that follow suggest several possibilities both personal and political, all based on the assumption that the boomers' place in history has more to do with Act Two than with Act One. This is unknown intellectual territory, left unexplored in large part because of the protracted reluctance which senescence-phobic boomers have thus far shown in facing up to their biological destiny. They have found it hard to recognize that the best that they have to give lies before, not behind them. And needless to say, nothing is guaranteed in human affairs — nothing good and nothing bad. That is why some of us write books, hoping to provide an influence that might not otherwise be there. Boomers, so uniquely obsessed with themselves — their tastes, their values, their choices — have been condemned as narcissists since they were in kindergarten. But with a bit of Socratic help, narcissism can be the beginning of self-knowledge, even self-criticism. And a good, critical knowledge of the self — one's strengths and vulnerabilities, one's irrationalities and shortcomings, one's false hopes and true needs — is the best basis for moral action. By sheer weight of numbers, an elder culture we will have, but which will it be? The boomers' sad demise or their finest hour?

As boomers become the older generation, those in the media who chart their progress are eager to applaud them for nothing so much as not growing old. The literature of active aging has become a cheerleading genre in its own right. Journalists and advertisers compliment boomers for sticking at their careers, touring the world, keeping fit, winning prizes, staying sexy. *The AARP Magazine* decorates its cover with senior celebrities, still virile, still nubile, still making it — in brief, extending their middle age by another 10 or 20 years. The subtext is clear enough.

Holding age at bay for as long as possible is the only good choice seniors have. Stay in the race, keep the party going. Still others hope to see this most affluent of senior generations shop its life away by turning it into an unprecedented merchandising opportunity, as if becoming a market validates people.

But my interest is in another possibility: that the final stage of life is uniquely suited to the creation of new social forms and cultural possibilities, because, as naturally as the leaves drop from the trees in autumn, age offers us the opportunity to detach from the competitive, high-consumption priorities that dominated us on the job and in the marketplace. At that point, life itself—the opportunity it offers for growth, for intellectual adventure, for the simple joys of love and companionship, for working out our salvation—comes to be seen as our highest value. What I offer here is an appeal for the building of a new, humane social order based on that insight. That is what I have always assumed it means to be *countercultural*. It would be fruitless to make such an appeal if we were not experiencing an irresistible, long-term demographic shift toward societies dominated by seniors. There would then be nothing to work with but fond wishes and desperate rhetoric. But that shift is taking place. Boomers in growing numbers are aging beyond the acquisitive values that created our industrial system. I merely suggest we make the most of that fact by taking on a task worth living for and fighting for.

Start with what you have. That was among the key ideas of countercultural protest. Start here—in this neighborhood, this house, with these people. Don't waste time on blueprints and head trips. Start with the means, the wit, and the resources at hand and build out from where you stand toward something better. Youthful boomers had a good deal to start with. They had the prosperity of the postwar era and the unusually permissive child-rearing ethos of the time, the willingness of parents to be generous and indulgent. They had access to higher education on an unprecedented scale. That gave them freedom and a common ground, a gathering place that could be used to thrust their demands upon the public. They also, paradoxically enough, had conscription, a lever of power that allowed them to resist the war in Vietnam by hitting the warlords where it hurt the most. Those advantages played a significant part in amplifying protest.

Now, in their elder years, they also have quite a bit more to start with. They have their voting power — a resource those below the age of 21 did not have in the 1960s. Above all, they have a special claim upon the national treasury: Social Security and Medicare. As important as these programs are in bread-and-butter terms for the senior population, they are something more. They are the model and linchpin of the ethical commitment we have become accustomed to calling *entitlements*. Too accustomed — so that people overlook how much good can be done by a few good social programs even in this oversized, flabby, often Kafkaesque social order. In my own writing I have lashed out many times at the impersonality, the faceless, unfeeling, bureaucratic impaction of urban-industrial society. This planet-straddling empire of industrial cities we have so blindly created is inhumanly wrong in a thousand ways. And yet it has granted millions the empowering right to say "I'm *entitled*." That is a good beginning. The fact that both Social Security and Medicare need to be reconfigured and expanded means there is unfinished business on our social agenda. And whose business can that be but that of elders themselves?

As the guardians of these entitlements, elders bear a special responsibility. By building upon these programs, they can become the creators of a compassionate economy that will at last put our national wealth to some better use than war-making, wasteful production, or corporate profiteering. Those were very largely the targets of protest in the 1960s when it seemed there was no way forward but rallies, demonstrations, civil disobedience, and maybe a bit of bomb throwing. But now, at another stage of life, a different possibility presents itself, the chance to make a society that will bring independence, health, and long life to everybody. Read that sentence again and appreciate what it means: independence, health, and long life *for everybody*. After centuries of privation and unjust privilege, this is what history now offers us. It is really little more than many European societies and the Japanese have already undertaken to achieve, in every case recognizing that a growing population of elders demands such a change.

In truth, the United States is a laggard in this movement toward a robust welfare state, and our resistance to that goal weighs heavily on other nations. The American corporate community has used its inordinate power to configure the global economy as an extension of its own mean-spirited social ethic, a policy orientation that impoverishes people throughout the developing world, starting with its homeland where, in the period 1974 to 2004, it has, according to the a 2007 survey by the Pew Charitable Trust's Economic Mobility Project, for the first time in the nation's history driven the earnings of working people below those of their fathers. A century after the first labor laws were passed in the United States, American firms are once again setting up sweatshops, beating down unions and putting children to work where they can get away with it — mainly in Asia and Latin America. The influence of our neoconservative corporate community is now an impediment to humane reform, environmental health, and social justice everywhere. It has imposed a free-market orthodoxy and a grinding Social-Darwinist ethic on the world at large. It has vastly widened the gap between rich and poor and is ruthlessly exploiting the planetary ecology. Worst of all, the American corporate community has by example, by competitive pressure, and by investment encouraged other societies as consequential as China and India to imitate its myopic standards.

What I propose here simply calls for extending the spirit that underlies the senior entitlements to our society as a whole — and above all the concept of *entitlement* as a rightful claim upon the wealth we have all created. That may not seem like much in the way of a utopian alternative, but given the fierce and benighted ideological agenda of the corporate elite in our political life, it will be a fight to accomplish that much. If boomers can change the self-serving entrepreneurial and neoconservative values that now dominate our lives, they will have made a historic contribution not only to their own society but to the modern world at large. In their own interests, boomers have every good reason to take on the task of taming the world's most dynamic, most market-oriented economy and to bring it under the guidance of an elder culture that sets a new criterion for wealth and progress. Do that, and we will have placed wisdom and nobility at the center of our lives.

CHAPTER 2

Boomers — Act Two

I lift my voice aloud,
make Mantra of American language now,
I here declare the end of the War!
Ancient days' Illusion!
and pronounce words beginning my own millennium.
— Allen Ginsberg, "Wichita Vortex Sutra"

When I wrote *The Making of a Counter Culture* in 1969, I was as fascinated with the political ebullience of college-aged, and even high-school-aged, youth as the rest of the world around me — the *young demographic*, as the marketing industry would soon refer to them. The rising influence of teens and twenty-somethings in the United States and Europe was the big story of that decade and the next. It was as if a war-weary parental generation was looking to its children to plant the ruined world with flowers. Everything from hair styles to social ideology seemed to be falling under the sway of the exuberant young. But what middle-class parents saw happening among their progeny as they reached their high school and college years was not encouraging. It was not satisfaction, and it was not gratitude. The prevailing intellectual style of the time on campus and in the coffeehouses was an existential angst that asked whether life was worth living — or was it an exercise in absurdity: pushing the rock up the hill only to see it roll back down? There was a good deal of such melancholia among the early Beats of the postwar period, a surly life-is-a-lousy-drag sullenness that seemed out of keeping with their country's recent good fortune. Why were such gestures of disaffiliation catching on with the young? What place did morbid discontent have in prospering America? Was this not the land of limitless discretionary income, where not a single bomb had dropped and where nobody was going hungry? As mothers and fathers would soon learn: that was not going to be good enough. A dark disquiet was brewing in their pampered children.

The American version of Sartre and Camus might have been lightweight and skewed toward adolescence, but the inarticulate angst of Holden Caulfield, the rebellious young hero of J. D. Salinger's *Catcher in the Rye*, had a quality that formal philosophy rarely achieves. Embodied in the experience of a teenage runaway, Holden's clear-eyed contempt for the adult world could speak to a larger and younger public. One of the most widely assigned high school texts of the 1950s, the novel, both in its wistfulness and in its premature cynicism, overlapped with the impulsive need of the young to make their own life. Norman Mailer, writing in 1959, shrewdly recognized that explosive connection early on in the period. For Mailer, the American existentialist was the *hipster*. The hipsters were "white Negroes," as Mailer put it, "a new breed of adventurers, urban adventurers who drifted out at night looking for action with a black man's code to fit their facts...an elite with the potential ruthlessness of an elite, and a language most adolescents can understand instinctively, for the hipster's intense view of existence matches their experience and their desire to rebel."[1]

A college instructor at the time, just beginning my teaching career, I recall how astonished I was to see the change that came over my students through the early 1960s. It was as if someone had pushed a button, and within a few short years the universities were turned upside down. The students I had before me were nothing like the college population I remembered from my own undergraduate experience. Just to set a time line: when I arrived on campus as a freshman, World War II vets on the GI Bill were finishing up on their post-docs and exploring the job market. Many were already married and raising families; they were on their way into lucrative careers as doctors, lawyers, weapons engineers, marketing analysts, and junior executives. My postwar years at UCLA were lived out under the shadow of Senator Joseph McCarthy's reign of terror. In that period, as the pressures of the Cold War set in, it took courage simply to sign a petition or attend a political rally. But now, as I entered my teaching career, seemingly overnight students were talking revolution and behaving as if they were willing to defy all official rules and parental conventions. Many of the brightest were vanishing from the campus, walking out on their parents' expectations in search of some better alternative.

In the United States, the baby boom was the largest population bulge in the nation's history — too large a number to be fairly contained either then or now by any simple generalization. As one might expect, this young demographic exhibited a spectrum of values and choices. Most of these babies would grow up to follow in their parents' footsteps. They would be as patriotic, as pious, as law-abiding, and as complacent about the inherited ideals of their society as their parents and grandparents before them. But a sizeable number — nobody can say how many, but enough to make for good-sized rallies, marches, and rock concerts — would find reasons to voice significant discomfort with just about everything in sight: education, family, foreign policy, national priorities, middle-class conformity, corporate misconduct, race relations, gender identities, the work ethic, sexual mores. "Young people speakin' their mind/Gettin' so much resistance from behind." At times they seemed to be acting out Marlon Brando's line from the 1954 film *The Wild One*. Asked what he is rebelling against, Brando, playing a surly, leather-clad biker, answers, "What have you got?"

I realized at the time that the wild ones among my students were a minority of their generation. In fact, the disaffiliated were a minority of a minority. The college-aged population might have been larger than ever before, but it was still a minority of the nation — and of the world — as a whole. And even among those who showed up at the universities, only a minority participated in the protest politics of the time. But however small their numbers, they knew how to draw attention, and not simply by their boisterousness. The quality of the issues they were raising demanded a response. They had drawn a bead on the phoniness and hypocrisy of their society, on its greed and injustice and moral numbness. *Generation* is the most unwieldy of social categories, little better than the people who happen to be lined up together at a bus stop. Yet, almost of necessity, we do isolate eras, movements, and groups out of the steady and seamless flow of time and give them names, faces, identities. The parents of the boomers have been called *the greatest generation*, but not everybody went to war in the 1940s or suffered the worst trials of the Great Depression in the 1930s. We speak of the *flaming youth* of the 1920s, but that term did not describe more than a small minority of boisterous college kids, then an even smaller fraction of the total population. How many young women of that era would claim they were flappers, how many young men habituated speakeasies? The style of a generation is not a matter of statistics but of innovation. Historians, always on the lookout for the novel and flamboyant, are often guilty of overlooking the mainstream, the average, the ordinary — perhaps because nothing interesting is happening there. Changes in the cultural taste and moral awareness of society always begin in the lives of a minority, and that minority may become the soul of a generation.

Perhaps I would have viewed the youthful disaffiliation of the time differently, and probably with less hope of rapid social change, if I could have foreseen how many members of the younger generation would eventually wind up as cultural conservatives or evangelical Christians, how many would settle for lucrative business careers, how many would find the thrill of a lifetime at a NASCAR rally. In all the generalizations and high hopes I offer here, I have tried to remember that George W. Bush, Karl Rove, and Newt Gingrich qualify as boomers — as do many architects of the Iraq war. So were the piratical traders at Enron and World Com. Boomers have been the main market for SUV gas-guzzlers and the most competitive parents in history when it comes to getting their children into the best schools. But that does not change my assessment of the dissent I saw around me through the 1960s and 1970s. That period will be remembered in the history books as a time of significant political unrest, as much so in the United States as the years of the Progressive movement at the turn of the 20th century or the New Deal of the 1930s. The protestors might have been young and at times frivolously high-spirited, but the issues they addressed were weighty. More importantly for the years to come, many of the ideas they championed are as bright and promising today as they were in the days of Woodstock.

The hopes I invested in the protest of that period had much to do with my own situation. I was at that time developing serious reservations about the basic sanity and sustainability of urban-industrial culture. I cannot say where these reservations came from, certainly not from my very conventional, working-class, Catholic background. Maybe dissent was in the air and I caught a good, strong case of it, especially after I settled in the San Francisco Bay Area. After all, the world was living (as it still does, though we assume with a bit less urgency) under the threat of thermonuclear annihilation. What clearer sign could there be that our technology was rapidly running away with us, setting mindless priorities that lacked all prudence? Under pressure of the anti-communist mania which had become the total foreign policy of the United States, the scale of our institutions, both governmental and private, was overwhelming any meaningful democratic control. The power of governing elites — the military-industrial complex — was growing, unchecked, by the year. The social reality that we were expected to adapt to — an unsavory mix of marketing lies, mysteries of state, and technocratic obsessions — was becoming ever more claustrophobic.

It was the surrealistic incongruity of it all, the sheer crazy-making inanity of business and politics as usual, that was most troubling. I had spent a good deal of undergraduate time imbibing existential negativity, bemoaning the bad faith and moral treachery of humanity and expecting the worst from those who controlled the bomb; perhaps that had deepened my sensitivity to the absurd. And now I found it all around me. The era that brought us the theater of the absurd also brought us the society of the absurd. All Mort Sahl had to do to produce mass hilarity was to stand in Sproul Plaza in Berkeley and read the newspapers. Following a war that was fought against the ugliest of racist ideologies, racism persisted. In the midst of the unprecedented affluence that followed the war, poverty persisted. In the ethos of the Cold War, the very civil liberties that supposedly set us apart from fascist and communist totalitarianism were being undermined by right-wing demagogues. With more knowledge at our fingertips than any society had ever enjoyed, we were drowning in duplicity and mystification. Though technology had given us more power over nature than humanity had ever enjoyed, it was becoming frighteningly clear that we were doing the planet more harm than good. DDT was being sprayed in the open air of public parks and residential neighborhoods across the country. Television bubbled over the delights of limitless consumption (this was, after all, the era that invented the credit card), but in our schools, children were learning to duck and cover when they saw the sky catch fire.

Has there ever been such a heady mixture of social contradiction and moral ambiguity? Had any previous generation ever faced a larger agenda of weighty issues? The very ideals for which revolutionaries of the past had fought were being brought under critical scrutiny. Radical spirits had long embraced science as the heart and soul of enlightenment; they had seized upon technology as the secret of universal prosperity; they had turned *progress* into a secular religion. But here I was, wondering what difference it made who owned or controlled the means of production if those very means had become a Frankenstein monster over which leaders had less and less control.

Where to look for a sane alternative? At the time, my own thoughts were reaching back to the origins of industrial society, to the great Romantic movement that had pitted the poets and philosophers of the later 18th century against the momentum of modern history. I believed that Blake and Shelley, Goethe and Wordsworth had more to teach us about life and the world than the experts at the RAND Corporation. The young Romantics of that distant time were the first to rail against the gargantuan growth of cities, the concentration of power in ever fewer hands, the rape of nature that was then just beginning, and above all against the dominance of a narrow, desiccated form of rationality that purported to be master of all that it observed — "Single Vision," as William Blake called it. So it was that I quoted Blake as the epigraph for *The Making of a Counter Culture*: "Art Degraded, Imagination Denied, War Governed the Nations." Consciousness was at the core of the Romantic political style — as it was once again among the young protesters of the 1960s. As zany as their politics might sometimes seem, it struck me that they had it right: The materialistic obsessions and blinkered consciousness that dominated both the capitalist west and the Marxist east were corrupting our souls. More than we needed new laws and new programs, more than we needed a change in governance, we needed a new quality of experience, something we would have to learn from artists and visionaries rather than politicians. We needed a culture that would *counter* the reality principle that ruled our souls.

The forces of youthful dissent achieved a good deal in just a few years' time between the mid-1960s and mid-1970s. They succeeded in stopping a disastrous war in Vietnam and in bringing down a crooked and deceitful president. They championed new initiatives for equality and justice: a women's movement and a gay liberation movement to take their place alongside movements for racial justice. They planted the ideal of multiculturalism squarely in the mainstream. They transformed the sexual morality of their society and deepened our awareness of the irrational forces that lurk in the depths of the psyche. And, not least of all, they launched an environmental movement to address the future of the planet. All to the good. Even so, by the mid-1970s, it became clear that much would remain undone. The magnitude of the countercultural changes some had sought was too great. That would require more thought, more strategic planning, more maturity than a single generation still in its youth could manage. Then, as the younger generation moved out into the world to seek careers and form families, their dissenting energy faded. The youthful élan that had offered us these new beginnings was passing. Some called it *the big chill* And by the 1980s, a well-financed and well-generaled conservative backlash was on the scene, working to restore the "economic royalists" of corporate America (as Franklin Roosevelt had called them as far back as the mid-1930s) to their place of privilege and to build an even bigger warfare state. Intellect, once the monopoly of the left, began to gravitate to new, right-wing think tanks. Competitive individualism and free-market orthodoxy, the discredited worldview of the 1890s, suddenly reappeared as hot new ideas. The future, it seemed, had lost its utopian luster.

Life Beyond the Young Demographic

Throughout the 1960s and 1970s, there was heated debate about the intellectual and ethical significance of youthful protest. The media fed avidly on the antics of the young, while many pundits dismissed all they saw as ephemeral, narcissistic posturing. Conservatives were particularly dismayed at what they saw unfolding. Eventually, in a grand judgmental summation entitled *The Closing of the American Mind*, Allan Bloom, a major neoconservative mentor, would look back in contempt on the entire, turbulent era, blasting it as a betrayal of absolute values. Multiculturalism, Bloom believed, was a fatuous offense to the glories of western civilization; feminism was an absurd attack upon the natural order of the family and the biology of gender relations; the language and behavior of young dissenters were uncivil and subintellectual; their lenient, liberal professors were guilty of a poisonous, anything-goes permissiveness. Bloom could see nothing redeeming in the "histrionic morality" of the 1960s. A "period of dogmatic answers and trivial tracts," it was "an exercise in egalitarian self-satisfaction." For the universities, it was a period of "unmitigated disaster," in which pusillanimous and guilt-ridden academics, instead of cracking down on bad taste and bad thinking, encouraged the muddled self-indulgence of students who were little more than a mindless "rabble." Above all, it was the vulgarity of the era that offended him, the lack of respect for excellence and the great creative achievements of the western heritage. The result, he felt, was a corrosive cultural relativism that "succeeds in destroying the western world's universal or intellectually imperialistic claims, leaving it to be just another culture." For Bloom, the concept of *lifestyle* sums up the sins of the era. "'Lifestyle' justifies any way of life, as does 'value' any opinion.... Lifestyle was first popularized here to describe and make acceptable the lives of people who do attractive things that are frowned upon by society. It was identical to counter culture.... Counterculture, of course, enjoyed the dignity attaching to culture, and was intended as a reproach to the bourgeois excuse for a culture we see around us. What actually goes on in a

counter culture or a lifestyle — whether it is ennobling or debas-
ing — makes no difference.... Whatever you are, whoever you
are, is the good."[2]

Strong words from a learned man. Bloom could wield the
authority of great minds with self-assured dexterity — Plato,
Locke, Rousseau, Nietzsche, Hegel. He brought these to bear
with impressive effect in his biting critique of youthful dissent.
And it must be granted that the angry irreverence of the time, as
expressed in slogans, posters, graffiti, and street theater, does not
stand up well against the measured words of intellectual giants.
But what conclusion would Bloom have reached if he had lev-
eled the same erudite criticism at those on the commanding
heights of society — the Pentagon warlords, the RAND Corporation strategists, the "best and the brightest" in the West Wing,
the corporate beneficiaries of the military-industrial complex,
all those whose decisions enforced the chauvinism, the racism,
and social injustice at which the dissent of the 1960s was aimed?
Would he also have awarded them a failing grade for their vio-
lations of reason and decency — or would he have given them a
gentleman's C?

Bloom, a committed conservative, was not alone in finding
the 1960s an elusive critical target. Though the counter culture
was rebellious enough to offend the political right, it was not
ideologically rigorous enough to please the left. Many old-line
lefties were as harshly dismissive as Reagan right-wingers. Even
those who were in the thick of things still had a hard time making up their minds. In a 2006 interview, Country Joe McDonald,
whose "Fixin' to Die Rag" was the anti-war anthem of the period sung to crowds that numbered thousands, confessed that
he had no idea what all the demonstrations accomplished — if
anything. "There was a lot of bull thrown around about revolution and a lot of drug taking and sex happening," he observed.
But he wondered if it made "much of a difference." Other veterans of the period found the radical politics of the time so mis-

conceived that they made an about-face and turned staunchly conservative. Peter Collier, an editor of *Ramparts* in the 1960s, and David Horowitz, once a fiery New Leftist, made that transition. The title of their 1989 book, *Destructive Generation: Second Thoughts About The Sixties*, captures their change of heart. The counter culture, so Collier and Horowitz concluded, was little more than "an Oedipal revolt," an outburst by adolescents "who never grew up politically."

Now, looking back, I think a lot of what has been said pro and con about the 1960s — a calendar decade that has assumed a personality of it own — was foolishly overwrought. The scene was chaotic, a lot of people doing a lot of things — some of it smart, some of it witless, some of it astute, some of it delusionary — but none of it officially initiated or under central control. And that as much as anything else was worrisome to people in high places. The mandarins of corporate America were being mocked by the children of prosperity and the values of the sacred marketplace rejected — but not in the name of any familiar ideological tradition. The attack was a disconcertingly playful confabulation with anarchist social theory, voluntary primitivism, Zen-Taoist mysticism, occult lore, Tolkienesque fairy tales, with all of it fueled by a randy, adolescent prankishness. Conservatives especially were troubled by the brashness and disorder of the time. Many of those who would later flock to the Reagan backlash — horrified evangelicals, Young Americans for Freedom with their high respect for God and country, neoconservatives nursing visions of a worldwide Pax Americana — probably still carry troubling memories of the sexual openness and disrespectful rhetoric they saw around them, and perhaps regret they missed out on the fun and games when they had the chance. If one cares to lint-pick, there was plenty to denigrate. There was certainly no lack of ideological extremists, loud-mouthed bullies, radical poseurs, and devious opportunists moving through the ranks of the protest movement. Bloom, for example, drew a great deal of his spleen from a few obnoxious activists he had to deal with and some distasteful incidents he lived through on his campus. He was especially offended by the uppitiness of black power leaders and even more so by the insolence of militant feminists, who, he felt, failed to appreciate the chivalric side of machismo and seemed to have no idea why God had endowed them with a womb.

Yet self-righteous vituperation and strident anger were hardly the only ingredients in the bubbling political stew of the times. The Port Huron Statement of the Students for a Democratic Society is as fine a manifesto as any ever written, and the authors on whom young dissenters drew — C. Wright Mills, Paul Goodman, Noam Chomsky, Jacques Ellul, E. F. Schumacher, Herbert Marcuse — were hardly lightweights. Admittedly, there were new modes of expression, especially the rock music of the period, that were troublingly unfamiliar to the cultural mainstream, but, given the chance, they could be persuasively incisive. Works such as Stanley Kubrick's *Dr. Strangelove* (especially Terry Southern's mordant screenplay) and Allen Ginsberg's "Wichita Vortex Sutra" brilliantly capture the craziness in high places (both east and west) that was threatening the world with thermonuclear devastation. Despite its cool demeanor and consoling euphemisms, the "mad rationality" (to use Lewis Mumford's phrase) that dominated postwar politics was a far greater offense to civilized values than the fear and fury in the streets. That is what one must listen for in the whirling words of Bob Dylan's "Subterranean Talking Blues," once so suspiciously jarring that disk jockeys would not put it on the air. Even when the poetry and lyrics of the time were awkward or just plain bad, they voiced a desperate frustration. The very quality I most admired in the dissenting politics of that period — its lack of monolithic organization, the absence of heavy leadership, the spontaneity and improvisational imagination that invited everybody to speak their piece — made it impossible to reach a firm conclusion about occasional outbursts of misconduct. Making evaluations of a social phenomenon as messy as *The 1960s* is like trying to make a single, unqualified judgment about the Protestant Reformation or the French Revolution that neatly balances the moral grandeur against the lamentable extremes. That is certainly more than I can do. That was why, in writing on the period, I limited myself to cheering on a few prominent ideas and the people who championed them. But inevitably that carried over into a permissiveness on my part that other commentators could not accept.

Now what I most regret overlooking in my critique of the 1960s is an obvious demographic fact that has remained subliminal until recently. Like all the rest of us, boomers grow old. There is more to this generation than what it did between the ages of 18 and 24; it did not evaporate before reaching the age of 30. No generation deserves to be judged before it has run its course. Given time, a big younger generation becomes a big older generation. Maybe we overlooked that fact because of the infatuation with youth that boomers ushered into history. When they were young, boomers had the attention of the world, so much so that when they stopped being young, it was as if they vanished in a puff of smoke. *Old boomer* was a contradiction in terms. Who could imagine Bob Dylan going gray or Mick Jagger getting wrinkled? But to dismiss those who have stopped being the younger generation is to subscribe to the very obsession with youth that boomers themselves created — with the help of the adoring media and an opportunistic marketing industry.

Yet, if anything, a big generation takes on more cultural influence with age; in its senior years, it brings a hard-won maturity to its politics. It also finds its way to values that lie beyond the immediate demands of family and career. In memory, it carries forward what it once was and finds time to ponder its place in history. As a Gray Panther leader of the 1960s once said, "Being retired is like being back on the campus," which is at least a chance to take stock and review. What comes of that review can be wisdom, and, given the size of the demographic, the wisdom of elders may have more power to change the world than the passion of youth. Maybe, in the light of its peculiar historical experience, every older generation has been different from those that came before. But there is no question that this older generation of boomers, born into an era of unprecedented affluence and apocalyptic anxiety in the wake of the worst war and the worst economic debacle of modern times, will be different enough to change the bad habits of the corporate and military elite who have done such a remarkable job of reconstituting themselves over the last generation.

Nothing distinguishes the baby-boom generation more than its capacity for holding center stage. What would one expect of so large a generation? Its slightest whim, whether in the marketplace or in the voting booth, was bound to have major social implications. So, too, the ideals that shaped its most important decisions in life. Boomers grew up being scrutinized and analyzed as if they possessed some privileged knowledge of the future, something their parents could not see or understand. The counter culture played upon that attribution. Hence, the fascination with code words, song lyrics that could not be heard over the roar of the amplifiers, psychedelic fonts that were nearly illegible. As a result, they got into the habit of smug self-assertion. And too often they were taken at their own narcissistically high evaluation. In their teens and twenties, large numbers of boomers opted to identify themselves as champions of dissent and cultural innovators. Saving the world is a heavy assignment for the young to take on, but boomers at least enjoyed an inspiring precedent: the rebellious exuberance of youthful generations past. They were not the first younger generation to assign themselves an idealistic role; there had been young revolutionaries and red-diaper babies before them. In the United States, at the end of the 19th century, Progressivism was a movement of the young, mainly the young professionals who were graduating from the new land-grant universities. During the days of the New Deal, there were young communists and Trotskyites on many university campuses. The association of youth with radical change has been with us since the days of the French Revolution when the entire western world seemed to be at the threshold of a new era which only the young could understand. It was the revolutionary Year One. The young William Wordsworth, on a walking tour of France as the nation fell to the Jacobins, came home singing, "Bliss was it in that dawn to be alive, And to be young was very heaven."

Now boomers face a more daunting challenge. We have no precedent for an insurgent older generation. If anything, the stereotype for the senior years faces in the opposite direction, toward stodginess and passivity. Age has always been the time to leave the stage and ring down the curtain. For that very reason, it is essential for boomers to have a clear sense of their unique place in history. In creating an elder culture, they have no better place to start than with the unfinished business of their youth. With their attention focused on the new and the now, many boomers may have overlooked the fact that they arrived on the scene with an identity they inherited as much as created. Like every generation before them, boomers have been molded by circumstance. History writes the script for our lives, and in the case of the boomers, the script has been an eventful one.

Not by Size Alone

What accounts for this remarkable destiny that now offers boomers a second chance to reshape history? Numbers alone were never the decisive aspect when it came to the ethos of disaffiliation that flourished during the early baby-boom era. Moral daring counted for more. In Europe, where the postwar generation was not as large as in the United States, the young were nonetheless rocking the ship of state, raising many of the same issues as their American counterparts — which created the exhilarating impression of a coordinated worldwide movement. Maybe the young always have the advantage of claiming innocence; nevertheless, even though those in authority were quick to dismiss what they saw and heard as an outburst by spoiled kids, there was no honest way to dismiss the indictment they were drawing up of their society's failings.

As the children of parents who suffered through the Great Depression and World War II, boomers were born into a traumatized world that cried out for renewal. And renewal there would be. It took the most obvious form imaginable: sex. Not sex as boomers would later experience it, a playful, guiltless romp, but as an act no less life-affirming. The reproductive outburst of the 1940s and 1950s that brought the boomers into the world was a defiant celebration of life following years of harsh privation and genocidal violence. Later, boomers would march in the streets shouting, "Make love, not war." But that is exactly what their parents sought to do, by deed if not by word after living through the worst of wars. They made love, and they made babies. Soon enough, war caught up with them again — a Cold War that seemed destined to last forever — but not before they had launched one of the biggest reproductive binges in the history of the western world. The role boomers would later play in launching a sexual revolution has become part of their legend; but sex would never mean to them what it meant to their parents. There have been generations so defeated by war, plague, famine, and atrocity that reproduction dropped sharply, as if people had given up on life. To bring children into a world overshadowed by Auschwitz and Hiroshima was an act of stubborn courage, a commitment to life that was as brave as any revolutionary act of defiance. In a very real sense, boomers drew in idealism with their first breath, inheriting their parents' faith in the future.

Not only did they inherit a world that demanded great change, but it was a world that offered the means to make that change — especially in the United States. No one before World War II could have guessed how fabulously rich an industrial society could become. It was the fate of the United States to show the postwar world the full productive capacity of industrialism. America, the arsenal of democracy and unscathed on its own soil by the war, ushered in the promise of a world beyond scarcity and, with it, a revolution of rising expectations. Rarely has any great war ended on so hopeful a note. Industrial technology, now equipped with more ingenious inventions than at any time since the harnessing of steam, would rapidly attain such dizzy new levels of economic growth — first in the western world and later in the century in Asia — that it became possible to imagine the abolition of poverty, and with that an end to every kind of injustice. Indeed, it is my intention to return to those high hopes in the pages that follow. But at the same time the very power that offered that promise threatened to put an end to history. No generation has ever experienced such a deep fear of extinction as Americans born into the post–World War II world. The threat was more than that of the bomb. Industrial power imperiled the ecological limits of the planet. Used unwisely, such power might, just as surely as thermonuclear war, destroy the intricate web of life that sustains us. Never before had it been so imperative to ask the most basic questions of economics and ethics. How much is enough? What can the Earth afford? How shall its abundance be shared?

Now, as boomers arrive at their senior years, an even more extraordinary factor intervenes to shape their lives. It is one thing to be a big generation; it is quite another to be a long-lasting generation. Boomers are both. Medical science has placed us within sight of a life expectancy that may surpass 100 years before the end of the 21st century. Add the newfound powers of biotechnology, and we may see human longevity extend to lengths known only in myth or science fiction. Every new generation born from here on will be a smaller part of the total population, but every child born is apt to enjoy a longer, healthier life. Put those two facts together, and the demographic logic is undeniable. Every society in the world, and especially those that join the global economy, is destined to tilt in the direction of age.

Endgame

The most important line of demarcation in contemporary politics may have to do with one's vision of history. Where do we stand as a society in the turbulent flow of events? Conservative thinkers believe a good dose of unrestrained entrepreneurial energy will solve all problems. Others, myself included, believe that urban-industrial society is playing out its endgame. It has arrived at a boundary condition where more of the same will not save us. Beyond that boundary lies either a downward spiral into economic and environmental chaos — or a new postindustrial world whose guiding ideas and inspiring ideals will be very different from those we have been following for the past three centuries. What follows in these pages is an effort to redefine those ideals and to present them as peculiarly the values of an aging society. Issues of this magnitude cannot be settled by a few statistics. They are matters of philosophical commitment based on what we have learned about people, their vices, their virtues, their resourcefulness, and above all their moral wisdom.

Throughout the modern era, western society has looked to its ability to redesign nature for security and prosperity, just as the nations of the western world once looked to war to achieve national greatness. We have been living out a Faustian bargain, a love affair with power: the power of our monkey cunning, the power of brute force. We have spent several generations beating our fellow human beings and the natural world into submission: native peoples, slaves, the working class, the land, the rivers, the forests, everything from the backward billions of our own species down to the microbes and the molecules of living systems. Perhaps our insatiable appetite for power made sense as long as human beings lived in helpless fear of famine, plague, and the annihilating forces of nature. But industrial and scientific power has served its purpose; it has given us more than we need, so much, in fact, that we are running out of space to bury the excess and out of time to repair the damage. Dr. Faust may still have wonders and amazements up his sleeve, but we can no longer assume they will bring us more blessings than liabilities. The simplicity and innocence of our quest for domination has come to an end. Something new, something that goes beyond power and plenty, must take its place as the goal of history — something that has to do with finding a greater meaning for human life than shopping sprees and space shots.

My experience of the 1960s left me with no clear idea what that something might turn out to be, but I knew it had to do with questioning the rightness and rationality of urban-industrial society. That was a question none of the major ideologies of the past had ever dared to raise. On both the political left and right, capitalists, Marxists, and socialists were committed to expanding the empire of cities that now girdles the Earth. All were convinced that industrial power was the whole meaning of progress, the only defensible way to use our skills and resources. All that mattered was who ran the system. *More* — more merchandise, more profit, more growth, more of everything — was the goal of life, and technology was the means to that goal. Alongside that pursuit, everything else was defunct, irrational, backward. This was the culture I saw being challenged in the 1960s by the voices of a new generation. Eventually, the phrase *counter culture* took on a life of its own, usually becoming more superficial and purely sensational as it was passed along. Often it was understood to have more to do with hair styles or ragged jeans or light shows. Definitions like that did not have to be trivial; the counter culture did express itself in its peculiar taste in dance and music; it had its emblems and gestures. The motley, thrift-shop chic of the period was a celebration of cheap living and a rebuke to expensive mainstream fashions. But too often the values that underlay the emblems and gestures went unappreciated. At least for me, the deeper meaning of the counter culture surfaced in the literature, music, and films that explored the meaning of sanity. *Catcher in the Rye, One Flew Over the Cuckoo's Nest, Catch 22, The Naked Lunch, Dr. Strangelove, The Bell Jar*, the beat poetry of the 1950s, the acid rock of the 1960s, the psychiatric theories of R. D. Laing and the Mad Liberation Front, the psychedelic art of the underground press — works like this probed the limits of the official reality principle. Even the satirical magazine *Mad* that went out to the teens and pre-teens of the period was premised on the craziness of the adult way of life. One has to return to the early Romantic period to find the same fascination with madness and what it reveals. The boomers' early years were a time of protest, but the protest went beyond conventional political issues of justice, equality, and peace. At its most radical, it took its politics to the depths of the psyche. Change consciousness and you change the culture. Change the culture and you change values. Change values and you change politics. That was the counter culture I cared about. The manifesto that spoke to me was Shelley's proclamation: "Poets are the unacknowledged legislators of the world."

Now, as I look back, I can see how difficult it was to formulate such a critique in political terms, especially when those who sought to do so were as young and frequently as gauche as boomers then were. Challenging the values of urban-industrial culture requires more experiential depth than one can expect from the very young. The project of transforming perceptions and values still seems to me the way forward toward a humane society, but this cannot be done with push-button rapidity by jolting the nervous system, whether with drugs or very, very loud music. Rather, it is best done by moving with the grain of nature. Life in its normal course alters our consciousness more than any narcotic, especially if we are given the chance to reflect on our experience. The greatest transformations any of us undergo arise out of the rhythms of ordinary life: the trauma of birth, the trials of adolescence, suffering serious disease, facing the loss of loved ones, confronting our own death. Aging turns many of us into totally different people. If we confront the experience with full awareness, aging can prepare us to learn what so many great sages have tried to teach: to be mindful of our mortality, to honor the needs of the soul, to practice compassion. Conscious aging opens us to these truths; it is a mighty undoer of the ego. It sweeps away the illusions that once made wealth and competitive success, good looks and fine possessions, seem so important. Granted, age comes hard to some, especially a certain class of alpha male who may never find his way to wisdom because he can never give up on the rat race, never cease pursuing the glittering prizes, never stop doing battle with the young guys coming along. Granted, too, there are any number of old fools in the world. Just as youth can be wasted on the young, age can be wasted on the old. But was anybody who turns out to be a fool at 70 any wiser at the age of 20? At this crux in our history, my faith goes out to our countercultural capacities, meaning our ability to change course. Once I pegged that faith to what a big younger generation might be able to achieve. Now I would look to what a big older generation is far more likely to achieve, not simply on the basis of high ideals, but by working along the grain of demographic necessity.

Once again, I remind myself that nothing good or bad is guaranteed in history. The world will always turn out to be what most of us make of it. But there are moments in time when possibilities present themselves, and we must take our chances. I believe the new beginning that boomers fell short of achieving in their youth has become more possible and more practical with every year we have added to our life expectancy — a prospect nobody could have predicted. We have arrived at this juncture thanks to the productivity of our technology and to the demographic shift that technology has helped bring about. *Urban-industrial culture is aging beyond the values that created it.* The revolution belongs to the old, not the young.

CHAPTER 3

You Say You Want a Revolution

*Some would have us believe that Americans feel content-
ment amidst prosperity — but might it not better be called
a glaze above deeply felt anxieties about their role in the
new world? And if these anxieties produce a developed in-
difference to human affairs, do they not as well produce a
yearning to believe that there is an alternative to the present, that something can be done to change circumstances
in the school, the workplaces, the bureaucracies, the government?... The search for truly democratic alternatives to
the present, and a commitment to social experimentation
with them, is a worthy and fulfilling human enterprise,
one which moves us and, we hope, others today.*

— Students For A Democratic Society,
The Port Huron Statement, 1962

True revolutions have deep roots. They grow out of aspira-
tion and conflict that may reach generations into the past.
We date the baby boom from 1946, but the elder culture that
was destined to emerge from that brief reproductive outburst
connects with historical undercurrents that reach back centuries. Above all it connects with the subterranean meaning of
industrialization, an economic development we most readily associate with the harsh use of material power, Promethean technology, and maniacal self-interest. But there was always more to
that process, a hidden dream of human well-being that has only
now revealed itself.

Let us start where a new awareness of industrialism first began to dawn. In 1884, an English social worker named Arnold Toynbee delivered a series of lectures at Oxford under the title "The Industrial Revolution." The phrase, so familiar now that it is difficult to believe anybody had to invent it, did not exist before Toynbee's lectures. He used it as a lens to look back 100 years to the 1780s, and in doing so imposed an identity on his period of history that has become the accepted interpretation of the modern world. In so many words, as if he were drawing a map in time, Toynbee told his audience

> You are here. The people of Great Britain stand in the midst of a wrenching historical transition that is tearing us away from the villages and farmlands of our agrarian past and transforming us into a nation of cities and factories, steam engines and dynamos, railways and steam ships, entrepreneurs and proletarian laborers. All this is part of one big picture.

In these pages we are about to make this "one big picture" bigger by showing how Toynbee's already ambitious idea of an industrial revolution has become something even greater and more life-enhancing: the beginning of the senior dominance.

When Toynbee was lecturing, people were familiar with the word *revolution* as it applied to great political upheavals. Revolution brought to mind the fall of the Bastille, the guillotine in the public square, barricades in the streets. But as Toynbee used the word, revolution meant something else: a grand convergence of impersonal factors — technological, social, and political — that came together without planning over the course of a century. By virtue of a single phrase, scores of seemingly disconnected events and social forces — wars, the struggle for colonial empire, domestic unrest, the rise of great cities, the migrations of millions, periods of hardship and repression — assumed a shape and a meaning. All this was the industrial revolution.

Was and is. Because that revolution is far from over. It continues; it envelopes us today. The world is still moving through its strenuous industrial adventure, an ongoing process now in its high-tech stage that embraces the entire planet and has transformed nations around the world into the sort of buzzing, bustling urban workshop that the midlands of England once uniquely were in the time of James Watt and Richard Arkwright. Understanding that process as it unfolds through its later stages is the key to understanding the boomers' place in history.

Just as we revise our reading of political revolutions, we also reinterpret social revolutions, finding in them elements that earlier generations missed. Take one well-known feature of the industrial revolution that will be of special interest to us here: urbanization. The industrial city was among the most obvious innovations of the period, but it had more dimensions than anyone recognized at the time. The new machines, ungainly improvisations of belts and shafts and gears, required factories; the factories, needing a local workforce, required cities. By fits and starts, without planning or foresight, the first industrial towns formed around the factories. And to begin with — especially in the first industrial nations — the cities were killing fields. People left their hamlets and villages seeking work in the factory towns; what most of them found was death. Through the first three generations of the industrial revolution, cities could not replace their own numbers. They grew because thousands were moving off the land and into early graves. Those migrants who left the countryside left behind their familiar diets, their folk remedies, their inherited immunity, their social support. They entered cities that were hellholes with no streets, no clean water, no sewers, no public health facilities, no garbage collection. And by the thousands they died an even earlier death than they would have died in their villages. In the wretched little factory town of Manchester in 1820, little more than a collection of shacks and shanties along unpaved roads, life expectancy was 17.

That figure reflects a high rate of infant mortality, so high that the earliest campaigns to clean up the cities and make them livable focused on children.

In a very real sense, this is where the boomers' extraordinary life expectancy begins — in the misery and squalor of industrial towns that cut life short, killing children by the thousands. It was the deaths of children in the slums and tenements of factory towns that launched the great public health campaigns that have wiped out the worst epidemic diseases. In London during the 1830s and 1840s there were years when half the recorded deaths were children below the age of ten. Babies became the first humanitarian concern of that period. Their deaths inspired do-gooders to launch the sanitarian and health-of-towns movements that cleaned up the cities. The drive was on for clean water, better nutrition, professional nursing, decently clean hospitals, and eventually inoculation. More babies survived. And though nobody foresaw it at the time, that was the first step in the direction of mass longevity. Save a baby in the cradle, and the baby will have a better chance of surviving into adulthood — to the age of 30…or 60…or 70. Babies were the target, but the unforeseen result was a growing number of older people.

Did society want a growing number of older people? Nobody thought of putting the question that way. It was just…happening and seen as good, a measure of progress. Thus, by 1900, life expectancy in the United States and most urban-industrial societies had reached 45 years. The cities were finally replacing their own numbers. In another century, by 2000, the life expectancy of baby boomers would reach 70. At no step along the way did anyone raise the warning that all this sanitation and public health was prolonging life and so saddling society with more elderly dependents than it could afford. Nobody advocated tearing out the sewers or eliminating the water-treatment plants so that people would die younger, just as we hear nobody today advocating that we encourage more smoking and put more toxic additives in food in order to send more people to an early grave. Step by step, reform by reform, the industrial revolution was becoming something greater, a longevity revolution for which industrial power was the means, not the end.

The Longevity Revolution

The longevity revolution comes at us in ways that override all the doubts and reservations that pundits and experts of every political stripe now entertain about affordability. It is, quite simply, unstoppable. Revolutions of the past, those that were fought on the picket lines or at the barricades, were often easy to defeat; the powers that be simply sent in the troops or the cops and beat people into submission in the name of the rule of law or property rights. But the longevity revolution is being fought on a thousand fronts — not against humanity, but against disease and risk. It is the unceasing war against filth, danger, germs, unwholesome food, bad hygienic habits. It moves forward almost by stealth, with the irresistible logic of progress, and not simply along the lines of medical science where genetic research is now promising to eliminate disease at the embryonic stage of development. Name a problem that threatens to harm people, and for sure there is a group somewhere working to diminish that risk. Committees form to promote safe sex, mothers band together to punish drunk drivers, manufacturers devise superior ways to guarantee auto safety, employers ban smoking in offices and corridors, farm workers organize to eliminate toxins from the crops they harvest, school officials undertake to serve healthier food in the cafeteria. All of this flows forward like a mighty river fed by a thousand tributaries.

Everything we do to make life safer, healthier, and more secure is part of the longevity revolution. Put it all together, and you might almost conclude that there is a committee somewhere coordinating all these efforts as part of a campaign to make sure more people live longer. But there is no such committee. There is, instead, a consensus among people of goodwill to make life better. The longevity revolution has no headquarters, no charismatic leaders. It consists of small, scattered groups trying, each in its own way, to meet some need. How does one defeat a revolution like this? Can we imagine some political leader taking the position that people are living too long or that we are producing too many healthy children? Try to imagine an argument against long life and better health that any politician of any ideological orientation would ever dare to voice.

The aging of the modern world is not some stroke of unaccountable bad luck that has saddled us with an impossible fiscal burden. Although nobody seemed to notice it until the day before yesterday, all industrial societies are aging with the momentum of biological necessity. That is the true measure of their progress. Unless we can imagine the modern world giving up entirely on medical science and technology, then progress toward ever greater longevity is *inevitable* — as inevitable as the continuing refinement of computers and telecommunications. And unless we can imagine people giving up on life and health as commonsense goals, then longevity is *good*.

Both words are important. *Inevitable* is what you cannot sensibly fight *against*. *Good* is what you fight *for* in life. Put inevitable and good together, and you have a historical movement. In the modern world, nothing inspires people to greater deeds than belonging to a movement, especially if they believe they are riding the wave of the future. For the past two centuries, revolutionary spirits have asserted their claim to the future loudly and violently, as if they were not really certain about their destined success. In the 20th century, we have seen some very ugly politics grow out of movements that insisted *their* nation, *their* race, *their* class, or *their* economic system owned the future. The movements have come — and gone — marching away into the past, often leaving a bloody trail behind them. We have learned to treat movements with skeptical caution. But there is one leaderless, unplanned movement that has secretly owned the future all along: a quiet, gentle, life-enhancing movement called longevity. Few have recognized its cultural importance because its power springs from the simplest of the heart's desires, a prayer to which all but the most despairing have given voice. *Let me live another day.* At its core, the longevity revolution is as simple and as human as that.

Viewing history from this angle, one might almost say there was an unseen purpose to the industrial city. Workers came to cities to find jobs; entrepreneurs came to make money. But all the while, the city was doing something else. It was concentrating misery, making the suffering and privation of its population hideously visible — especially the suffering of children — so that it could be registered as a humanitarian concern. Unlike the death rate in scattered villages and farms, the urban death rate stood out in high profile; the city's many dead could be counted and their ages averaged. The result was a spreading sense of horror. In *The Ghost Map*, a study of the great London cholera epidemic of 1854, Steven Johnson highlighted the paradox of the modern city.[1] The epidemic was made possible by urban conditions of that period, the era when the city was a death trap. Tens of thousands people died before their time. But it was precisely the squalid overcrowding of London that brought people together in such a way that the disease could be demographically charted and its source discovered. Two sanitarians of the time, a physician and a clergyman, drew up the first death-density map and located the cause of the spreading infection. They made a guess: cholera is spread by a waterborne microbe — and they were right. The battle against urban epidemics was launched, a giant step toward mass longevity.

The cities highlighted a new issue in human affairs: *premature death*, the number of young who were cheated of life. It would be no exaggeration to say that industrial society discovered childhood as a phase of life deserving sympathy and understanding. Reformers of the period lamented the plight of waifs and urchins, they protested against hungry babies and children in the mines and mills. Writers waxed sentimental over abused orphans and exploited ragamuffins. Thanks to novelists such as Elizabeth Gaskell and Charles Dickens, the plight of children in the factory towns became a major public issue. Most of what was done to improve life in the way of health, education, and welfare was justified by the benefits brought to children. And so death became an issue in ways that could not help but shift the demographics of society at large.

The more that people of goodwill learned about the deplorable condition of cities, the more action was taken. Industrialism took on a second, subterranean agenda that seemed to be nothing more than common decency. In this way, the industrial revolution, disrupter of nations and killer of thousands, began to segue into something far more morally significant: an extension of life expectancy that would not be recognized until more than a century later — in fact, not until our own time, when we are so amazed to discover that we are collectively aging toward gerontocracy. Where have all these old people come from? Answer: from the continuing effort over the past two centuries to save the children.

The improvements that would eventually yield a steadily growing senior population originally had little to do with the old. The old were in fact the worst victims of industrialism, primarily because they were not deemed worth saving. They belonged to that class of unwelcome dependents called *the impotent poor* — those who could not provide for themselves. Whenever seniors hear themselves portrayed as a powerful vested interest in our electoral system, they should look to the past for the truth of the matter. As comfortable as many middle-class elders may be today, they share with all older people a long, sad history of bleak mistreatment they would do well to remember. For generations the old have suffered wrongs inflicted on them by harsh public policy and often by their nearest and dearest. With the exception of some traditional societies where elders may be honored — if for no other reason than that there are so few of them around — not many societies have treated their seniors as more than troublesome dependents who are expected to stand aside and let life pass them by. That has certainly been the case in the modern western world, where the old have been seen as the claim of the dreary past upon the bustling forces of progress.

Initially and for the next century or more, the new industrial economies took an especially savage toll among older workers. The men burned out early at the heavy and dangerous work they did in the factories and mines, on the railroads, and in the oil and timber fields. The women grew old before their time in the sweatshops and mills. Even if older workers kept their health and strength, industrial accidents, for which there was no compensation or adequate medical care, might cut them down at any moment. During the early generations of the industrial revolution, the aged, unless they belonged to the propertied classes, ordinarily ended lives of hard labor assimilated to the status of *the poor*. Even if they had worked all their lives, they were expected to die as paupers. The workhouse and the county home were little better than concentration camps for the elderly. There they were fed on gruel and bedded down at night on straw or bare wood. Yet they were expected to earn their own keep at tasks that atrophied the mind as well as the body: picking oakum, grinding bones. If the elderly wished to avoid the humiliation of public assistance, they had no place to turn for care after they left the payroll but to their children. Even if they were charitably classed among the *deserving* poor, they were still viewed as a burden. If they suffered, they suffered in silence.

For what power did they have, a scattered minority living in their children's homes or in state institutions that cut them off from one another? For the elderly, distance of any kind could be a formidable barrier; they were apt to find themselves too physically weak to take on the task of vigorous protest. After all, they might go hungry to bed every remaining night of their lives, their share of the family's meager rations going to the children or to the breadwinner who had to keep up his strength. Try finding a picture anywhere in our history that shows a well-fed elder who was not a plutocrat. The old are always shown as bent, toothless, withered, and painfully lean — and *old* might mean under 50. One might have assumed it was obvious that the more babies you save, the more wretched elders you will one day have. But that simple connection went unrecognized until our time when, at long last, the most exploited and disadvantaged class in the industrial world — save for outright slaves — found the power to make its presence and its needs known.

The Late-Blooming Power of Elders

Whatever happened to Ma Perkins? How many readers remember her at all?

In the years before World War II, whenever I stayed home from school, I recall the radio playing in the background while my mother laundered and ironed her way through the day migrating from soap opera to soap opera. *When a Girl Marries, Life Can Be Beautiful, Backstage Wife*…the shows were never better than a mediocre pastime, but their *dramatis personae* make a revealing contrast with what we have today in domestic melodrama. Almost invariably, these radio shows featured older central figures like Ma Perkins, Grandpa Hubbell, David Harem, Just Plain Bill, Scattergood Baines, Stella Dallas — not to forget Papa David Solomon, once regarded as the wisest soul in the US. The principal characters were usually middle-aged parents, but hardly a problem arose in these make-believe radio homes without the grandparents being brought in for a calming word. Not that their advice was always taken either in real life or on the radio. They did not rule the roost. The main reason they had to be in the story was because people remembered them being there — under the same roof or just down the block. Most radio soaps were located in small towns with a distinctly rural flavor: River's Bend, Silver Creek, Rushville Center. In the mind's eye, they were romanticized in the mode of Norman Rockwell magazine covers. But the tales they told of extended families in which grandma and grandpa played a significant role were an accurate depiction of an America that was fast disappearing.

By the 1930s and 1940s, this convivial, small-town America was already fading into the faux-nostalgia of Garrison Keillor's Lake Woebegone, a sort of hick-chic fantasy scene where neither Keillor nor his audience ever lived. With the end of World War II, as the boomers' parents began to look for the suburban amenities, the United States was fast becoming a society in which small towns, farming communities, and wise, old grandparents faded to the margins. One looks in vain for characters over 50 in television soap operas; all the shows have gotten younger and sexier. If there are old folks around, they are cranky codgers or randy, over-aged seductresses clearly out of their league. In that respect, the shows are very different from the original soaps of radio days. With the coming of the baby boom, children, adolescents, and young marrieds (or cohabitors) became the staples of popular culture.

Meanwhile, the nation's elderly, still badly scarred by the Great Depression, were continuing their steady decline to the bottom of the society where they would be among the last to enjoy postwar prosperity. In *The Other America*, Michael Harrington's 1962 landmark study of poverty in the richest country in the world, the old ranked with inner-city blacks and Appalachian whites as the three classes left furthest behind by the affluent society.[2] As late as 1975, when Robert Butler published his classic study of the elderly, he began by identifying old age, especially as the oldest old knew it, as a *tragedy*. He called his book *Why Survive?* and did not come up with an encouraging answer.[3] It was a bleak title for a bleak condition of life. During the first half of the 20th century, as they saw whatever moral stature and authority they once held steadily slipping away, elders were certainly not prompt in fighting back. Then, in 1947, Ethel Percy Andrus, a retired California educator, founded the National Retired Teachers Association, a support group with a special concern for health care. At the time health insurance for the elderly was practically non-existent, which made the burden of medical bills a major cause of old-age indigence. In 1956, Andrus, determined to find insurance for her group, joined forces with a savvy New York insurance agent named Leonard Davis who had managed to negotiate a health-insurance contract for an organization of retired New York teachers. Together, Andrus and Davis worked out a senior health-insurance policy that was to be sold through a new organization, the American Association of Retired Persons. Given the limited choices available, AARP's health-care policies for the elderly were an immediate success, and even more so the AARP Drug Buying Service, a mail-order pharmacy that was among the first voices raised against the inordinate cost of pharmaceuticals. The pharmacy soon branched out into a highly profitable, general business in sundries. By the mid-1970s AARP's insurance company, the Colonial Penn Group, organized as a holding company by Davis, had become one of the most profitable companies in the country.

Until Andrus's death in 1967, AARP maintained a serious commitment to political lobbying on a broad front. But once Davis took control of AARP, the organization assumed a very different, less public-spirited character. It was Davis's emphasis on marketing that soon lent senior politics a narrow and peculiarly commercial character, as if it were all about bargains and deals. Even as Medicare was being enacted in 1964, there were politicians who mockingly characterized seniors as voters who really have nothing in common beyond their love of hotel and airlines discounts.

Davis may have used AARP's mailing lists and publications to speak out on issues like entitlements, but the political side of the organization was becoming little more than a come-on — and not a particularly ethical one. After *Consumer Reports* ran a severely negative review of Colonial Penn's business practices, Davis found himself in trouble with the post office for abuse of nonprofit mailing privileges. The postal authorities actually wanted AARP to be prosecuted for fraud. Then in 1978, the television news magazine *60 Minutes* ran an exposé on Davis that shook AARP free of his control. *Sixty Minutes* characterized AARP as secretive, dictatorial, and vastly overblown, with little interest in anything greater than selling its wares. Following Davis's departure in 1979, AARP rapidly evolved into a true lobby — "America's most powerful lobby," as one historian has called it — replete with an internal factionalism that makes it anything but a monolithic voice.

Discounts and insurance may seem like an unlikely beginning for a political interest group, but this oblique origin reveals how laggardly seniors have been in becoming a power bloc. The story also has a peculiarly American quality. AARP was created by the very market economy whose conservative defenders now wince with pain whenever they observe the growing cost of entitlements. But if anything besides advertising and merchandizing first gave seniors a sense of their new power, it was the entitlements themselves. For once the benefits had been given, they became precious turf that would be defended. They could not easily be withdrawn; they could only be augmented as the senior generation increased its numbers.

Not only did Medicare and Medicaid have the obvious result of allowing the elderly poor, the sickest part of our population, to visit a doctor; these two programs allowed the elderly to take advantage of new medical breakthroughs that lengthened their life span decades beyond their working lives. Between 1953 and

1982, the number of indigent seniors who consulted a doctor in any 12-month period rose from about 60% to 85%. These are the elderly who once would have died off most rapidly; now they have gained access to costly procedures that will keep them alive long enough to require still more costly procedures. It is astonishing that neither our political leaders nor any of our brainstorming futurists foresaw the enormous fiscal and electoral implications of that simple fact. Perhaps the prospect of limitless economic growth blinded them to the ultimate potential of Medicare to generate deficits.

By the mid-1970s, the first full-entitlements older generation was on the scene, enjoying the modest but solid benefits of both Social Security and Medicare. With these seniors we saw the first indications of political insurgency since the days of the New Deal. These are people who retired with more years to look forward to than any previous generation and were out to make the most of them. They wanted the freedom to spend what they had saved, perhaps on pleasant weather, perhaps on a new home in a retirement community. It was almost as if the elderly had collectively decided to kick back and enjoy a leisure and security their parents and grandparents had been denied. I suspect they were amazed to learn, as they soon would, that there were critics in the country who believed they had no right to either leisure or security, that they had no entitlements at all. But thanks to the organizational and lobbying efforts of groups like the National Council of Senior Citizens, the Gray Panthers, and the revised AARP, and to the publications and programs that have grown up around those groups, this cohort of elders realized that they had become part of a significant demographic transition that carried a good deal of electoral weight. So much so that AARP was coming to be identified as a menacing political lobby that might one day soon hold helpless politicians up for ransom with its iron command at the ballot box. Of course, it makes little sense to speak of a demographic group of 50 to 70 million people related by blood to the remaining 200 million people in the country as a *special interest*. But even if it did, when it comes to the politics of greed, senior Americans have hardly been aggressive in asserting their interests.

The Attack of the Greedy Geezers

Nevertheless, the feistiness with which senior citizens began to defend their entitlements in the 1980s earned them a great deal of contempt and opposition. Conservative critics found a name for them: *greedy geezers*, a term that included those who had saved enough of their own money to retire in comfort. In states like California, Arizona, and especially Florida (where the Silver-Haired Legislature, a senior lobby, was being described as a "political powerhouse"), even liberal political activists began to castigate the elderly for voting to defeat bond issues and social programs that would benefit children and adolescents. As these critics saw it, the senior population was committed to pursuing an "anti-youth agenda" in favor of "Aid to Dependent Seniors."[4] Minority group leaders have charged that the non-white poor, concentrated in an "immigrant belt" that includes California, New York, Texas, and Illinois, are especially burdened by the costs of "publicly subsidized welfare" for seniors. In the coming century, they foresee "the prospect of young minority workers supporting the mostly white elderly." The Brookings Institute demographer William Frey predicted a "coming war" over entitlements dollars between states dominated by the "old white" and the "young diverse," a warning that has been echoed frequently by the far right on Fox News and in anti-immigrant circles.[5]

In the same way that organized labor was once regarded as a potentially tyrannical force able to use the ballot box to achieve its own selfish ends, entitlement critics began characterizing seniors as a threat to the democratic process. At the extreme there was the economist Lester Thurow, who raised the fearful prospect that retired Americans (whom he regarded as a "revolutionary class," but not in any good sense of the word) were "bringing down the social welfare state, destroying government finances, altering the distribution of purchasing power, and threatening the investments that all societies need to make to have a successful future." Writing on "The Birth of a Revolutionary Class" in *The New York Times Magazine* in May 1996 Thurow predicted that "in the years ahead, class warfare is apt to be redefined as the young against the old." He warned that the grandparents of America might achieve what no foreign foe has succeeded in doing: they might destroy the democratic way of life. Democracy, he stated, "is going to meet the ultimate test in the elderly. If democratic governments cannot cut benefits that go to the majority of their voters, then they have no long-term future."[6] Was he perhaps proposing that after retirement age, elders should be disenfranchised?

If we were to believe the conservative think tanks that are providing so much ideological firepower to the campaign against Social Security and Medicare, we might almost assume that entitlements were foisted upon an unsuspecting nation in the dead of night by a cunning conspiracy of grasping elders. The truth is quite the opposite. Senior power is a recent development in the modern world; it is still far from an equal contender when it comes to dealing with the well-funded financial services and insurance lobbies that stand behind the effort to privatize entitlements. Until the Great Depression of the 1930s, the elderly had little voice in the political life of any nation — and even then, their power and organization did not compare to that of the labor unions or the various conservative lobbies that opposed all publicly funded old-age pension plans. There are no power brokers meeting behind locked doors in Washington plotting the next move that will make everybody above age 65 fabulously rich.

Boomers, Know Your Enemy

Indeed, powerlessness may have been the socially and economically mandated condition of the elderly since the beginning of our species, a reflection of the scarcity that made the support of the older generation a heavy burden. Unless they were rich or royal, the old were always driven to the margins, shadowy figures never quite in focus, people on their way out of the human story. For that reason, the history of old age has received only oblique documentation. What we find if we look is a long, sad, and outrageous tale. In the 1960s, activist boomers rushed to the support of every exploited minority on the scene. But how many of them even now realize that they are joining the ranks of the world's most maligned and victimized class? If they take the time to study the lives of those who came before them, they will soon learn who their allies and who their enemies are. Nobody of any political stripe wants to risk the charge of granny-bashing, but the facts are clear. In the United States, gaining even a modest degree of security in retirement has been a struggle against business leaders, political conservatives, and free-market economists for whom money is the measure of all things.

Again, it is important to turn to lessons of the past to which boomers have given too little attention. Just as each year we pause to review what the experience of African Americans, women, and other once-oppressed groups can teach us, so too elders have a history they can draw upon as they assume ever greater power in the 21st century.

In 19th-century America, caring for the elderly was understood to be the voluntary responsibility of families or charities. The only other possibility in sight was the niggardly private pension plans available from a few employers, mainly the railroads. *Voluntarism*, as this approach was called, was the alternative to government intervention in a free-market economy. Voluntarism, which remains a much-favored idea on the political right, was not expected to make the lives of retired Americans comfortable. Far from it. In the voluntaristic perspective, it was assumed that the senior years of most working people would be meager and cheerless. The companies they had worked for owed them nothing once they were off the payroll, an assumption rapidly coming back into fashion under the global economy. The well-to-do are always the first to tell us that there just is not enough to go around. Thus, if the elderly had not put aside an adequate nest egg during their active years, they were regarded as failures who had simply lost out in the great race for success. In a competitive world, what then could they expect? Those who spoke of granting the elderly any sort of pension simply did not understand the mechanism of the free market. For was it not obvious that if anything better than squalid dependency awaited the elderly at the end of life, that would only discourage thrift and self-reliance?

Generosity was not only deemed unaffordable by business leaders; it was regarded as morally wrong. The fear and trembling that old age inspired in the early industrial period was not even denied; it was celebrated. Conservative ideologues openly touted the fear of dependency as a character-building force; it was the "chief discipline in the interest of wholesome living." As one economist of the period insisted, "The ultimate test of the wisdom of the various forms of public provision for destitute old age must be, not merely the comfort and gratification of the individual concerned, but the influence on the moral fiber of the community."[7]

Throughout the 19th century in the United States, the elderly were haunted by the threat of the poorhouse, a place of minimal comfort and moral degradation. The poorhouse embodied the prevailing response to senior indigence, namely that public assistance should be the absolute last resort for the desperately needy. In New York, that last resort would have been the notorious Blackwell's Island, a dismal tenement not all that different from the facilities used for criminals and the insane. The terror of the place was meant to deter the undeserving from seeking care. In the view of one conservative social commentator writing in 1909, the "fearsome prospect of old-age dependency" was a "most powerful incentive which makes for character and growth in a democracy."[8]

The earliest, and ultimately unsuccessful, effort to organize American seniors to defend their interests came in the 20th century. In the early 1920s, the fraternal Order of Eagles tried rallying seniors to campaign for some kind of state-based, old-age pension program, either at the state or federal level. Bills were brought before Congress, but none had enough political muscle behind it to overcome the entrenched resistance of the business community, which was committed to an ideology of competitive individualism. Businessmen insisted that any compulsory pension plan was un-American and would surely "undermine the self-respecting character of our people." They saw pension plans as the "entering wedge of communistic propaganda, ... an insidious experiment in paternalistic government which would sap the self-respect and destroy the moral fiber of thousands of people, besides costing taxpayers millions of dollars." It was only after the invisible hand of the marketplace had become a mail fist hammering the country ever deeper into the Great Depression that social insurance began to look like a better way.

Even so, the approach to Social Security that was taken by the New Deal was agonizingly modest and far short of what was being called for by Franklin Roosevelt's opponents on the political left. For one thing, placing the age of retirement at 65 was a bit of black actuarial humor; in the 1930s, when the life expectancy was 61, few people would live long enough to claim more than a few years' worth of benefits. Meanwhile, Huey Long, the great Populist voice of the era, was demanding a retirement system that would "soak the rich." Long was backing a program that would tax billions away from "predatory wealth" to pension off every American over the age of 60. At the same time, Dr. Francis Townsend, a California physician who was appalled by the number of grandparents who were committing suicide to avoid burdening their depression-ridden families, had rounded up millions of signatures from senior clubs across the country supporting his demand for a pension of $200 a month for retirees at age 60. Townsend's petition represents the first major show of elder power in the United States. As sensitive as he was to these rivals, Roosevelt felt free to reject Townsend's plan as a "dole" that would give most Americans more money in retirement than they had ever earned in their youth.

Though Dr. Townsend was mocked by the experts, he held to his plan, arguing that it was "only incidentally a pension plan." This is characteristic of senior politics; the programs proposed have always been quite sincerely understood as offering some larger benefit to the society as a whole. In Townsend's case, pensions were to be available only to those who gave up their jobs so that younger workers might find employment. Moreover, pensions would be paid in colored money that had to be spent promptly or it would lose value. Getting pension dollars into rapid circulation was meant to function as a sort of pump priming for the depressed economy. Townsend spent considerable time delineating the plight of the jobless young, assuming that his followers would share his paternal sympathies. As the doctor pointed out, with competition from the elderly eliminated, young workers would be able to demand better wages.[9]

In 1937 when the Roosevelt New Deal launched the Social Security program, conservatives still regarded the elderly as burdensome parasites who could not pay their own way. Social Security "will destroy initiative, thrift, and individual responsibility," proclaimed Alfred Sloan, CEO of General Motors, who of course needed no pension plan. Even after Roosevelt got his Social Security program through Congress, right-wingers challenged it in the courts as unconstitutional. When the case was finally settled in favor of supporting the Social Security Act by a 7–2 vote, Justice Benjamin Cardozo gave it his judicial blessing in a famous pronouncement: "The hope behind this statute is to save men and women from the rigors of the poorhouse as well as from the haunting fear that such a lot awaits them when journey's end is near."

In the mid-1960s, when the Great Society programs got under way, nearly 30% of America's elders were still living below the poverty line, three times as many as the rest of the society combined. *Poor* almost invariably implied *old* in everybody's mind. Thanks to the extension of Social Security during the fiscally conservative Eisenhower presidency and the creation of Medicare under Lyndon Johnson, that association finally began to change — to such a degree that, in our own time, it is possible for conservative critics to write books that portray the elderly as almost sybaritically well-off. But again, the motivation behind the Great Society was as much to serve the interests of the younger as of the older generation. What LBJ did to aid seniors — Medicare, the Older Americans Act, the Administration on Aging — was welcomed as a way to free footloose, upwardly mobile children from being tied down by the needs of their parents. The economist Max Frankel, who was present when President Johnson signed Medicare into law, relates a telling anecdote: "'My mother thanks you,' I said to LBJ. 'No,' he replied, 'It's *you* who should be thanking me.'"

At the time Medicare was passed, there was no powerful senior lobby pressing for these reforms, nor any senior vote that politicians needed to view with respect. Rather, this was a latter-day ripple of the great postwar boom when the rising economic tide was lifting everybody's boat. The young of that prospering period voted enthusiastically to pack their parents off in mobile homes or to retirement communities, "glorified playpens for the elderly," as the elder-activist Maggie Kuhn called them. One might almost argue that the principal financial beneficiary of Medicare was the medical industry, which has continued to cash in on the program ever since. How else could the elderly afford the wonders of life-extending medicine? These are patients that might otherwise never have arrived at the doctor's office. True, billions of dollars flow into Medicare every year, but none of it is paid out to seniors. The money spent for whatever costs seniors incur under Medicare never passes through their hands or bank accounts; it goes directly to doctors, hospitals, and the pharmaceutical industry — and their stockholders. The Medicare program should be seen as an income-transfer program that passes billions into the hands of the country's richest class: physicians, health-care entrepreneurs, and drug and insurance companies and their investors. As it has turned out, entitlements entitled more than the elderly. Doctors felt entitled to be paid their fees; children felt entitled to have their own rich family lives and lucrative careers. It was not the ruthless use of political clout that gave senior Americans the chance to better their lives. If many seniors came to value the added independence they derived from Social Security and Medicare, that was a happy side effect of programs intended to let the younger generation get on with its own design for upscale living.

But there is one thing Social Security and Medicare have done that reaches beyond the elderly: they have landmarked a standard of living in the United States that has been fast disappearing from the private sector. Like flies embedded in amber, the entitlements that elders still enjoy remind us of a time when every good job in the United States included such benefits. How many boomers envisioned a day when the drugs they would value most would not be LSD or Ecstasy but blood-pressure medications and diabetes pharmaceuticals? And if elders had managed to pay off the mortgage on their homes or made a few smart investments to add to their nest egg, they might even wind up with enough retirement income to live out their lives in comfort — a radically new phase in the otherwise dismal history of old age.

Sabotaging Entitlements: How To

The last major adjustment in Social Security came in the early days of the Reagan presidency. The fix is usually credited to Alan Greenspan, who, with broadly based, bipartisan support, headed off what was then an authentic threat to the system's immediate solvency as the baby boomers approached retirement. Greenspan's national commission decided to raise the Social Security payroll tax by 2%, thus producing a trust-fund surplus that would see the last boomer into retirement somewhere in the middle of the next century. The surplus, as might have been predicted, was seen at once by Congress as a revenue windfall: money that could be borrowed cheaply and spent, wisely or not, as Congress has seen fit to spend it. As a result, the trust fund and the surplus it was created to safeguard have given rise to a bit of paranoid folklore on the part of right-wing critics.

Because the surplus is used to buy special, low-interest Treasury bonds, there are those who insist the trust fund is a hoax, containing "nothing but IOUs" from the government that will some day have to be redeemed with tax dollars. Or, as it is sometimes phrased, there is nothing in the trust fund but "mere pieces of paper," as if the entire global economy were not based on pieces of paper called stocks, bonds, promissory notes, deeds, contracts, etc. But of course the IOUs in the trust fund are Treasury bonds, the world's most secure financial paper, a promise to pay on which the federal government has never defaulted. For that very reason, investors around the world value having US Treasury bonds in their portfolios and fully expect them to be redeemed, just as every investor who holds municipal, county, state, school district, or water department bonds expects to have them paid off in time.

Brokering government bonds and investing in them is a standard kind of business, hardly something that should amaze or appall financially knowledgeable types, many of whom are so severely critical of entitlements they have no qualms about maligning the single most reputable and honest government bureaucracy we have. They know full well that bonds are routinely issued to cover necessary expenditures that cannot be financed by private money; they know that all government bonds must be redeemed by taxation. Conceivably the Social Security surplus could have been restricted in some way — say, to home loans. But what else did anybody expect to come of the money in the trust fund but that it would be loaned out — or *put to work*, as we like to say in a capitalist economy? Nobody leaves money lying idle. Or did those who raise these foolish objections expect the surplus would be tied up with a pink ribbon and kept in a giant piggy bank? Given the fact that the nation's retirement account is the highest of public trusts, its use was bound to be made as non-controversial as possible — a restriction that ruled out letting the Social Security administrators pick and choose equities. Instead of quibbling over what stocks the Social Security Administration should and should not be allowed to buy (tobacco? oil? strip mining? junk foods? foreign companies?), the money is used to fund the things approved by the people's representatives, which lends as much of a seal of democratic approval as one can imagine.

And when the bonds are redeemed — starting about 2017 — they will be paid off with income tax dollars collected on a graduated basis. This means that at some point in the future, the better-off will pay more to meet our Social Security obligations than the lesser-off. Those who side with the rich will howl at the prospect; this is exactly the sort of income-transfer program conservatives hate. But they know their outrage will be useless, because by then millions of boomers will be under Social Security and may even be using their voting power to improve the benefits they receive. And how bad will that be? It will do no more financial harm to those in the upper brackets than the taxes levied on the well-off in other countries, sometimes referred to as "our competitors," who have been paying for a more expensive welfare state for years.

Greenspan's reform (which also included a gradual rise in the retirement age) was a remarkable achievement, given Ronald Reagan's anti-tax commitment. Who could have predicted that Reagan would open his mouth and swallow one of the biggest tax increases ever adopted in peacetime? But so he did without batting an eye and with no apologies. The reform met almost no opposition — except on the neoconservative right of the Republican Party, which was quick to recognize the precedent that was being set. If saving the New Deal's flagship program was such a high public priority that the likes of Reagan and Greenspan were willing to jettison conservative principles, what was to prevent this kind of fix being adopted every time Social Security required fiscal rebalancing? Was this not a dangerous invitation to write more blank checks for the funding of other big government programs? It was from that point forward that more extreme critics on the right wing embarked upon a desperate campaign to undermine Social Security.

Even while Greenspan's commission was devising a fix for Social Security, the Cato Institute, a major conservative brain trust, was unfolding what it lightheartedly called a *Leninist strategy* for sabotaging Social Security. Acknowledging the deep popular support Social Security enjoys, the Catonians decided that an ideological assault was out of the question. Anti-entitlements critics dare not declare what is in their hearts, namely that they find Social Security morally obnoxious, a violation of the ideal of competitive individualism. The favored technique has been to avoid strong, doctrinaire statements about taxes, big government, and social programs in favor of convoluted statistical analyses that make Social Security appear financially unsustainable. This was done by simply turning a blind eye to the reasonable reform Greenspan and company had achieved — and by associating Social Security with the far more serious fiscal problems faced by the other senior entitlement, Medicare. The programs are, of course, funded separately and differently, and so each has a different fiscal character. Medicare has its own battle to fight. It is up against a deeply rooted insurance industry that is determined to maintain its profits; it also has to cope with the rising and unpredictable cost of medical care. The fact that Medicare was and still is in need of substantial adjusting should never have been confused with Social Security's secure status. But by conflating the two programs, militant fiscal conservatives continued hinting that entitlements are a menace to the economic stability of the United States — this at the same time that the Reagan administration was raising the military budget to record deficit levels.

Thus, the right-wing opposition presents its hostility to Social Security, not as a matter of ideology or ethics, but as pure mathematics. At times it almost seems to bemoan the supposedly sad state of the system. At the same time, it advocates modest, purely voluntary private alternatives for pensions around the edges of Social Security which it hopes will draw off entitlements supporters who cannot do the math.[10] Nevertheless, this approach, focused especially on the media, has been remarkably successful in muddying the debate over the future of Social Security. Lost in the welter of crooked statistics is the fact that Social Security is the *only* government program that is funded as much as 30 years into the future. In contrast, try asking where next year's Pentagon budget is coming from.

Here is where the greedy geezer stereotype plays its most important role. It is meant to provide some emotional juice to fuel the purely statistical arguments raised against Social Security. A key part of this strategy has been to characterize seniors as avaricious and irresponsible, an intolerably selfish interest group. With remarkable speed, elders went from stereotypically lovable grandparents to the scourge of the nation. The most intemperate assault on senior entitlements has come from the Concord Coalition, a right-wing pressure group founded by Peter Peterson, an investment banker who was Secretary of Commerce under President Nixon. Peterson has been campaigning against entitlements since the 1980s. Anybody who believes the senior vote can have its way in American politics would do well to study what Peterson has been able to accomplish with a few well-placed millions from the brokerage community with its deep vested interest in privatizing Social Security. Author of two book-length jeremiads on entitlements, Peterson helped direct what may be the most effective lobbying effort since Prohibition. He has certainly had little difficulty commanding the generous and friendly attention of major American media, none of which seem to have had time to check his predictions with the Social Security Administration.[11]

In May 1996, the *Atlantic* magazine published an excerpt from one of Peterson's books. It summarized his many-sided attack on entitlements: senior entitlements are unsustainable, undeserved, unprincipled, and unfair. Indeed, like all self-made men who have presumably made it through life without asking for favors, Peterson found the very concept entitlement obnoxiously un-American. But more striking than any statistic he offered were the illustrations the *Atlantic* chose to accompany the article. In these nasty cartoons, seniors appear like some parasitic species, geriatric layabouts living it up on the sunny shores of Florida, stealing the food from their children, and devouring the national treasury. One especially vicious illustration depicts a cadaverous geezer in a hospital bed studded with IV tubes; the life-giving fluid being injected lavishly into his arm is...money. If anything, such an image tells us that for some critics money is the equivalent of our life's blood.

As anti-entitlements critics would have it, the old are a curse in every respect. They are too numerous, they insist on living too long, but worst of all, they are just plain *bad*, a failed generation of weak, self-indulgent freeloaders. Peterson, for example, not only condemned entitlements as "a fiscal meltdown" but castigated the entire baby-boom generation — the geezers to

come — for its "unseemly" and "ruinously dysfunctional" way
of life, this in spite of the clear fact that boomers will be staying in the workforce well into their seventies. He believed "we
now face public budgets strained to the breaking point by demographic aging which will crowd out all forms of capital ac-
cumulation, private and public, material and human." As if he
could imagine no worse fate for the nation, he asked how we
would like to be living in "a nation of Floridas," amid a "gray
wave of senior citizens that fills the state's streets, beaches, parks,
hotels, shopping malls, hospitals, Social Security offices, and senior centers." (Bear in mind, Peterson is himself old enough to
qualify as one of these obnoxious pests.) Tirades like this echo
the fears raised in the early 20th century about Asian immigration — hungry, alien hoards that would, so nativist fearmongers
warned, soon overwhelm the American population. In the case
of the Yellow Peril, the usual proposal was to lock the intruders
out or send them back where they came from. The dreaded Gray
Peril offers no such options. Still, one shudders to imagine what
entitlements critics have in mind for our senior population. Peterson is among those who have most forcefully proposed the
rationing of health care. By this he means finding some way to
deny dying seniors the expensive medical care that might keep
them going another few weeks, months, or years at the expense
of some health insurance company's profits.

This Leninist approach, dedicated to the steady erosion of
entitlements, has found favor among conservatives and is still in
force. Part of that scheme is the alternative that President George
W. Bush campaigned for so strenuously at the opening of his
second term in 2005. Had that proposal been approved by Congress, it would have changed the law so that workers under 55
could divert as much as one third of their Social Security payroll
tax to a private portfolio: "an account with your name on it," as
Bush liked to say, "an account you will own that nobody can take
away from you." Of course the only people trying to take Social

Security away were Bush's own people. These included at one point a nominee for Social Security commissioner who outspokenly regarded the system as "a sacred cow" that should be "led to the slaughterhouse." The president's proposal also included a deceptive new formula for price indexing that would undercut cost-of-living increases and so diminish benefits. Tried out by the president at town meetings around the country in 2005, the plan was seen for what it was, especially by seniors in attendance. Wrapped in vague promises of high earnings on the stock market, privatization would be a poison pill for Social Security. Whatever younger workers contributed to private retirement plans would be subtracted from the Social Security payroll tax; that would move the system toward insolvency at an even earlier date. To avoid that in the near term, privatization proposals often call for the government to borrow over $600 billion to make up for the shortfall, a massive, ongoing contribution to the fiscal deficits that are now bankrupting the public sector. Though the president's reform was dead on arrival in Washington, it was included in all his subsequent budget proposals and is bound to rise from the grave whenever neoconservatives gain enough power on the political right to force the issue. But their time is running out. As more boomers retire, the chance of taking away their Social Security benefits diminishes.

The irony here is acute. In their haste to wreck entitlements, Republicans, once the voice of fiscal conservatism, have signed on to run sky-high deficits. Under their leadership, the fastest growing part of mandatory government spending is not Social Security or Medicare, but interest on the national debt. Meanwhile, as doctrinaire right-wingers continue seeking for ways to kill Social Security, the corporate community is defaulting on pension plans as fast as it can, dumping them into the hands of the Pension Benefit Guaranty Corporation, the federal agency that will soon take over pension obligations from private companies throughout the economy.

This, then, is the situation boomers inherit as they move into retirement. They face an anti-entitlements opposition that is still intact, still well funded, still planning new campaigns to appease its free-market mania. They face relentless if senseless conservative hostility, as well as liberal anxiety about the nation's growing debt — largely the result of tax cuts and war. At the extreme, they will have to deal with insistent predictions in the media of fiscal meltdown and rumors of generational warfare. Is there a way forward that speaks to these fears and offers a chance to transcend our inherited notions of progress, wealth, success? Can elder power become a countercultural force?

CHAPTER 4

Elder Insurgency

Old age will only be respected if it fights for it, maintains its rights, avoids dependence on anyone, and asserts control over its own to its last breath.

— Cicero, "On Old Age," 65 BC

Bob Dylan...John Lennon...Janis Joplin...Joan Baez...Mick Jagger...Jerry Garcia. They remain the luminaries of the 1960s, young at the time and now (if still alive) growing old with the generation they helped shape. But how many boomers remember Maggie Kuhn? Not many, I suspect. And yet she may be the one figure from that period who has the most to teach us about building an elder culture.

Maggie Kuhn, a gentle but politically savvy senior citizen who had learned her politics from the Quakers, was 65 years old when she founded the Gray Panthers in 1972. She must have seemed amusingly irrelevant to the youthful boomers of the day, if indeed she registered at all amid the distractions of sex, drugs, and rock-and-roll. The experience that radicalized Kuhn was being fired by the YWCA because she had reached age 65. That struck her as outright discrimination, though of a kind few people had yet registered, certainly not the college-aged young. Of all the disadvantaged minorities whose needs found a place in the protest politics of the period, the elderly were well down the list. The political style of the time was to reject the older generation — all older generations, including the Social Security crowd. An elderly Doctor Spock may have found an honored

71

place in the anti-war movement, but there were not many others of his age who were asked to share the stage. After all, the prevailing image of old people then was both sad and comic. They were crabby, hopelessly conservative layabouts who used up their time playing canasta, lounging on the sunny beaches of Florida, or strolling the golf course. The slur became so commonplace by the late 1980s that the *New Republic*, a reasonably liberal weekly, felt free to illustrate critical reports on Social Security with images of greedy geezers who were leeching away the wealth of the nation.

Move ahead 20-some years, and here are those same boomers, now approaching the age at which Maggie Kuhn launched the Gray Panthers, and much in need of her wisdom. If boomers require a model for elder power in the years ahead, her vision of an intergenerational alliance fills the bill. Given the enduring strain of Social Darwinism still so prominent in our society in this era of globalized competition and corporate avarice, nothing could be more countercultural than an ethic of mutual aid that reaches across the generations, seeking health and long life for all.

What kind of political activist was Maggie Kuhn? She was an authentic elder, convinced that the old have a unique role to play in shaping the future. She rejected *sociogenic aging* — age as defined by calendars and legal rules. "We must act," she said, "as the elders of the tribe, looking out for the best interests of the future and preserving the precious compact between the generations." Elders, she believed, are the guardians of a heritage that belongs to the young as well as the old. As she put it, "The old, having the benefit of life experience, the time to get things done, and the least to lose by sticking their necks out, [are] in a perfect position to serve as advocates for the larger public good." From the very beginning, Kuhn saw her network of friends and allies as part of a comprehensive agenda, with resistance to the Vietnam War at the top. The name she chose for the group she formed was "the Consultation of Older and Younger Adults for Social Change" — not exactly a catchy choice. Early on, a television interviewer came up with something better: Gray Panthers. The name stuck — and so did the motto: "Age and Youth in Action."

At the time, that was a daring — some would have said a quirky — new idea. Anybody involved with seniors in the 1960s and 1970s assumed this was a sadly dependent population. Elders were those you did something *for*, rather than citizens you worked with. Kuhn knew how to court publicity; she knew her grandmotherly image appealed to the media, and she made the most of it. But she despised the condescension that came with public recognition. "I am often portrayed as a cute old lady by the press," she complained. "They love to describe my 95-pound physique, my half-moon bifocals, and my wispy bun. It is much harder for people to see the determination that lies beneath my sense of fun. Why are old people so often treated like children?" she lamented. As she saw it, real independence for seniors begins with responsibility. "We wanted to go beyond the national groups for 'senior citizens' that had already been established, the highly successful American Association of Retired Persons and the National Council of Senior Citizens. These organizations, we felt, didn't encourage older people to take control of their lives or to concern themselves with large social issues. Fighting for services and privileges for their members, many organizations for the old fell into the special interest pit, as if the old were saying to the young, 'We worked damned hard and we're going to get ours.'"

Kuhn's mildly critical swipe at *special interest* seniors reminds us that not all elders can be lumped together in a single demographic category. She was in fact inventing a new political agenda very much at odds with others of her age whom she found narrowly focused on defending their Social Security checks. In her own time, the elder insurgency she sought to foment lacked one major political feature: numbers. The demographics of the country had not reached the tipping point that would give elder voting power dominance. That day would come when the young dissenters with whom she associated her cause became the nation's largest senior population. Meanwhile, her influence has not vanished. The Gray Panthers live on, still advocating policies that serve the needs of all social groups and causes. And in their book *Aging Nation*, leading gerontologists Robert Binstock and James Schulz struck a decidedly Kuhnsian note in advocating that the next generation of elders "form a coalition with advocacy groups for children and other key organizations concerned with the welfare of family members of all ages." They asked, "Will American society witness, due to the necessity of family economics, the return of three-generation and perhaps even four-generation households? A coalition of advocates could vividly pose many such questions."[1]

Not only would such a coalition embody a sense of generosity and justice befitting the boomer generation; it would also be the best way to defend and extend Social Security and Medicare. As Maggie Kuhn saw so clearly, elders must become more than a special interest. Theirs must be a noble, far-sighted cause. They must be the spearhead of a compassionate economy that spreads its benefits to everyone. Universalizing entitlements is the best way to guarantee their survival. But how do we get there? To some degree purely impersonal historical forces will draw us in that direction. But it always helps to know what may be blowing in the wind. How might Maggie's compact unfold as boomers become the next older generation?

Stage One: The Elders' War of Independence

Revolutions are born of necessity; ideology comes later. Until the world hurts them enough, people can bear with a remarkable load of disadvantages and hardships. But when the necessities of life are threatened, they rise up even against impossible odds. The longevity revolution is apt to follow that course. In the case of the world's industrial economies, the hardships will not reach the extremes they have in other, much poorer societies. Neither police brutality nor starvation will be significant factors. But there will be indignities and privations enough to weld senior citizens into a political force in any country that lacks a welfare state offering decent health care and financial independence.

Over the next several years, we can expect to see a protracted and increasingly tedious debate over the public cost of aging boomers. (More about this in the following chapter.) Militant conservatives will announce ever more dire predictions of fiscal disaster, insisting that the cost of senior entitlements will bankrupt the nation; they will bury us in an avalanche of obscure statistics; they will continue to present proposals for still greater privatization of entitlements. The debate will at last grow intolerably boring as it stalls time and again, bogging down in half measures and devious improvisations meant to look better than they are. And then, as if by magic, it will become unmistakably clear that there is no way to fund the benefits of longevity except through tax-based public programs — big government, if you will. Even during the great conservative backlash that swept Ronald Reagan into office, it would have been fatal for any politician to suggest otherwise. When Reagan himself once hinted at the possibility of privatizing Social Security, he had to begin backpeddling the next day.

Conservatives may continue to grouse and scold, but at some point they are bound to recognize that welfare-state programs like Social Security are beginning to work in tandem with the interests of corporate America. This has nothing to do with good will or compassion on the part of corporados; it is a matter of financial necessity stemming from the pressures of globalization. Our corporate leadership is surrendering the responsibility for pensions and health care it so generously assumed in the post–World War II era. With every passing month, major

companies are shedding the benefits they once paid, often defaulting into the government's hands. In effect, the federal government's Pension Benefit Guaranty Corporation (set up under
a far-from-liberal President Richard Nixon in 1974) is becoming
the private sector's unofficial Social Security Administration. As
ultra-conservative as the George W. Bush administration may
have been, the one big-ticket domestic program it rushed to
add to Medicare was a prescription-drug benefit. So eager was
Bush to appeal to senior voters that he was willing to cram this
ill-conceived bill down the throats of congressional Republicans. True, the program was skewed to benefit the pharmaceutical industry — it prohibited Medicare from exercising any cost
control over the price of prescription drugs — but it nonetheless gave a major industry an interest in a huge federal program
meant to improve the health of elders. More important, it set up
a framework for bargaining with the drug industry as the act is
amended in years to come. When that happens, given enough
pressure from boomers determined to put an end to corporate
greed in health care, the pharmaceutical giants may wind up
taking more of a beating than they ever expected.

As the private sector closes out its health coverage and retirement programs, first for its retirees and then for all its employees,
there will be nowhere to turn but to the government — a lesson
Europeans have long since learned. Indeed, many of America's
rivals in the global marketplace are carrying far heavier benefit
loads, which ought to leave us wondering why American corporations claim to be at such a competitive disadvantage. China
may be shortchanging its elderly population, but not so the Japanese, the Germans, the Swedes. For the past two decades we
have been hearing dire warnings that the Japanese will soon be
weighed down by the cost of their growing, elderly population.
One Japanese economist made a dire prediction: "As Japan gets
older, less new investment will follow. A decline in the number
of young people will decrease the savings rate. In summary, a

probable consequence is a sharp decline in young labor, a decrease in the savings rate, and a decrease in capital formation. All these factors will contribute to the shrinking of the Japanese economy."[2] And yet it is the Japanese who have put the US auto and electronics industries to shame, taking markets away from them in their own country. In any case, whatever its official ideological position on big government, corporate America will be happy to see these burdens taken over by the public sector and assimilated into Social Security and Medicare. And once the business community has opted out of the debate, the nation's ideologues will soon have to follow suit and simply stop agitating for things only opportunistic brokers and insurance companies want to sell at prices no boomer with any sense will be willing to pay.

As other industrial nations have come to recognize, health care, paid vacations, and generous pensions are part of the social infrastructure, as much so as well-paved roads, efficient sewage systems, and clean water. Because these amenities are part of the logic of progress, they will have to be afforded in the same way we have paid for other big-ticket items in the past. The building of the railroads, the settling of the frontier, the interstate highway system, wars both civil and foreign: nobody has any idea how much these projects have cost, but they all got paid for one way or another. In this case, paying what the benefit of longevity costs is an ethical imperative, an obligation our society owes to every older generation to come. Just as the nation paid for the boomers as they grew up — laying out the cost of their health and education, the building of bigger homes in the suburbs and the commuter lifestyle that suburbia entailed — so it will pay for their retirement because nobody will have the power to say no to a large and self-assertive generation that was brought up to believe it is entitled to the good things of life.

Conservatives who snipe at entitlements, pretending to be taking the side of the exploited young against the greedy old, overlook the fact that the demographic of aging has a special characteristic. To take one example, entitlements, as Laurence Kotlikoff and Scott Burns, leading figures in the generational accounting movement, saw it, are little short of "fiscal child abuse." Their indictment was dramatic. "This is not just a moral crisis of the first order. This is the moral crisis of our age. We are collectively endangering our children's economic futures without giving them the slightest say in the matter. We are doing this systematically and with malice aforethought."[3] But what an odd, unhistorical way to frame the issue. Entitlements are hardly the cause of a moral crisis; they are the nation's response to the moral crisis of old-age indigence, a social wrong we have put a half century or more behind us. If they did not exist, we would be living with a population of penurious elders who, in the absence of personal savings, would have to be supported by their children. Moreover, the reference to *children* inspires images of helpless toddlers going without food. In fact, the children of the boomers, supposedly the main concern of generational accounting, are already in their middle age and quite capable of defending their interests. If they have not drastically reformed entitlements, that might be because they see their own need for them in the near future. Elders are not some adversarial ethnic, racial, or class-based group; they bear the names *mother, father, grandmother, grandfather.* The young are the children of the old and have every reason to make common cause with them. The bonds that tie the generations are, in reality, those very *family values* that conservatives purport to champion. Seen in that light, young and old are hardly locked into an antagonistic relationship. They are in the same boat. What this generation denies its elders is the deal it will have to live with when it retires. One need not be a rocket scientist to recognize that pooling the risk and sharing a common responsibility is the most economical and fair course. Up against demographic odds like this, what can even the most conservative do but throw in the towel?

Phillip Longman, another leading generational accountant, put an even more ominous spin on the longevity revolution. Advocating policies that would encourage more reproduction, he warned that "in a world of falling human population only fundamentalists would draw new strength. For the deep messages of the Bible and Koran and all the world's ancient religions are relentlessly pronatal. And so too are the fundamentalist ideologies of fascism and racism.... Population growth underlies our modern concept of freedom."[4] This would seem to mean that Egypt and Indonesia are freer than Holland.

The generational accountants are right in believing that, at some point, diverting resources to the welfare-state sector to meet the needs of an aging population is apt to serve as a brake upon entrepreneurial dynamism and the usual measures of economic growth. Economic growth, after all, requires investment and expansion. As Laurence Kotlikoff put it, "Every dollar the Treasury has to borrow is a dollar denied to the private sector for investment. Over time, that diversion of resources will curb economic growth and leave America poorer." But of course he means poorer by the standards of the past, leaving health and longevity out of account. This is already happening in Japan, whose population is aging faster than that of any other industrial society. As Japan registers the demand for the social services it must provide for its seniors, there is less capital to pump into the dynamic high-tech ventures that have kept the economy booming for so long. Because the Japanese are reluctant to run budgetary deficits, the fiscal choices involved in aging have shown up more dramatically with them, but it is only a matter of time before all of Japan's rivals face the same choices. The business community may feel considerable ideological unease about the reordering of priorities that comes with an aging society, but, ironically, it has only itself to blame for the result. As long as capital flows toward profitable returns in health care, pharmaceuticals, and biotechnology, smart investors are helping make us an older society. If we were ever to discover an eternal-youth pill, it would become the hottest investment on the street. But how would we pay the cost of entitlements for a race of immortals?

Stage Two: The Senior Dominance and the Health-Care Economy

As the number of seniors grows, their collective voting power will increase — at least in democratic societies around the world. Authoritarian nations — like China — may find effective ways of warehousing their aging population while they spend on more accelerated development. But where seniors have the numbers to dominate the ballot box, that will not be an option. Voting is, to be sure, a modest form of political action, but older citizens have ways to amplify their power at the ballot box. They have more money to contribute to political campaigns than most younger voters and, perhaps most important of all, more time to make available in the political process. As the active years extend deeper into old age, we may expect to see more seniors working as campaign volunteers and lobbyists. We can also expect to see them running for office. Accordingly, the influence of their needs and values upon the political agenda is bound to increase. While there is a wide range of opinion in the senior population, overwhelmingly their values clearly lead toward expanding welfare-state benefits and all goods and services related to those benefits.

Meanwhile, thanks to continuing progress in public health, nutrition, modern medical science, and biotechnology, we will find ways to extend life expectancy even further. As the number of senior citizens in the population increases, the need for and the cost of medical care will rise. Both the need and the cost will act as incentives for research and investment, encouraging still more medical progress. Research in longevity will become an ever livelier field. Health care (insurance, pharmaceuticals, hospitals, nursing homes) will become a major enterprise, steadily attracting more capital, technical talent, and entrepreneurial skill, until it becomes as important to the economy as a whole as railroads, automobiles, and high tech have been in the past. As new techniques are discovered and applied, more people will benefit from the advances. Accordingly, the ratio of older to younger in the population will increase.

Entrepreneurial values contribute to longevity in other ways, some of them highly ironic. These days enlightened employers, seeking to hold down the cost of medical insurance, take pains to look after the health of their workers. They offer heart-healthy foods in the company cafeteria, encourage regular physical checkups, perhaps open a gym on the premises to provide aerobic training. If the employer does not offer such care, insurers might, sending out literature or lecturers to pitch for better diets and exercise and to warn against smoking. No doubt the result is real immediate savings. But it is also an even longer life span. The same healthy practices that save money on the payroll lead to a larger, more long-lived retirement population. So the cost of entitlements rises and with them the payroll taxes that employers must pay — at which point, the very companies that did so much to encourage good health may complain about the cost of Social Security. They may even contribute to one of the conservative think tanks that clamor for an end to entitlements. But if the cost of entitlements results in so great a fiscal burden, then employers would do better to discourage a healthy lifestyle. Why not serve lard sandwiches and French fries in the cafeteria and provide free cigarettes?

Short of such measures, it is difficult to see how longevity and entitlements can be kept from circling round and round and increasing with each cycle. Moreover, if we include in our calculations the effects of any single major biotechnology breakthrough in reversing the aging process (a subject we will take up in later chapters), the circle might begin to accelerate, producing more older people who would extend their careers not only in literature, art, and finance, but also in medical science, thus increasing the medical expertise of our society. With each turn of the circle, more experienced and qualified scientists would give us more research in longevity and, very likely, more significant results.

In the ongoing debate over entitlements, liberals have charged conservatives with cutting back on senior entitlements in order to finance upper-income tax breaks. Conservatives, of course, hasten to deny the accusation, but were they more candid about the matter, they might frankly insist that holding down the taxes of the entrepreneurial class is a defensible concern. As they see things, unless the rich get richer, the wealth will not trickle down. Conservatives might then warn that the capital we need to launch new industries is being used to keep the elderly ambulatory. Are hip replacements and cataract surgery worth what they are costing us? The high-tech future on which investors have their eyes fixed will at some point be gravely compromised if Medicare expenditures continue to grow. And what else can they do but grow? Currently, health care absorbs about 15% of GDP in the United States. Some experts warn that this figure may grow to 29, 30, 40% over the next generation. Well, suppose that happens. Which is of greater value: adding another 100 megahertz to a microprocessor or adding another ten years to our life expectancy? On what basis do we answer such questions? There is surely no law of the marketplace that dictates that General Motors or Microsoft must make more money than Kaiser Permanente or Merck Labs. As Jonathan Cohn, editor of the *New Republic* argued, "As a nation we are creating more wealth — wealth that can easily be directed to health care rather than to, say, sport utility vehicles, either in the form of higher insurance premiums or (heaven forbid!) higher taxes."

In his book *The AARP*, an incisive analysis of the coming health-care economy, Charles Morris targeted the "counting conventions" that shape our view of service industries and of health care in particular. "There is a brawny illusion," he wrote, "about manufacturing and other goods-producing industries that makes them seem more 'real' than services.... When an older person gets a hip replacement...it does not appear so obviously on the radar screen as an increase in wealth." His conclusion was clear: "The argument that a continued shift away from traditional heavy industry toward health care will somehow impoverish the country is a compound of nonsense."[5] Among the hidden prejudices of market economics is the assumption that a productive economy is made up of healthy, young people; it reflects their needs, not the needs of the old. That is why a gadget like the iPod is hailed at the top of the network news and on the front page as a great achievement, while innovations like the MRI or interventional radiology go nearly unnoticed outside the pages of professional journals. What justifies such a discrepancy? It surely makes no financial sense. When news of the market is reported, no one makes a distinction between profits from things for the young and healthy and things for the old and infirm. The raw statistics of the matter are neutral. What we have here are simply different consumer groups spending their money on different goods. One group spends on digital novelties and designer jeans, the other spends much more on cataract surgery. As boomers shift more of their money toward their needs, we will at some point come to recognize that a health-care economy can be as prosperous as any other.

Indeed, as a foundation for our long-term industrial future, an economy based on health care offers distinct advantages. Health care has become intensely technological and so puts our best technical brains to work on obviously necessary tasks like saving lives. It is labor intensive, hiring people at both the skilled and unskilled levels at jobs in all parts of the country. And while there are a few services, like record keeping or X-ray analysis, that have been outsourced, these are marginal aspects of health care as a whole. True, one can now schedule surgical junkets to India or Thailand, but that is only because those without health insurance are looking for cheap prices. It is doubtful, in any case, that any of these offshore services will hold up over the long run in the face of inevitable malpractice suits. As for productivity, I suppose one might consider the *product* of Caesarean surgery to be one human unit, but the very idea is absurd.

At some point, plain common sense must intervene to tell us that health care makes a more defensible use of capital and resources than the high-definition (and high-expense) television we are under increasing pressure to fund. If health care raises the nation's tax bill, people will adjust in the same way they once got used to paying for clean drinking water and street lighting. They will spend less on something else in order to have a safer, healthier life. Perhaps families will cut back on season tickets for the local baseball team. And what great harm will that do? Money that now pays a mediocre shortstop several million dollars per season will flow toward paramedics, nurse practitioners, or brain surgeons. The shortstop may have to make do on a mere few million a year.

By the time health care begins to consume 40 or 50% of US GDP, we will have learned to see the benefits of such an investment. We will want what the money is buying us. Rather than regarding healing as a costly liability, we will accept what physicians and physical therapists, aerobics teachers and pharmaceutical researchers, dietitians and psychiatrists offer us as the supreme value in life. We will wake up to the fact that health and longevity are, at last, the highest stage of industrial development. We will be used to seeing more of our scientific brainpower at work in biotech than in computer animation, more caregivers than aerospace engineers. Caring will become a prominent occupation, even a profession — the signature occupation of the elder culture. I have met young people at retirement facilities specializing in elder care as gerontological doctors, nurses, counselors, and all-purpose helpers. It is not difficult to imagine this turning into a growth industry, a category of service employment that cannot be sent offshore or technologically eliminated. As the longevity revolution unfolds, we may look back upon all that came before, from heavy industry to high tech, as a dark age of deplorable waste when people did not know what really mattered.

Make a historical comparison. In the years following the Civil War, both the federal and state governments poured countless millions of dollars into subsidizing the railroads that settled the west. In today's money, those millions would amount to trillions. These were public moneys, paid out either in land or cash. The subsidies were so rich that it was all but impossible for those who won contracts to lose on the deal. They went forward with the task under no cost control or official supervision. Indeed, many of the entrepreneurs who reaped the benefits of the period knew next to nothing about railway engineering; they could buy all the brains they needed to do the job. At the time nobody protested that the government could not afford such generous grants of land, money, right-of-way and tax favors. Universally, political leaders and the public recognized the immense value of the railroads, so they paid whatever it cost to transform the country from a rural to an urban-industrial economy and to do so as rapidly as possible.

Now think of Medicare in the same category as an economic launching pad using public money to subsidize the next great phase in the nation's development. And if the nation put still more money into health care to train more physicians, build more research facilities, and construct more hospitals, it would be doing an even better job of hauling us up to that level. While waste and corruption should never be tolerated (as it was when the railroads were being built), the money we lay out for health care should be seen, not as a regrettable cost, but as an investment in economic progress.

I learned my most persuasive lesson in health-care economics from a woman named Mamie. I had just finished a lecture at a California retirement community. My lecture subject for the day was the rising cost of health care. No news to this audience, which was used to hearing economists and politicians lament what the senior population is already costing us and how much more the retiring baby boomers will add to the bill. But I came that day with a different message. When I hear that the nation's medical bill is going up, my deliberately provocative response is: "So what?" Who wants to live in a society where life expectancy is declining? The only problem I see about longevity is that the billions we pay to live longer and stay healthier are not buying fair access to good medicine for everybody. Would that the projected 20, 30, or 40% more of our national income we will be paying for health care in the future bought *all of us* 20, 30, or 40 years of extra life and reasonably good health. I would regard that as the best bargain in sight. When I was finished, Mamie was the first person to come up and shake my hand. She was 84 years old, bright eyed, smiling, and looking not the least bit burdened by her years. "Thank God somebody finally recognized how much I'm worth," she exclaimed. "What you see is a high-maintenance body. There must be 50 people making a living off of me. Why, I'm a walking medical gold mine."

Mamie saw my point. She blithely rattled off her medical record. Cataract surgery, hearing aid, dentures, quadruple heart bypass, double hip replacement, gall bladder removal, podiatric care, arthritis…I had to admire her sense of humor. It showed that she was glad to be alive, despite the ailments. And I was glad she was alive too, because, as she went on to tell me, she spends most of her retirement time at volunteer activities with children and shut-ins, valuable community service for no pay. Calculated by the hour at a fair wage, she is probably paying back a lot of her doctor bills.

As the Mamies of the world multiply, America, along with all the industrial nations, will become a health-care economy with the same spontaneous consensus that led us to span the continent with railroads in the 19th century. Money spent on and money made from health care is already fast becoming a major economic indicator; in the future it may become the major indicator. Caring for Mamie will account for more and more paychecks. Providing the medical miracles, pharmaceuticals, and prosthetic equipment she needs will earn more and more businesses and investors fat profits. Discovering ways to solve the tricky biological problems of aging will become a primary attraction for our best scientific and technological talents.

It is not just the elderly who are transforming us into a big spending health-care economy. Treating AIDS and cancer and saving premature infants incur among the highest medical costs, often beyond what insurance companies will pay. Young and old, we are in this together, wanting ever more of what modern medicine can give. Recently, it was discovered that CT scans can locate cancer at a very early operable stage. Some physicians now think mass scanning for everybody above the age of 30 might be a good idea. The only drawback? Cost. But can anybody doubt that, once the word gets around, lifesaving cancer scanning will come to be seen as a medical necessity worth more to most people than sport utility vehicles? In 2001, New Jersey, under a Health and Wellness Promotion Act, mandated that HMOs provide free annual physical examinations to every adult in the state. The testing includes pap smears, mammograms, blood tests, and sigmoidoscopies. The program will result in higher taxes to cover the costs, money that will be paid to health professionals for their services. It will also result in all the health-care costs that New Jersey residents will incur by living longer because of the tests. After all, without the program, many of them would have died sooner rather than later, some of them well before they got to their retirement years. Is this a better or worse way to use the wealth of New Jersey residents than building a new sports stadium? Does it make the state richer or poorer? How do we calculate the wealth of nations?

The time is not far off when boomers who once spent lavishly to repair their cars will spend more to repair their physiques. The *raw material* of our economy will be ailing and aging bodies; the *product* will be better health, longer lives. And if for-profit HMOs will not pay for that product willingly, they are likely to be forced to do so — if necessary to the point of driving them out of the business of life and health. Like every other economy, health care obeys the first law of money, which is that "money keeps moving." Having most of our money moving through the hands of doctors and nurses, physical therapists and pharmacists, hospital administrators and nursing home attendants frankly makes more sense to me than spending it on cars or computer games. It is both environmentally sustainable and morally defensible. As of the early 21st century, the people of the United States are spending $630 billion annually on casino and lottery gambling, a figure twice as high as the amount we spend on Medicare — and that does not factor in the possibly billions more that Americans funnel into illegal gambling for the benefit of organized crime. A January 2001 report on *60 Minutes* estimated that as much as $400 billion may be wagered each year on professional football, much of it by way of illegal Internet websites. In the near future, the amount spent on *gaming*, as it is euphemistically called, will rise as more concessions are made across the country to Native American casinos. Bear in mind, whenever you hear worried reports about the rising cost of Medicare, how much of our wealth is being fed into slot machines.

There are elements in the business community other than the pharmaceutical companies that are beginning to wake up to the profitable prospects of the coming health-care economy. In July 2006, a group of private-equity firms (Merrill Lynch and Kohlberg Kravis and Roberts, among them) laid out $33 billion to make a highly leveraged purchase of Health Corporation of America, a major hospital chain. Health-care consultants and market analysts recognized this as an effort to cash in on the aging of the baby-boom generation. The cost of health care in the United States already totals $2 trillion a year. At least a third of that amount goes to bureaucratic overhead such as processing insurance forms, running labs, and hospital administration — and that is where the profits are. As boomers retire, those figures will rise. As one health-care consultant, David Lazarus, reporting in 2006 on future investment opportunities, put it, "Everyone in the industry is waiting for the Baby Boomers. The presumption is that we're all going to be in the hospital soon."[6]

The fact that big investors are willing to go into the hospital business ought to be a convincing reply to all those who see money spent on health as a dead loss. It surely will not be for those who own the means of treatment. But this is also a warning. If health care remains as privatized as it now is and with as little cost and quality control imposed by government, consumers will be at risk of seeing bookkeepers and shareholders determine even more about their treatment than we see today. The result will be ethically compromised medicine, involving the closing of low-earning hospitals, shorter stays in the hospital, lesser-skilled personnel, poorer equipment. That is invariably what happens when welfare-state programs are mingled with market values. It will be the boomers' responsibility to make sure the health-care economy they are entering will not be simply another for-profit business.

We might have achieved that goal as long ago as the mid-1990s when Bill Clinton made health-care reform a major element in his presidential campaign. That opportunity was badly botched when Clinton used the occasion as an opportunity to have his wife barnstorm the country taking soundings on an issue that had already been much discussed and whose solution was obvious. This was a clear waste of time that allowed the insurance industry to mount an effective counterattack. Instead, Clinton might simply have revised Medicare, making it available to every American citizen regardless of age. That is the position that has been taken by the AFL-CIO. Private insurance companies might stay in the business, but they would have to compete with Medicare. This they could have done by offering an upscale, privatized option for those rich enough to afford high premiums. There is business to be done at that level, as the British learned when Mrs. Thatcher opened the National Health Service to private insurance.

Stage Three: The Rise of the Compassionate Sector

Whatever position the law may finally take, those who retire from the workforce, whether voluntarily or not, will include an increasing number of healthy, active, highly skilled men and women. By the time they begin their retirement, they may even be the beneficiaries of breakthroughs in biotechnology that bring them a life expectancy that stretches beyond 100 years. There they will be, retired by the millions, with nothing but time on their hands.

Leaving so much skill untapped is the one cost of retirement that nobody is likely to regard as affordable. Finding ways to recycle this enormous pool of senior energy — one commentator calls it "quite possibly this country's only increasing natural resource" — is apt to become an industry in its own right and is, in fact, already under intense study by social scientists and policy makers. The job boom of the 1990s in the United States was largely related to the increased recruitment of retired workers, many of them at bargain-basement wages — and with no need to provide them with a pension or health-care plan. As naturally as water flows downhill, we will soon find ourselves improvising a postindustrial economy in which increasing numbers of older Americans work voluntarily as the spirit moves them, at occupations — perhaps vital occupations — that are nothing like employment as we have known it. They will have only the most tenuous connections with standard hiring, ordinary scheduling, or a conventional paycheck. Transferring over to so divergent a pattern of working life may take some painful adjustment, but in fact it should be seen as a sign of our economy's ever-increasing productivity. Needing less labor to produce the necessities, let alone the wasteful luxuries of daily life, we will have more leisure than we have yet learned to handle gracefully.

Some among the well-to-do have taken volunteering quite seriously as a personal ideal, but voluntarism can also function as a rhetorically effective riposte to liberal proposals for government relief, welfare, and public works. We should recall that voluntarism entered American politics as the pet project of President Herbert Hoover, who believed all social problems might be solved by grass-roots generosity. He was himself the embodiment of conscientious, unpaid public service. But his high hopes revealed their limitations after the Crash of '29. By no stretch of the imagination could a disaster of such dimensions be solved by the Salvation Army or Catholic charities. It was at that point that the first federal entitlements were initiated under the Roosevelt New Deal.

Yet the very fact that presidents as conservative as Hoover, Reagan, and the first George Bush turned voluntarism into a talking point in their domestic agendas has sparked ambitious social thought about what is now often called the *Third Sector*. In Europe, where the third sector is frequently regarded as the first sector in its importance, the name more often used is Civil Society Organizations. CSOs or Third Sector groups are the sum total of all volunteer and service work — most of it nonprofit — that takes place outside the marketplace. More and more, such organizations fill in the growing gap between government bureaucracy and private companies, offering more attention and protection than people can find elsewhere. This would be the main locus of all the volunteer work we might expect of retired elders; it is almost perfectly designed for their abilities, values, and availability. When all the people, the projects, and the assets currently involved in the Third Sector in the United States are pooled, we arrive at some strikingly large numbers. As of the beginning of the 21st century, there are a million and a half nonprofit, Third Sector organizations with combined assets of $500 billion. These organizations account for 10% of the nation's employment; the money they spend for social projects is greater than the gross national product of all but seven nations. The rising number of able and experienced elders in our society will make itself felt in the workforce in many ways, not least of all in the Third Sector, employment that eludes all the usual careerist and financial motivations and which will gradually alter the nature of work throughout the society.

Despite its size, economists give little attention to the Third Sector, mainly because it tends to operate in informal ways that produce few statistics. This is not what modern economics was created to study. Its focus is on major industries, major cash flows, international markets — the big, exciting stuff that leads to billion-dollar fortunes. In contrast, the Third Sector pays little in the way of taxable wages and produces nothing that can be measured as *output*. In that sense, the Third Sector is a great theoretical challenge to economic theory. It is comprised of all the work, all the funds, all the resources that hold communities together in such fields as education, day care, health care, legal advocacy, sheltering and feeding the homeless, drug rehabilitation, and elder care. Yet, one looks in vain for some recognition of its value in standard economic texts or in the financial pages.

In other lands, the situation is very different. In France, where, as in all the European nations, unemployment has been rising inexorably, the volunteer workforce is seen as one important way to employ people in what is called the *social economy*. The French have been willing to offer a guaranteed income to those who agree to contribute time to that economy. The idea is not far removed from the now-familiar American welfare reform that puts people to work at community service jobs like cleaning up the streets and parks or wiping the graffiti off walls, work that often goes unpaid in the United States and thus amounts to a form of servitude. But again there are hopeful signs of change. In 2007 the Conference Board, the business-intelligence service that collects the nation's leading economic indicators, issued a call for new policies to recruit, train, and above all retain retired talent for nonprofit organizations where turnover has become almost crippling. Along with Civic Ventures, it announced awards for programs that seek to utilize older workers in nonprofits and to make such employment more appealing. Among the innovations that were rewarded were flexible hours, help with telecommuting, and grandchild care for elders who would otherwise be tied down with child-minding responsibilities.

Conservatives like to see voluntarism as an alternative to government. But the two can work in tandem, exchanging resources and inspiration. Government can empower the Third Sector, often in very simple ways. For example, it could channel what is now welfare money through nonprofit and voluntary organizations to allow them to expand their workforce in the community. It could create a *shadow wage* that allows tax deductions for the value of the time one contributes to volunteer work. When we identify the retired as volunteers and assume that they are willing and able to work for nothing, we may be badly mistaken. For Social Security recipients who are dependent on family to pay their full cost of living, a paid job, even a modestly paid job, makes perfect sense. There are several million Social Security recipients who now must scramble to supplement their meager government stipend. What they find are usually catch-as-catch-can, part-time jobs at meager pay. It would clearly make far greater sense to pay retirees to work at something they know or to assume long-term caregiving responsibilities for members of their own generation. But by far the neatest, least bureaucratic way to achieve that goal is simply to give them higher Social Security payments so they will be free to volunteer. Would this run up the bill for entitlements? Of course. But it would be payment for useful services that must be done one way or another. We are rich enough to pay compassion the wage it deserves.

While this is a speculative scenario, it does not assume more than the continuing demographic thrust of a growing elder population and a few commonsense economic necessities. Even with minimum forethought and a near total lack of imagination, how else would we expect things to turn out in the years ahead? This is what the aging of the modern world is likely to bring us. But add a modicum of ethical energy and some honest idealism, and think of how much more might come of those same inevitable changes. In the same way that the forces of industrialism inspired the great social movements and ideological crusades of the 19th century, so the force of longevity may carry over into utopian designs that will at last touch our industrial power with as much moral character as the cry for social justice that saved earlier generations from wage slavery and corporate feudalism. But in this case the victory will not be that of a class or a race or an ethnic group, but for all who grow old, all who must come to terms with mortality.

The Crunch

We should not assume that the scenario outlined here will play out as a smooth transition. Indeed, the rise of the elder culture will take place against stubborn conservative resistance. The battle lines in that confrontation were drawn as far back as the 1980s, when a president supposedly committed to strict fiscal restraint authorized military spending that ran the national debt into the stratosphere. Some 20 years later, in 2002, Vice President Dick Cheney, a veteran of that giddy, spendthrift era, drew the lesson that had become the basis of neoconservative policy: "Reagan proved that deficits don't matter." Provided, that is, that the deficits are all military — and so great that they crowd out even long-standing social programs. When old-line conservatives heard those words, they must have realized they were not living in Kansas any longer. The balanced-budget, cautiously international conservatism of Barry Goldwater and of Robert Taft before him, had been swept away, replaced by a big-government, big-spending, militarized ideology ready to bully the world into a new imperial order. That was the green light to begin pouring red ink.

So there is bound to be fierce opposition from right-wing elements who will insist that we cannot afford the vast expansion of entitlements we have been discussing. For indeed they have done their best to validate that message of fiscal doom, spending more and more public money on military bases and salaries, extravagant Pentagon hardware, and especially on private contractors, a new, privatized militia which is turning the security of the nation into a splendidly lucrative mercenary business. With a recklessness that was truly breathtaking, the Bush administration committed the nation to a colossally expensive and interminable war — *and* at the same time it cut taxes. The result has been a ballooning national debt, more and more financed by foreign investors including Sovereign Investment Funds under the control of governments like China or the Arab emirates. According to one calculation made in 2006 by the Government Accounting Office, the United States was running a deficit in the funding for major social programs (like senior entitlements) of $46 trillion. That is an increase from $20 trillion in 2000 due mainly to the fiscal policies of the Bush administration (the big tax cuts) and the cost of wars in Iraq and Afghanistan. More and more each year, we are living off the forbearance of foreign investors. Is this prudent? Is this safe? The issue has hardly been discussed. Instead, the neoconservatives have rushed forward with credit-card budgeting whose goal is to starve the public sector and so drive everything — war-making, education, health care, infrastructure maintenance, law enforcement — toward privatization, public services offered for private profit. Thus, the American public is left to believe that the world's most dynamic and prosperous economy cannot afford to insure its children against illness or provide them with a decent public education — or offer any of the amenities other societies make available.

But there is bound to come a moment of truth when elders, driven by necessity, will demand that the money be made available to fund the entitlements that represent their very survival. And where will that money be found except in the pockets of corporate America, where it has been stashed away in ever-increasing amounts since the days of the Reagan presidency? When the crunch comes, the elder culture, with its ever-growing voting power, will find the leadership it needs, politicians who will, perhaps opportunistically, perhaps sincerely, recognize an electoral groundswell when they see it. And we will hear the old populist battle cry: "Soak the rich!" Just as Franklin Roosevelt imposed a wealth tax on the "economic royalists" of the 1930s, demanding that they foot the bill for the programs needed to end the Great Depression, so an insurgent elder generation will make the corporados pay.

Thanks to the devious fiscal policies of the Reagan and Bush presidencies, that contest will play out against the background of a towering national debt that has been created by cutting the taxes of the well-to-do and fighting futile wars in the Middle East. Even as the demographic numbers and the voting power of elders increase, voices on the right wing will insist that the cost of longevity is unaffordable. They will argue that in increasing numbers Americans must reconcile themselves to being poor or becoming poor because the money to meet their needs simply is not there. But of course it is there. It is there in the hands of those who have profited outlandishly from a piratical stock market; from trade treaties like GATT, NAFTA, and most-favored-nation arrangements with China; from the rising cost of oil;

from the manipulation of financial markets by bankers, brokers, and hedge-fund managers; from the exploitation of cheap labor in the global economy; from no-bid military contracting for an increasingly privatized army; and from countless corporate acquisitions and mergers that have done little more than run up stock prices. For the past generation, we have been practicing trickle-up economics at the expense of the working poor and the middle class, who have been bled white by the skyrocketing cost of oil, health care, education, housing, and credit. They have endured the dislocations and job losses of a global economy that has brought them little more than cheap and shoddy foreign-made merchandise at big-box stores. Who, then, will pay for the longevity revolution? Whatever the outcome, entitlements will be the battlefield on which the first great campaigns of the elder culture are waged.

How rich are the rich? And where do they keep their treasures? These are among the most closely guarded secrets in the modern world, deep financial mysteries enveloped in bureaucratic obfuscation and arcane accounting, and often protected by the banking and investment laws of other nations. How can the public know the true financial state of companies like Haliburton and KBR after they have moved their headquarters to Dubai or an island nation one can hardly find on the map? Are these even American companies any longer? This much is certain: The corporate community has been skimming the wealth of the nation for over a generation since the Reagan administration began deregulating as much of the economy as possible. It has been running sky-high profits in a more and more corporate-friendly economy, most recently growing fatter still on the wars in the Middle East. Untold billions have passed into their hands, little of it subject to honest bookkeeping. The global economy, working to beat down wages and living standards, has operated wholly in their favor, offering ordinary Americans little more than Wal-Mart bargains on shoddy, foreign-made goods. For conservatives, who insist that taxes must never be raised, those profits, whether gained by hook or crook, are sacrosanct, never to be reclaimed. Neoconservatives like to deny that there is any such thing as an entitlement, but they claim one for the corporate elite they serve: the right to unlimited and unreported profit. But that will be a feeble ideological defense against the needs and the voting power of the elder culture. At some point the corporados will have to decide if they want to be part of the American community, sharing in the responsibility for making their society healthier and wealthier — or a class apart, swinishly rich but without a country, continually scrambling to find somewhere to sequester their riches — possibly in a galaxy far, far away.

I suspect that when the crunch comes, it will resolve itself quickly — within a few, hard-fought election cycles. In much the same way that Americans of every regional and cultural variation joined the New Deal of the 1930s, we will see the same powerful, national consensus form behind the priorities of the elder culture. It will not be a matter of deep philosophical analysis, but a simple recognition of what justice, decency, and physical necessity demand.

Boomer Daughters in Revolt

Every political revolution has its moment of decisive drama: the point of no return — the Boston Tea Party, the destruction of the Bastille, the attack on the Winter Palace. The longevity revolution is not that kind of revolution, but it may have its defining moment of rebellion.

I will hazard a prediction. One of the first hard-fought encounters of the longevity revolution will arise from our society's most exploited class. It would probably take most people several guesses before they identified what that class is; there are many among our working poor who might qualify. But I have in mind the most invisible workers in the United States, a house-bound proletariat that remains unknown because it is exploited in the name of love and victimized in the name of duty. They are the private caregivers of our society.

Who are the caregivers of America today? Knock on any door. You are likely to find these silent heroes struggling to serve the needs of young and old alike throughout your neighborhood. They come from all classes, well-off and poor. They might be adult daughters who lovingly tend to an incontinent mother, or sons whose elderly fathers have difficulty admitting their dependency. They may be spouses caring for lifetime companions long after the romance has gone out of their marriages. Or they may be parents faced with months of care for a child diagnosed with incurable cancer. Sometimes in a public park or at a ball game or museum we catch sight of one or more of the disabled on a field trip. Perhaps they are temporarily in the care of special attendants, but behind every one of them there is a family somewhere who will take them back into care at the end of the day, resuming the demanding routine that is theirs for a lifetime. As of the beginning of the 21st century, 22.4 million American families — one in every four American households — are now looking after frail or disabled members over the age of 50. Each month, these families spend a total of $1.5 billion of their own money on the care of a sick relative or disabled acquaintance. Caregiving is being done by families because home care is presently the only alternative to cruelly expensive institutionalization. Until they are forced to face the harsh financial truth of their situation, few families realize that Medicare does not pay for long-term care services, which can run as high as $50,000 a year.

This is the fate that boomer women have found waiting for them, the role they are expected to welcome as a way of closing out their lives. For it is women — daughters or daughters-in-law — far more than men who are suffering the pressure of home-based caregiving. While caregivers come in many shapes and sizes, their gender is all but uniform. Ninety-nine percent of paid caregivers today are women, most of them ethnic minorities who earn minimum wage and have no benefits. As for the country's unpaid caregivers, they are also overwhelmingly female. For the most part, they are middle-aged women, hidden away in the privacy of their homes, working for no pay at all at a task of the most demanding character, work that is often a matter of life and death. The AARP estimates that three-quarters of the people looking after sick or disabled family members in those households are women; others place the figure at 90%. In 1992, H. M. Zal coined the new phrase, referring to women thrown into this role somewhere in their middle years as the *sandwiched generation*. No sooner do they finish raising their children than their ailing parents move in for care. As of 2000, the average age of daughters taking care of their parents was in the mid-50s; more than a third were over 65 and were destined to spend more of their lives *parenting* their parents than they had spent caring for their children. Imagine for a moment women in their fifties and sixties saddled with this role for most of the rest of their lives. When anti-entitlements critics step forward supposedly to defend "our children" from paying for the burden of entitlements, these women make their claim ring hollow. Far from being helpless babes in arms, many of those children are themselves on the brink of retirement. And many more are already so weighed down with home care that the last thing they want is to be saved from the entitlements monster. How many caregivers want to finish their exhausting day worrying over a retirement-investment portfolio — the alternative to Social Security favored by conservatives?

Women remain our society's default caregivers, those expected to provide tender loving care whether they like it or not. They must reschedule their workday, delay promotions, and sacrifice career advancement to take care of a loved one. Caregiving is often done at the price of depriving women of the education or career they were looking forward to after their children have left home. How many of them might have been gifted teachers, doctors, lawyers, or engineers? How much might they have added to the GDP had they stayed in the job market? In the years to come, these patterns of elder dependence will shift, but not in ways that favor voluntary home care. Not only are families shrinking, but in all the developed societies, women are waiting longer to have their first child; the average age is now close to 30. This means they will reach their senior years about the time their children are starting their own families. Even if they remain in good health into their seventies, they may be turning to their children — mainly their daughters — for several years of care when their children are in their forties with young children still at home. Instead of being sandwiched between dependent children and parents, caregivers, with fewer siblings to help out, will be overlapped and overwhelmed by responsibilities that can only grow more demanding and expensive.

One thing seems certain: As caregiving grows more gendered, it will become a hot button issue on the national scene. Sooner or later we are apt to see women of the sandwiched generation, those who are now subsidizing elder care out of their own bank accounts and thwarted aspirations, stretched to the limit. Their demand for help will take its place near the top of women's political agenda.

One characteristic of boomers has often been satirized. They *workshop* everything. That is, they get *into* things, turning every experience into a study, from death, divorce, and taxes to straightening up their desks. Identify something as a *problem* and, as if by magic, *experts* emerge and courses are scheduled at the university extension. It was inevitable that as caregiving came to be an unofficial occupation, expertise would grow up around it. The books, magazines, hotlines, websites, and counselors multiply by the year. The books bear names like *How Did I Become My Parent's Parent?*, *Are Your Parents Driving You*

Crazy?, *Caring for the Parents Who Cared For You*, *Coping With Your Difficult Older Parents: A Guide for Stressed-Out Children*, and *Caring for Yourself While Caring for Your Aging Parents*.

As the titles suggest, much of the advice has that kind of frankness we have come to expect from a psychologically so-phisticated — and saturated — boomer society. It is directed as much to the needs of the giver as the receiver. This is both honest and practical. Nobody who serves in a worthy cause these days is unaware of burnout and the toll it takes. Burnout is the result of assuming any task without some psychological sensitivity to its burdens and liabilities. So the books advise caregivers to de-fine the limits of what they can do, consider their own health, give themselves a break when they need it, let their frustrations hang out periodically, and seek assistance fast when they can-not cope.

Candor like this is a hopeful sign. What is bound to come of it is a prompt realization that the fiscally cheap solution of unloading elder care on families is not the best solution. This is saving money at the expense of middle-class and working-class families. Worse, it may be a way to destroy even the best-intentioned families by burdening them — especially the woman of the house — beyond endurance. The result of that will be not only poor care but resentment, hard feelings, strife, and abuse. As the elderly live longer, and as gerontological medical science advances, many of the problems of old age require more than amateurish, part-time attention. Caring for an ailing parent is no longer a brief stint; it may go on for 10 or 20 grueling and expen-sive years. The classic Victorian family dealt with aged parents by seating them in front of the fire, bringing them an occasional cup of tea, and waiting for them to stop breathing. The wait was usually not long. Maybe the love was there, but not the skill and patience that elder care now demands. Nobody in the past had to administer medication (injections, IV feeding, dialysis), take blood, stool, and urine samples, give physical therapy, prepare special foods, offer aerobic exercise, groom, dress, and bathe a fragile body, tolerate dementia, and deal with depression — one's own as well as the parent's. This is not a minor household chore; it is a full-time occupation. And beyond all this there is the vexation that comes with paying bills and collecting reimbursements, processing paperwork, and struggling with agencies and accountants. When it comes to the nitty-gritty details of elder care, it is hypocritical to envision such service as anything but a hard, bankrupting job.

As all the elder-care manuals emphasize, guilt is not the appropriate response for those who find themselves overwhelmed by an ordeal like this. The extensive care that the frail and infirm require is uniquely the result of modern medicine. Nobody in any previous culture was expected to handle demands of this magnitude while raising a family or trying to have a life of their own. We are keeping people alive well beyond any limit for which the family was designed to provide wholly self-reliant care. Most families still prefer to keep parents at home; they make the effort, but the sooner we recognize the emotional and financial limits of home care for the elderly, the sooner we will begin looking for better alternatives that are bound to take the form of public programs.

Private home care is usually praised as an expression of love. But let us be blunt. In the context of the longevity revolution, public policy that unloads the total responsibility for elder care on private households has nothing to do with love. It has to do with avoiding taxes for a crying social need. The true task of love is to find the best possible care for those we hold dear. And that will not always be home care, not if all the work and all the bills fall on the caregivers. Love means fighting for something better.

Full-time, full-scale home care is bound to become an urgent issue as women find themselves sinking ever deeper into the harsh responsibilities that come with longevity. They will demand relief — and they will surely get it. The revolt of the caregivers, when it comes, may be the turning point in the history of the elder culture, as distinctive and defining as the anti-war rallies of the 1960s and 1970s. But how different it will be — a rebellion embedded in family values, a giant step toward building a compassionate public sector, the most positive and personal of all political struggles.

As far back in the past as we have historical records, politics has been an arena of bitter conflict, where bare survival was often at stake and where parochial loyalty was the greatest cause many could imagine. With few exceptions, scarcity was the order of the day, and competition was the norm. Caught up in the daily turmoil, when did people have the time to attend to the private and the personal? When was it time to be human? The gap between the anger and struggle that fills the streets and the quiet yearnings of the inner life has been the curse of our species. But the elder culture brings us face to face with ultimate questions that must now be formulated as matters of public discussion: life, death, loss, pain, purpose, salvation. Elder power, wisely used, may be the point at which a very different politics becomes possible, perhaps necessary — the chance to explore the philosophical depths that have been there inside us all along and to find that elusive sense of fulfillment we call the meaning of life.

CHAPTER 5

Entitlements for Everyone

*There is no wealth but life. Life, including all its powers
of love, of joy, and of admiration. That country is richest
which nourishes the greatest number of noble and happy
human beings; that man is richest who, having perfected
the functions of his own life to the utmost, has also the
widest helpful influence, both personal and by means of
his possessions, over the lives of others. A strange political
economy; the only one, nevertheless, that ever was or can
be: all political economy founded on self-interest being but
the fulfillment of that which brought schism into the Polity
of angels and ruin into the Economy of Heaven.*

— John Ruskin, *Unto This Last*, 1860

During their years of youthful struggle, protesting boomers put up a good fight against a powerful opposition.
They took on the military-industrial complex in campaigns
that ranged from irreverent, publicity-grabbing prankishness
to militant civil disobedience — with a bit of amateurish bomb-
throwing at the extreme. They staged teach-ins on campuses, tied
up major cities and presidential conventions with mass demonstrations, invaded the offices of university presidents, set fire to
money at the New York Stock Exchange, blocked troop trains,
burned draft cards, stuck flowers in the gun muzzles of grim-
faced troops guarding the Pentagon — and even threatened to
levitate the building. At the height of protest, they succeeded
in driving two presidents from office and put a ragged end to

a misguided war. They put their weight behind civil rights and voting rights legislation; they helped open doors that had been locked against women and minorities; they made the university more culturally universal than it had ever been and launched an environmental movement that has found a permanent place in our politics. They also provoked a conservative backlash of unprecedented determination and cunning that has turned back the clock on many of their achievements and has set the stage for a new period of radical social change. In their elder years, how will they do in the rematch?

Since the Reagan presidency, three opponents that were among the principal targets of protest in the 1960s — the corporados, the war lords, and the universities — have regrouped and found ways to return to their old habits. Who would have guessed in 1975, after the war in Vietnam came to its humiliating end and the Watergate scandal played out to its dismal climax, that another, more powerful and profitable military-industrial complex would soon rise from the ashes, this time directed not by liberals but by neoconservatives committed to an imperial agenda? But that is exactly what has happened. Corporate America, resurrected during the high-flying 1980s from disgrace, has, through mergers and acquisitions that have come to be all but automatically approved, become more gargantuan than ever. It has fattened into a laissez-faire global economy where it is free to move offshore and find greater profits in lands where it can flout labor and environmental laws. Trade and tariff agreements like GATT and NAFTA — as much the gift of Democrats as of Republicans — have given multinational corporations the power to move capital and break unions while enjoying limitless investment opportunities in new booming economies like India and China. As if legal profits of record levels were not enough, lax regulation has permitted more corruption and scamming in the business world than at any time since the days of Calvin Coolidge. CEOs have once again become "the privileged princes" of the nation (as Franklin Roosevelt once labeled them), richly compensated even when they ruin the companies they head. They have become celebrities in their own right; their wealth, as well as their marriages, infidelities, divorces, and antics are shamelessly on display in the media. They are the Marie Antoinettes of the new world order — and without any guillotines in sight.

At the same time, the Pentagon, the chief agency of neoconservative chauvinism and the beneficiary of uncontrolled deficit spending, has accumulated more money and power than it enjoyed while it was stumbling through the Vietnam War. Now integrated with a growing number of private military contractors, its ties with the corporate world have become even tighter than in the past. Generals continue to circulate through the revolving doors that lead from Washington to lucrative jobs in private industry, now with more contracts to spread around and more expensive military technology at their disposal than they know what to do with. The war on terrorism has become far more advantageous to the Pentagon than the Cold War ever was, because it is a war that can never end nor even be clearly defined — and so its theaters of action have spread opportunistically across the planet as a new Worldwide Attack Matrix. Mercenary warriors have freed the military from the need to deal with the sort of troublesome conscripts that crippled the war effort in Vietnam.

As for the universities, though they are now more multicultural than ever in their curriculum and more open to technological innovation, the runaway cost of higher education has made them greater bastions of privilege than the schools that were seeking to offer a free-to-cheap college education in the post–World War II period. With an unaccountable irony, many boomers who once gloried in dropping out of the stifling irrelevance of academia have, upon dropping back in, become fiercely competitive about placing their children in *the best schools*, meaning those that offer the most prestigious careers. And so once again the universities have become corporations by another name, tied to the marketplace by their services to the business community, run by administrators who pride themselves on earning CEO salaries.

The changing character of the university connects with one of the major stories of the late 20th century: the rise of the right-wing intelligentsia — and an aggressive intelligentsia at that, determined to settle scores and win points with its liberal opposition. This is a significant cultural transformation, one that has placed considerable intellectual force on the side of corporate values. In the process, this has made the university less than friendly to the elder culture, if not outright hostile.

Viewed against its historical background, this is an astonishing change. Through the early and middle years of the 20th century, intellect was virtually a liberal monopoly. That connection dates back to the Progressive movement of Teddy Roosevelt's day. Progressivism, the most potent force for reform in US history, was a university-based movement of books and magazines, academic research, and investigative journalism. It bubbled with new ideas for empowering people against the raw power of city bosses and big business. Roosevelt himself was an intellectual, a man proud of his learning who spoke like a book, perhaps the only president we have had who ranked as a genius. Under the guidance of leaders like this, reformers of the Progressive era recruited academic specialists to serve on the new regulatory commissions that were then being established at the state and federal levels.

From that point forward, liberals developed strong connections with the universities, while conservatives — and especially the business community — came to distrust intellectuals as the main spokespeople for reform, if not (on the far left) outright revolution. Intellect was the enemy of wealth. Journalists (like the muckrakers) and novelists of the early 20th century portrayed conservatives as philistines who took no interest in ideas.

Sinclair Lewis's meathead salesman Babbitt became the emblem of his class; those who took the side of the moneyed few were the "boobocracy." A generation later in the 1930s, the second Roosevelt reinforced and augmented liberalism's intellectual credentials. By offering subsidies to the arts and literature through the PWA, the New Deal enlisted still more intellectuals for liberal causes; Roosevelt took pride in surrounding himself with a brain trust largely made up of university professors. As of the mid-20th century, the reigning minds in the universities (even the Ivy League schools), the media, and the intellectual world were generally well left of center. Liberals published most of the weighty journals of opinion and took the initiative in setting up think tanks where new ideas and social programs might be brainstormed.

But since the 1970s, the corporate community, as if racing to make up lost ground, has invested heavily in brain power. It has launched political journals, subsidized books, and set up foundations. Above all, it has drawn university students to its cause through well-endowed political clubs and organizations like the Young Americans for Freedom. The United States today abounds in conservative think tanks largely funded by corporate money. The media are filled with columns, op-ed commentaries, magazines, and books that quote — usually quite sententiously — from Edmund Burke or *The Federalist Papers* to justify their policy recommendations. The stilted literary style of conservative journalists William F. Buckley and George Will — big words, convoluted sentences, a smug tone — has spread among right-wing writers as a way to advertise the benefits of the best education money can buy. The number of conservative journals has increased markedly, even as it has become more and more difficult to sustain a magazine of any kind; few political publications can survive these days without foundation money or private patronage. Conservatives have been especially successful in drawing a popular following through radio and television. Fox

News, the roaring voice of the flag-waving far right, has become the most watched network in the country. It is now routine on television talk shows to feature experts from the Heritage Foundation, the Cato Institute, the American Enterprise Institute, the Concord Coalition, and any number of military, foreign-policy, and economic study centers — and to ignore or exclude views that fall to the left of the Democratic Party. This last — muzzling the radical opposition — is more of a victory for the right than gaining greater visibility for conservative views. It is no worse than the left once did in assuming conservatives had nothing of intellectual value to offer, but in either case the result is to narrow the choices before us. What the hunger for divergence was to the teach-ins, free universities, and underground press of the 1960s, the search for convenient and familiar dichotomy is to the media of the early 21st century.

It was only a matter of time before this rightward shift in the cultural climate would reach the universities and especially the business and economics departments which have become strongholds of free-market theory. Thanks to the universities, the infatuation with "the magic of the marketplace" (Ronald Reagan's term) has reached cult-like status. The word has come to summarize the entire course of modern history. *Markets* won the Cold War. *Markets* are the world's guarantee of freedom and prosperity. *Markets* are the panacea for all social ills. Just as Christian missionaries once went forth to convert heathen peoples to the one true faith, so neoconservatives, armed with corporate billions and the military of the world's only superpower, would bring the gospel of markets to a benighted humanity. By the very curriculum that is spread before them in the universities, students are taught that labor and socialist-oriented economics are defunct and social justice a thing of the past. Keynesian economics, the dominant mid-20th century school of thought in the field, is held to be irrelevant. In its place we have what Kevin Phillips, who was once a Republican political consultant, calls "market absolutism." He includes this satiric hymn in his excellent analysis, *Wealth and Democracy*

> We have seen the speeches and metaphors of conservative politicians, bankers, and journalists hailing markets as economic voting machines and corporations as the democratic selectees of the marketplace.... Such choruses swelled during the 1990s like an economic version of Handel's *Messiah*. The market and the people are one and the same. *Hallelujah*. Buying, selling, and consuming is true democracy. *Hallelujah*. Popular will is expressed through the law of supply and demand. *Hallelujah*. Populism is market economics. *Hallelujah*. Opposition to the verdict of the market is elitism. *Hallelujah*. The Nations and the Peoples shall rejoice. *Hallelujah. Hallelujah!*[1]

In this theology of market economics, it is important to note the stunning disconnect with political reality. In what sense is the liberal economics of John Maynard Keynes obsolete? There is not a nation in the world that does not hold its government responsible for managing its economy; there is not a political leader anywhere who is not willing to claim credit for achieving economic stability and growth — even when they fail to do so. These are the irreducible hallmarks of Keynesian policy, simple truths taught by hard-won historical experience: that no economy runs by itself, that the economy is a human creation subject to human values and desires, that there are no laws of the marketplace that trump common sense or social ethics. Nobody in elected office openly advocates laissez-faire, even if it holds a fond place in their hearts. And yet in the universities we have learned men and women insisting that democracy is inextricably tied to a free-market orthodoxy that would be the ruin of nations.

The soaring good fortunes of the entrepreneurial elite are well known. Similarly, the war on terror keeps the military brass in the news. But the role of the university as a key institution of the conservative backlash is less visible. For that reason I give it special attention here, mainly because campus conservatives, championing market values and at war with *big government*, are now contributing significantly to the campaign against entitlements. Boomers have a greater stake than they may realize in what the universities of the nation have to say about the elder culture.

Justice Between the Generations

Free-market economics and the elder culture are not a good fit. The truth is they are radically antagonistic. There is simply no way to meet the need for a decent retirement and first-class health care except by big government programs, well financed and well monitored for fairness and efficiency. All this — the taxes and the oversight necessary — rub against the grain of the market with its steadfast commitment to self-interest, profit, and competitive individualism. Yet by a marvelous historical irony, the generation that would become guardians of the entitlements was coming of age at just the moment that market economics was taking over the very universities which were the headquarters of the protest movement. Even while the counter culture was in the streets reviling everything about the society that corporate America had created — and especially the *multiversities* so tightly integrated with the military-industrial complex — the universities were gravitating toward the most conservative stance they have held since higher education was an upper-class privilege in the pre–Civil War era.

This sea change on the campuses began with the crucial field of economics. In 1968, the same year protestors besieged the Democratic Party convention in Chicago, Milton Friedman, then president of the American Economics Association, delivered a historic address at the AEA conference that is usually identified as the end of the Keynesian hegemony in his profession. The address aimed some shrewd criticisms at the policies that the New Deal had used to fight the Great Depression and which had become dear to liberalism. Friedman declared Keynesian fiscal manipulations — tax cuts, public works, welfare — to be useless or even counterproductive. All they do is encourage inflation. There is a "natural rate of unemployment," Friedman argued, and fiscal policy cannot change that. Best to let the market run by itself — meaning let it be run by corporate decision-making. However accurate Friedman's critique was, its effect was to unleash a backlog of free-market economic theory in his profession, the gist of which was that the federal government cannot do much to micromanage the economy. Large government programs like Social Security and Medicare that transfer income from one group to another are especially anathema to post-Friedman economics — not simply as a matter of philosophical preference, but as a matter of practical policy.

In the universities and at conservative think tanks, the opposition to entitlements has taken the form of generational accounting. The creation of (among others) the economists Laurence Kotlikoff of Boston University and Alan Auerbach of the University of California, Berkeley, generational accounting has become the academic arsenal for the war against entitlements. A single-issue school of economics, its focus is the nation's senior dependency load, meaning the way in which wealth is distributed over time between retired Americans and their working children. Run the numbers, say the generational accountants, and the result is horrifying, a grave injustice between the generations. For example, they calculate that Americans born in 1930 have paid a net tax equaling 30% of their income for what they have eventually received in return from entitlement benefits; those born in 1950 will have paid 33%, and so on. If current policies continue, Kotlikoff estimates that progeny of the post-baby-boom generation will be facing a net tax of 84% for entitlements alone! "What that's telling you," he warned, "is that current fiscal policy is unsustainable and generationally un-conscionable. We need to pay more and spend less today so our kids won't be taxed to death." Otherwise, the result will be a "fis-cal train wreck."[2]

The generational accountants can be credited with raising a valid issue that every nation must face frankly: the full, long-range cost of pension and health care programs. They have been especially concerned about those commitments — primarily programs offered to public employees by cities, counties, and states — that have become less and less adequately funded. The vice they have targeted is real enough. It is tempting for governments to promise their employees, especially police and fire fighters, generous pensions and health care in lieu of higher wages. That puts off the full cost of such services to some distant future date. But too often the cost of these future benefits is underestimated or the necessary funds are not set aside. Eventually the distant future arrives and public employees retire — sometimes at a very early age. Law enforcement officers in some municipalities can take their full pension at the age of 50 and still be active enough to seek another job. This is sometimes regarded as scandalous, but is it? It may be wise to induce police and fire fighters to leave their demanding and hazardous work at that age. Early retirement is more problematic for other public employees. Employees of the federal government can retire at age 55 with 30 years of service. In the first decade of this century, 30% of the 1.6 million full-time employees in the federal government can make the choice to retire, with another 20% eligible for early retirement within the next decade. As these fiscal chickens come home to roost, the tax-paying public will be in for a rude shock as the bill for retirement benefits falls due. The problem is not restricted to public employees; there are plenty of private-sector health-care and pension plans that have been just as reck-lessly underfunded or, worse, have seen their resources vanish. Looting the pension fund is a favorite practice among take-over specialists in the marketplace. But public programs always come in for the most publicity.

In fairness, it should be recognized that some generational accountants, like Kotlikoff and Scott Burns, have only one foot in the neoconservative camp. They are realistic enough to acknowledge that Social Security and Medicare will have to be preserved in some form. Unlike neoconservatives, they are not out to slash and burn. For example, some generational accountants would prefer to see the government provide matching funds for private retirement accounts which would be invested in a single, market-weighted global index fund of stocks, bonds, and real estate. The fund would be managed by Social Security — a proposal that does not sit well with the financial community. Social Security is far too big a player to be welcomed on Wall Street. They also recommend that Medicare be supplemented by "participant-specific" vouchers of varying amounts to be spent on private insurance policies. The healthy get less, the sick get more. Medicare would review everybody's medical record annually and decide how much each voucher must cover — a marvelous opportunity for errors and appeals. Beyond competition between private insurance plans (hardly a reliable device), it is hard to see where cost control enters the picture. Moreover, some generational accountants acknowledge that entitlements are not the sole cause of fiscal abuse. There is also George W. Bush's credit-card conservatism (spend and borrow, spend and borrow) which Kotlikoff takes severely to task. He calls for reversing the Bush tax cuts and overhauling the Medicare prescription drug law, root and branch.[3]

In the view of generational accountants, none of the entitlements reforms currently under discussion comes close to doing the job that needs to be done. They contend that even the most rigorous proposals for balancing the budget in the early 21st century will cost the next generation a crushing 70% of their income. And even then, they contend that those who are drawing on the Social Security trust fund, will, on the average, use up everything they contributed within the first ten years of retirement, including the employer contribution. After that, they will be living off a *subsidy* from current workers, all this assuming that no adjustments will be made until this state of affairs is upon us. But what is this subsidy? Is it not rather like the subsidy those same retirees, as parents, once gave their children when they fed them, clothed them, put a cozy suburban roof over their heads, built schools, playgrounds, and universities for them, hired teachers to educate them and doctors to medicate them? And with even a minimal sense of history, one might add that some previous generations suffered the Great Depression and two or three wars along the way, sacrifices that make paying one's taxes look like rather less than an ordeal by fire. It is hardly unfair or unusual for governments to spread the cost of programs that meet extraordinary public needs over several generations.

The tie that binds the generations cannot be reduced to a neat fiscal formula. The discussion of entitlements is complicated by a biological fact that does not yield to a purely economic analysis. It is called *family*, a category that has no standing among professional economists. Indeed, that bond is made up of those very *family values* that conservatives purport to champion. The people who are giving and taking, earning and spending are relatives. As nature would have it, with the passage of time the babies grow up, get old, and retire. What this generation denies its elders is the deal it will have to live with when it retires. Despite all the groaning and gnashing of teeth we hear from the generational accountants, it pays to remember that nothing worse is happening here than that life is going on. The demographic configuration changes, but the underlying obligation of kin to kin continues.

Like all entitlements critics, the generational accountants assume that money spent on health care is a dead loss, rather than seeing it as money that pays for useful services. Or they suggest that the problem exists simply because of opportunistic unions that are out to bilk the taxpayer. Worse still, they imply that there is simply no way to provide adequate health care and retirement benefits that does not lead to bankruptcy except through the market. That is both absurd and unfair. True enough, the cost of retirement and health care has become a major expense of modern life. But rather than declaring entitlements unafford-able, it might make more ethical and economic sense to declare the high-consumption, middle-class way of life (as we now pur-sue it) unaffordable — precisely because it makes necessities like retirement and health care seem so expensive. The public needs only to realize that in taking on the cost of retirement and health plans, it is making a choice that may make perfect sense. For ex-ample, if it wishes to offer benefits to its employees, it must pay for them. This means it might, for example, have to choose be-tween offering its police force a decent retirement and floating a bond measure to build a classy new baseball stadium. Which is the better way to use tax dollars? Whatever the answer, it is not a matter of economics, especially not of free-market economics, which has no means of dealing with questions of ethical value or moral choice.

The Decisive Ratio

The most persuasive argument conservative economists have produced to undermine entitlements is a simple but seemingly decisive ratio: the number of workers compared to the number of retirees. Generational accountants present this ratio and draw a simple conclusion. There are not enough young people to sup-port all those old people. Poor young people, carrying such a heavy load! And in fact that ratio is dropping toward 2:1, a figure that sounds worrisome, almost as if someday soon every work-ing couple in the country will wake up to find a needy senior camped on their doorstep demanding to be taken in.

Well, if a 2:1 ratio of workers to retirees is fiscally unsustainable, what should that ratio be? Ten workers for every retiree? Fifteen? Twenty? Protonationalists are not alone in recommending policies (tax breaks, subsidies, bonuses) to encourage larger families so that there will be more workers in the future — on the assumption, I gather, that it costs nothing to feed, clothe, and educate children and to keep them healthy. Anti-entitlements critics often tell us that when Social Security was adopted in the late 1930s, there were over 100 covered workers for each beneficiary — as if to imply that this was the intended ratio. Does that mean the late 1930s was a good time to retire? Back then, those who had any job at all were earning a bare minimum and times were hard. Many, like my family, were living on a WPA pittance. No matter how many people were on the job, there was not much money going into Social Security, and payouts were minimal. Or consider: In nations like Somalia, there are 40 younger people working for every person over the age of 65. Does that make Somalia a great place to retire? Hardly. Nobody gets a pension in Somalia, because the economy is simply too poor to support even a minimal dependency load.

Obviously, then, the ratio of workers to retired tells us nothing about the wealth of any society. And indeed, Social Security has never been based on that ratio. No sensible retirement plan could be. For suppose we could, by raw reproduction or immigration, achieve a ratio of 10 or 15 or 20 workers for every retired citizen. What would happen when those 10 or 15 or 20 younger workers aged into *their* retirement? After all, the young do get older. And older. And older. And at last they too retire — or are forcibly retired by their employers. What then? Would each of these once-young, now-old workers require *another* 10, 15, or 20 workers to support them? Currently in the United States, immigration from Latin America and Asia is supposedly propping up the ratio of workers to retired. But these immigrants will one day also be retired citizens. Do the math. Seventy million retired boomers times ten workers apiece equals a population of 700 million. And then, as each of those workers retires, multiply times ten, and then times ten — we would be talking about a population of billions. Along these lines, a retirement policy is impossible, all the more so if life expectancy keeps increasing. We would seem to be moving in the wrong direction.

Where is the error in this line of thinking? It shows up if we ask another question: How many children can a family afford? With only one wage-earner, can a family afford four children, six children, ten children — plus a stay-at-home mother? Of course the question is unanswerable until we ask whose family this is. Bill Gates, the CEO of Microsoft, could afford a family of thousands. But if the father is a farm worker, he may not be able to provide decently for one child. Again, the ratios tell us nothing.

Social Security is paid for by the total amount of money paid into the system. And how much we pay in depends upon how much we decide to save for the collective cost of retirement. That amount can be raised in any number of ways. AARP has been circulating literature that spells out eight different ways of keeping Social Security solvent, all of them reasonable and practical.[5] We might simply decide to raise the payroll tax by a few percentage points. Or we might remove the cap on how much can be taxed for Social Security. Currently, the cutoff is $90,500. Raise that to $150,000 and half the Social Security shortfall predicted for 2040 vanishes. Or we might include capital-gains earnings under the payroll tax. For that matter, if we raise the minimum wage, the payroll tax will bring in more revenue. Others have suggested renewing the estate tax and dedicating it to Social Security, or placing a special retirement surcharge on gasoline. In all these cases, more money will go toward Social Security. Obviously, money put into Social Security will not be available for other uses — like the lottery or video games or expensive running shoes. But that is the sort of choice all of us make when we decide to save more and spend less. Lawrence Kotlikoff believes, when it comes to health and retirement, we must "save until it hurts." And is not raising the Social Security payroll tax (if we choose that option) a way of doing that? The money goes into retirement savings before we can spend it.

The Ethics of Affordability

Citing the ratio of workers to the number of retired without any reference to the total wealth of the nation displays a radical misunderstanding of the industrial process.

Throughout their history, industrial societies have seen a constant gain in productivity, even as the need for assembly-line and manual workers has diminished. In the course of the 20th century, this same process of making work less labor intensive has reached out to include white-collar, retail, high-tech, and service jobs. Computerized systems can now do the work of hundreds of telephone operators, file clerks, junior executives, and administrators. Automatic teller machines replace bank tellers, electronic scanners replace grocery checkers, vending machines replace sales clerks. Firms like Wal-Mart take pride in finding ingenious ways to cut back on employment. Of course, Wal-Mart, like all employers, has no interest in sharing the benefits of their labor-saving systems. They seek to appropriate the money they save on paychecks as private profit. Nevertheless, the goal they are pursuing is the very meaning of industrialization: the substitution of machine power or managerial organization for muscle power and even brain power. We have at last reached the point where a few skilled technicians can run an entire automated factory or oversee a vast inventory of merchandise. Neither capitalists nor Marxists recognized this trend as, potentially, a universal blessing; both assumed that wealth could only be wrung from the sweat of the proletariat.

Thanks to industrialism, we can now feed the whole nation and have food left over for export with only 2% of our population working on the land. These fundamental facts of modern economic life are exactly what makes it possible for industrial societies to support a higher and higher dependency ratio — and not simply the elderly, but the disabled and the ill of all ages. It is also what makes more leisure possible for us than our grandparents ever dreamed of having. We now have entire industries — entertainment and professional sports — that are predicated on the assumption that people have more and more time to spend off the job. If that is a good thing for the economy, why should that leisure not take the form of earlier and earlier retirement? All we need do is decide that this is how we shall use our abundance, and suddenly what looks like a crushing cost becomes a welcome benefit.

Every society likes to congratulate itself for being the greatest there is. Americans do more of this than anybody else on Earth, a sure sign of insecurity. How to evaluate these patriotic claims? Let me propose something dear to the hearts of free marketeers. In assessing a people's character and values, free-market economists insist that *money* is the best measure we can find. The way a society spends its money tells you more about a people than any amount of flag-waving or official rhetoric. Indeed, in the United States, the official rhetoric often runs directly counter to our spending habits. We say we value education, but we spend more on war, gambling, and entertainment than we do on schools and teachers. On the Fourth of July, we grow teary eyed over veterans who have given their lives and limbs; we cheer them and praise them, but we then go on to spend more on season tickets than on medical services for maimed and wounded soldiers. So which tells us more about ourselves — windy proclamations or hard cash? Free-market theorists are surely right in telling us that the market reveals our values and is therefore a kind of voting. The trouble is: they never look at the result with a critical eye and say, as they should, "And this is disgraceful!" Let us hope boomers will provide that tag line.

Some societies are so indigent that people have barely enough to survive through the night. They may have to choose between the survival of the old and the survival of the young. No industrial nation has to make fearful choices like that. When it comes to basic necessities, industrial societies have more than enough discretionary income to be generous. That is one of the blessings that industrialism brings with it. It invents machines that can fill our lives with products. But there is one thing machines cannot do. They cannot choose for us. They can produce wealth, but they cannot tell us how it shall be shared. Only the human heart can do that. Affordability is an ethical, not an economic, category.

The NLE (National Life Expectancy): The Number That Matters Most

Economics is burdened with arcane indices and mysterious measurements that often do more to obfuscate than clarify reality. The measure we call GDP, for example, lumps all we make and spend into one catchall category. It makes no difference if the product is food or cigarettes, houses or prisons, provided it can be expressed as money. This is as close to a meaningless statistic as one can come. It is a calculus that places more economic value on playing basketball (for which people get paid millions) than on mothering the young (for which nobody gets paid anything). It lumps together the productivity of factories that pollute and the labor that must then be employed to clean up the pollution. Yet, when it comes to longevity, even this unrefined, motley calculation is interpreted in a skewed way. For, oddly enough, if the goods and services accounted for in the GDP relate to health care, they are arbitrarily seen as liabilities, losses, costs. If a mechanic repairs a mangled car, that is a positive item on the balance sheet; if a physician repairs a broken body, that is a negative item.

What our economics lacks is an index for life and health.

It is the task of the elder culture to introduce that human note into our social affairs. So let us invent such an index here and now, a simple number that elder power may one day enshrine in our political life — the NLE: the National Life Expectancy. Let us factor into the NLE a calculation for quality of life that will help us distinguish a reasonably healthy life expectancy from the bare survival of the very sick and perhaps terminally ill. We would then be able to say that in a society where the NLE is improving, true wealth is being created. And conversely, where the NLE is falling, there is no other indicator that will let such a society qualify as economically successful.

What, for example, do we say about the fact that the Swedes now have life expectancy of over 70 while the Russians have dropped below 65? Or consider wretched Zimbabwe, where life expectancy has declined over the last twenty years from 60 to 37? If Russia or Zimbabwe somehow managed to push their GDP through the roof — perhaps by inviting foreign investors into their countries to run a few select industries — would we call these successful economies? When life itself is at stake, notice how every other criterion of economic well-being pales in comparison. Are not all the other numbers — employment, interest rates, return of investment, profits, wages, prices — merely means to an end, namely a long and healthy life for as many as possible? Why have economists never given that goal more attention? Perhaps because it was never within reach until now. Until our time, industrialism has had nothing to do with health; maybe it had nothing to do with happiness either — at least as economists and entrepreneurs see things.

How does the United States rank with respect to the NLE? We spend more on health care than any other nation and yet lag behind several industrial countries in life expectancy, among them Canada, Great Britain, France, and Germany. This means that our supposedly "inalienable right to life" is being denied. That may not be the way the founding fathers understood the phrase, but what else should it mean in our time when more life is available than ever before?

And what would neoconservatives substitute for Social Security and Medicare if they had their way? Why, of course, the market — in this case, the stock market. Hence, the plethora of investment schemes and programs that right-wing think tanks have devised to make the retirement population more self-reliant. Typically, they propose that it should be every man for himself. Invest your own money and retire to live off your own earnings — if there are any earnings. For the watchful and well-studied few, privatized retirement plans may work well enough. But for most retirees, the Social Security portion of their nest egg is an extraordinarily good deal. Not that it provides the sort of glittering returns sharp investors may be able to make on Wall Street, but what Social Security does offer is good value for the money. What one gets is pension income, disability insurance, and survivors' benefits all in one package — and all of these inflation adjusted. The inflation protection is an important feature, something one pays dearly for in the financial marketplace. By the reckoning of one financial columnist, a working married couple that has contributed to Social Security over the course of 35 years would have to pay nearly $750,000 for an annuity that paid as much as their $3,000 Social Security benefit — if they could even find such a deal.[6] To be sure, that deal has to be paid for. It is tax based, but it is a benefit that will eventually be available to every retiree, a compact between the generations that is as secure as government can make it.

The loss people would suffer if we scrapped that compact is more than economic. It laps over into issues of social philosophy. It presents us with the question: *What is retirement for?* Does it not mean the chance — at long last — to work at what one pleases, when one pleases, for as long as one pleases, under conditions one chooses? The chance to do your thing? That means freedom, though not in any sense that entrepreneurs endorse.

It certainly need not mean the end of work; very few boomers seem to be seeking 20 years of idleness in their later life. It may mean the chance to be your own boss — an option that might include playing the market. The work may be self-employment or hired labor, or the chance to serve in the compassionate sector of the economy, but it should be understood that, thanks to the support of a generous Social Security and Medicare, people in their retirement are finished being pushed around, exploited, forced to do boring or degrading work. They are free to say, "Take this job and shove it!" Perhaps our entire work life should enjoy such autonomy; but surely this should be how we use our time and skill in retirement.

From the time children enter school in the United States, they are living by the performance principle, competing for rewards and promotions. Middle-class parents enforce that influence, wanting their children to *get ahead* in the world. That same drive carries over into one's adult career. For many, this may not be onerous; some find their way to a calling of their own. But how many spend their lives at jobs they would never have taken if they had the choice? If retirement has any ethical and psychological value, it is the opportunity it offers to live by our own lights, out from under the pressure of necessity. As of the mid to late 20th century, that was the prevailing image of retirement we saw in the media, though often the advertisers could not think of anything better to represent freedom than golf and card games. Yet even in these clichéd forms there was the sense that people should finish out their lives in a very different, far freer, more personally gratifying way. This did not, of course, have to be a life of trivial pursuits. It might be the beginning of great changes.

It is precisely this freedom that corporate America is out to quash. Far from wanting a workforce that determines its own destiny and is free to make authentic (if often eccentric) personal choices, it seeks to keep our growing senior population money-worried and insecure. The only way it offers out of that condition is to revert to Commodore Vanderbilt's advice. Vanderbilt, as corrupt and ruthless a robber baron as the world has seen, was once asked what words of wisdom he had for impoverished workers who lost their jobs. His answer was, "Let them do as I have done." That is what the corporados would like to see: a nation, if not a world, made over in their image, focused on money, scrambling to manage an investment portfolio, eagerly following the ups and downs of the market, trying to outsmart the professionals. As for those who fail at the effort, well...are they not obviously unfit? Let them suffer the consequences of their incompetence.

At the height of our industrial development, when life could be easier and more rewarding for everybody, those who hold the commanding heights of the global economy have decided to make things harder, more insecure, more demanding. And for what? The chance to become the biggest and the richest, the multinational corporation that can take over the most and can pay its officers the highest salaries.

Right now, as you read, in every major city there are people in expensive clothes sitting around walnut-burled tables in high-rise buildings talking money. Not inventions, not innovations that will make their society healthier and happier — just money. Before they leave for a $200 lunch, they are thinking of ways to game various markets, rig various deals, finesse various angles, promote various products, and develop public relations campaigns that will cover their tracks and make them richer. These, too, include boomers, of course, putting into practice what they learned at the best business schools in the country. They are discussing how to jack up the price of credit, banking services, phone calls, cable television, rents, air transport, electricity, oil, prescription medications — preferably in ways the public will not notice or, if they do, will have no way to challenge. They are brainstorming mergers, takeovers, buyouts, leveraged deals, hedge-fund maneuvers, real-estate killings, and clever bankruptcy strategies that will produce nothing but money. With the help of million-dollar lobbyists, crooked accountants, and well-financed grafters in Washington and the state capitals, they are finding legal ways to hide dirty deals and enormous profits from public scrutiny. All this is what preoccupies the most richly rewarded people in our society. For every useful, helpful, life-enhancing project they undertake (there are always a few), there are a hundred schemes and scams that serve only to keep the wealth trickling up. Has anyone on any board of directors of any major corporation ever looked around the table and said, "God! Aren't we pathetic!"?

The Soul of the System

When we debate institutions and social programs, almost inevitably we get caught up in administrative technicalities and budgetary minutiae. How will the program be run? How much will it cost? Who will pay? Distracted by these details, it is easy to overlook the fact that every system has a moral core — a soul that animates its daily life. Even when we devise institutions by way of confused debate, somewhere inside that debate there are ethical commitments that derive, not from research or statistical analysis, but from living experience. Conservatives who reject big government are drawing upon an American pioneer mystique that once spoke to the experience of a frontier society and so has become embedded in the folklore of our society. In those early pioneering days, self-reliance was a necessity of life — as it is in all newly settled societies.

Many Americans still honor a worldview where it is every man for himself. But as every historian knows, those who struggled to settle the American frontier had one overriding objective in view: to replace risk and uncertainty with a more benign social order, and to do that as rapidly as they could. Once the land had been settled, the cities that followed were creations of government. As the basic amenities of life were laid on, taxes were levied to pay for schools and public services, and a federal marshall was brought in to drive off the gunslingers. That was how the West was won. The harshness of the individualistic frontier was assimilated to collective action that established a civilized condition of life. And what was happening in frontier America was happening across the urban-industrial world. Throughout western Europe, the late 19th century saw the beginning of humane reforms that would spread the wealth of nations more equitably. The *public sector* was being born and with it the hope of a new social system that transcended the inherited ideologies of the past. The welfare state, as it came to be called, arose from the candid recognition that there was at last enough to be shared by all; therefore, the squalor in which toiling millions were living must end. The wealth of the nation was, after all, a collective creation. Workers had contributed as much as entrepreneurs, if not more. "Without our toil and muscle, not a single wheel would turn" ran the words of a workers' fight song. The soul of the system was fair shares and compassion for all, a simple expression of everything that was finest in our religious traditions, all that was best in ourselves. Necessities before luxuries, a generous standard for all before opulence for the few, a decent start in life for children, a helping hand for the unlucky and disabled, a dignified independence for the elderly. It was on that foundation of moral sentiments that the first social programs were raised.

Through its first two centuries, industrial society was agitated by dreams of ideological perfection. Conservatives elaborated competitive individualism and the free market into a comprehensive system of ethics, politics, and economics. Radicals invented grand designs for collective ownership under the paternalistic state. If we have learned anything, it is that ideological purity, whether of the left or right, is unattainable. Attempting to achieve such purity leads to fanaticism and coercion.

Gradually, as social upheaval calmed, the ideological fevers that once blazed so hotly in modern politics cooled, giving way to a general realization that a mixed economy fares better than the theoretical dreams of conservatives or radicals. So the trend of capitalist and collectivist societies over the past century has been toward economies in which the public sector plays an ever larger role in keeping the economy stable and relieving the severest kinds of poverty. In return for the freedom to do business in innovative, risky, and frequently disruptive ways, capitalists everywhere have agreed, even if grudgingly, to have safeguards built into society to prevent the worst forms of instability and suffering. Even from the entrepreneurs' viewpoint, the arrangement makes perfect sense. It spares the business community from the responsibility of spreading a safety net under the economy and allows it the latitude to do what capitalists claim to do best: invent, innovate, wheel and deal, and run risks for the sake of increasing social wealth.

Modern societies everywhere have generated a substantial welfare state. In every industrial society, there are still well-to-do people; the entrepreneurial spirit continues to be generously rewarded; the market continues to have its ups and downs. But there is also an abiding commitment on the part of politicians left, right, and center to maintaining a shared, high standard of living. No more Great Depressions, no more starvation wages. There may still be debates over how generous the public sector can afford to be, how much money shall be spent on schools and health care, how long paid vacations and leaves of absence should be, how generous pensions can be. But there is no significant disagreement that these amenities should have a permanent claim upon the wealth of the nation. Out of a long history of welfare-state reforms, we have inherited a vision of what industrialism might become: a stable, healthy society that places a higher value on social justice than on competitive acquisition.

Or at least that has been the trend. Then, in the late 20th century, two major exceptions appeared: efforts to turn back the clock and to achieve a conservative purity that had no evidence to show for itself when it came to decency or sheer practicality. Great Britain since the Thatcher government and the United States since the Reagan presidency have seen a concerted effort to return to the primitive capitalist style of the 19th century. In these societies — though more so in the United States — social programs have been systematically starved while public policy has reverted to free-market orthodoxy. Margaret Thatcher's goal was "to kill socialism," Ronald Reagan's "to get the government off our backs." In both countries, the countervailing power of organized labor was severely weakened, substantial amounts of public property were sold off, and social programs were privatized. Under the administration of George W. Bush, even the military establishment, once the indisputable responsibility of government, has been extensively privatized into a mercenary force. At the same time, dismal forms of Social Darwinism long outmoded in the rest of the industrial world came roaring back into fashion.

The results of this neoconservative backlash in the United States would have staggered the imagination of even the staunchest conservative during the post–World War II era. Children of what we now quaintly call the *working poor* are sent to bed hungry; sweatshops have grown up in the back streets of our cities; major employers like Wal-Mart impose working conditions and carefully contrived hours that depress wages and eliminate benefits; over 40 million people live without health insurance; single mothers, denied welfare support, are forced to take minimum-wage jobs. In cities across the nation, public schools, libraries, parks, health clinics, and emergency rooms in hospitals are being cut back or closed down as unaffordable. More and more of these basic social costs must now be paid by private giving. To its credit, the American public has proven to be remarkably generous in its charitable donations. But of the nearly $300 billion Americans gave to charitable causes in 2006, more than 70% came from individuals, not corporations.[7] Even so, charity is no fix for the economic instability of the global market. Working-class families are required to bear the brunt of economic fluctuations in distant parts of an international economy over which they have no control. They are expected to stand by and watch jobs move to cheap-labor markets and to let their standard of living rise or fall as the market dictates. Take one measure of change: since the Reagan presidency of the 1980s, the number of homeless and derelict people reported to have died in the streets of exposure, hunger, and disease has risen to well above a hundred a year in major American cities. Ask what the soul of such a system is. Answer: the ethic of the robber baron, the economic royalist, the "greed is good" corporado.

Neoconservatives see such a social system as a legitimate way of breaking the will of the labor force and of punishing the poor. In their eyes, requiring the population at large to suffer the insecurity of the marketplace is a supreme good. Let workers compete for jobs, if not their very survival. It will encourage initiative and resourcefulness — the very qualities that made America great. Ronald Reagan called it "freeing" people of dependency. Above all, fighting for one's daily bread forces everybody to be more like the corporados: watchful, self-reliant, tough. Like all Social Darwinists of the past, the corporados regard themselves as the very flowers of civilization. If we were to follow their principles, we would have to cease believing in those binding forces of family, community, and mutual aid that hold our society together. All would be replaced by selfish interest and the profit motive.

Viewed in this context, expanding the welfare state no longer looks like so modest a goal. Rather it is an effort to salvage the moral truth we have learned from two centuries of industrial history: namely, that the world does not belong to the ruthless and cunning few but to all of us — to the poets and artists as much as to the entrepreneurs, to the weak and infirm as much as to those blessed with health and agility, to the meek as well as the bold. As they take possession of the entitlements that promise them health and independence, it will be elders who must make that case for their society as a whole.

Odd Political Animals

As the pre-boomer stereotype would have it, elders become more hidebound and cautious as they grow older. Thus, they are usually thought of as natural allies of the conservative right: property-conscious, tax-resistant, backward-looking, fearful of change. But elders are odd political animals. When it comes to entitlements — the main battleground between conservatives and liberals today — it is the older generation that stands on the firing line. They are the chief beneficiaries of the welfare state that conservatives are out to dismantle; no group is more dependent upon big federal programs and the redistribution of wealth. If it were not for the entitlements programs, anti-government conservatives would have had little trouble riding roughshod over every social program in the federal budget. Since the election of Ronald Reagan, right-wing political leaders have been presenting themselves as "revolutionaries" bent upon destroying every last vestige of the New Deal and the Great Society and returning the nation to the care of corporate America circa 1890. In that struggle, it is no longer the much-weakened labor unions, or liberal groups like Americans for Democratic Action, or the civil rights forces that have thus far thwarted their effort. It is the senior citizens of the country sheltering behind the bastions of the nation's largest social programs.

Boomers who are now aging into their promised entitlements will continue to anchor the welfare state in America — if not on ideological grounds, then because of their bread-and-butter daily needs. That is what conservatives find so fearful about aging boomers. Elders are not a public to whom competitive individualism can be made even minimally appealing. Every morning when they awake they are one day further away from the Social Darwinist ideal — which does not mean they will be softies when it comes to defending their own interests. On the contrary, as every politician who stumps America's retirement communities discovers, senior citizens are apt to be tough-minded about the stake they hold in the nation's wealth. They will not be easy to slap down; they cannot be fired or driven away in disgrace. What have they got to lose that can be legally taken away from them?

In another generation or so, we may look back and recognize the Reagan–Bush era as the last gasp of market economics. Greed ruled in that era because it was the last period in our history when entrepreneurs could pocket so much money without sparing a thought for the public interest. But by the early 21st century it has become clear that our society has more serious things to do with its wealth than to play financial games that enrich the few at the expense of the many. That is, of course, a point that has been raised by many groups at various times. At one point, it was raised by organized labor in its demand for a fair share of the profits; at another point, the civil rights movement crusaded for equal access to jobs and education. Each of these made our society fairer and more humane; but again and again the drive for profit and power has rolled back the gains. Now it is the turn of boomers to demand a reappraisal of priorities, this time in the name of all who expect to enjoy the benefits of good health and long life. Though they are apt to be the last to realize it, even the corporate leadership of our society has a stake in that cause. Striking an intelligent balance between the public and private sectors has everything to do with the prosperous survival of the market.

Among radical ideologues, it has always been assumed that revolutionary change arises from the dispossessed and wretched of the earth. The obvious candidates for that role have been workers or ethnic minorities. The inherited ideologies make no allowance for age, least of all old age. Perhaps that is because so few people survived into old age in the 19th century, and those that did arrived at that status depleted of resources and strength. Since they were no longer in the workforce, they were regarded as dependents of those who were. Their interests were those of the families that fed and housed them. Or, if they possessed material wealth, they were assimilated into the ruling class.

But now, as the number of older citizens increases, they become a significant political factor in their own right, bringing a distinctly new set of values into our public life. They are not values born of ethnicity or gender or class, but of existential condition. If their orientation is not *radical* in the traditional sense of the term, they may nonetheless be a force for great change. At the very least they may launch a kind of elder populism, committed to large-scale public programs and compassionate policies. But they may become more. They may at last give political standing to those questions about life and death we have always relegated to the realm of personal philosophy. Of course it is a cliché, but no truer words were ever spoken than "You can't take it with you." It sometimes seems that becoming a success in the American marketplace means acting as if you *could* take it with you. In that sense, nobody could be more greatly at odds with our business ethic than a generation of wise and empowered elders. In the later years of life, philosophy becomes as precious as bread and more meaningful than money.

In another hundred years, history books will find a new meaning in the culminating stage of the industrial revolution. They will see beyond the machines and the technological systems, corporate power and global markets. Instead of glorifying our brute power over nature or the great wealth accumulated by a fortunate few, they will see the longevity revolution as the point where our culture tilted senior-ward and generated a very different social order. They will see the period we are living through, the years in which boomers grew old and accepted age as their opportunity to make their finest contribution, as the time when people everywhere finally discovered what the trauma of industrialism was all about. Not profit and productivity, not getting and spending, but *life*. More of it and of a healthier quality. More of it and of a more thoughtful character. More of it and more spiritually fulfilling.

CHAPTER 6

Utopia Revisited — An Exercise in Cultural Archaeology

Instead — and this I did with all my will and apparently indefatigably (but I will one day drop with weariness) — I invented a different practical world than this world that made no sense and took the heart out of me. Instead of resigning, I reacted, in moments of despair, by thinking up something else, and behaving as if this more pleasing landscape might indeed come to be the case.

— Paul Goodman, *Making Do*

A s clear as the economic numbers make it that entitlements can be made available to our entire society, people generally remain unconvinced that we can afford such a utopian order of things. The age-old experience of scarcity is too deeply ingrained. Yet the boomers grew up in a society brimming with imaginative designs for building a post-scarcity economy involving a radically new redistribution of wealth. We turn now to those designs, a journey through the sort of practical nostalgia that boomers are able to draw upon in creating an elder culture.

We begin with affluence, the foundation of the baby boom, the distinctive quality that marked the divide between young and old in the post–World War II world. It was what white, middle-class kids were born to and what the other (mainly nonwhite) America aspired to. When the parents of the baby boomers looked back, they recalled the gray days of the Great Depression, a debacle so severe that only a catastrophic war could end the hardship by substituting bloodshed for joblessness. Now, when their children look back, they see the distant and receding glitter of the Great Affluence, a time when a single secure, union-negotiated paycheck could feed and clothe a family of four or five, buy a multi-bedroomed house in suburbia, finance a tail-finned monster of a car, and guarantee a college education for all the kids. And, oh yes, employers usually threw in a pension plan and health insurance. Understanding where the Great Affluence came from — and why it vanished so abruptly — is a key theme of boomer history and the basis of elder power.

The mid-1960s stand as the high-water mark of the Great Affluence, the brief interval during which it became commonplace in discussions of public policy to assume that the future promised limitless levels of material productivity. There was plenty to buy, and for more people than ever before the money to buy it. Even while the war in Vietnam was forcing its way into the nation's attention and Black Power violence was raging in our cities, so much that was good seemed possible. For the first time in history, there were societies, led by the United States, that had crossed the fateful frontier between scarcity and abundance. At long last, thanks to the productive thrust of the war effort, the industrial revolution was paying off. More than simply producing a postwar tidal wave of consumer goods, the American economy had proved what human technical ingenuity could accomplish from here on out. In discovering the secret of the expanding economy, American know-how stretched the boundaries of feasibility. It was that realization, as much as the sheer quantity of merchandise one might find on display in the shops and stores, that lay at the foundation of the Great Affluence and remains among the most precious memories boomers have to contribute to the longevity revolution. They lived through an era when utopia seemed like a realistic prospect. Now, as they approach their senior years, with all the worries for independence and security that come with their stage of life, they have the chance to bring back that prospect and to make it the baseline for a searching discussion of humane economic priorities.

Utopianism was among the features that most distinguished the radicalism of the 1960s from earlier eras of protest. In times past, the principal left-wing ideologies spent little time envisioning the new society they hoped to create on the far side of the barricades. Their focus was obsessively on the evils of capitalism; imagining better things to come seemed like a luxury. It was too much like building castles in the air. Revolutionaries sometimes spoke of "creating a new world within the shell of the old," but they gave little more than a vague sketch of what that new world would look like. True, there were radical catch phrases: "From each according to his abilities, to each according to his needs." But what *abilities*? The ability of the artist, the inventor, the entrepreneur? And what *needs*? Needs of the body, the psyche, the soul? Marx and Engels had no time for such abstruse queries. They dismissed the utopian socialists of their day as buffoons who distracted the proletariat from the main task at hand — which was making the revolution.

In contrast, young radicals of the 1960s were eager to envision new possibilities and even to undertake living experiments. These usually took the form of communes, collectives, extended families, ashrams, or perhaps just a shared crash pad. Some of these improvisations were staged in cities as cohousing ventures, others sought to put down roots in rural hideaways. Efforts like these came in for a good deal of ridicule from intellectuals, academics, and older lefties of the time. They were viewed as dreamy impracticalities or empty gestures, and indeed many were embarrassingly short-lived. What critics overlooked, however, is that utopianism energizes the imagination; it is the best medicine for what Paul Goodman called "the nothing-can-be-done disease" so characteristic of American politics during the boomers' childhood. Losing that sense of practical idealism has been among the most crippling deficiencies during the arid conservative backlash that has been with us since the 1980s. Conservatives, committed to entrepreneurial interests, would have us believe we are powerless before the supposedly iron laws of the marketplace. There is nothing to do but to wait for the money to trickle down. From their viewpoint the free market is utopia.

Lights That Failed?

There will always be those who elect to bail out of urban-industrial society, to return to the land, to live modestly in a society of friends and neighbors. *Hippies* was the word reserved for boomers who made or tried to make that choice in their youth. Remember the idealized scenes from *Easy Rider*? The two wayfarers crash with a wilderness community where everybody owns everything in common, works in the communal kitchen, and spends more time getting high than cultivating the land. I recall a few groups like that. Lots of free time and no work ethic. Today I suspect one might find more Jesus people living in small groups of like-minded families where they hope to protect their children from the corrupting secular world. The degree to which that option stays available is a good measure of a society's health. Where intentional community is prohibited, we have a sure sign of totalitarian control.

For about ten years during the 1970s I tried to keep track of the utopian experiments I came across by way of correspondence or occasional visits where I was welcome. Some groups put out ratty-looking, offset newsletters; their participants sometimes wrote articles or went on the road holding meetings and soliciting support. I wound up with boxes full of reports, pamphlets, letters, handwritten essays, theoretical plans, and wishful blueprints, some of them heart-warmingly idealistic, some incredibly zany. There was one visionary of the time whose idea of utopia was to take kids into the wilderness, shoot them up with dope, and then wait for them to mutate into superior beings.

Another group that called itself Drop City sought to cover the New Mexico landscape with geodesic domes, then the architectural emblems of utopia, made of cast-off auto body parts. In the course of that ten-year period, all but a handful of the communities I was tracking evaporated, but a surprising number endured. Timothy Miller, who has studied the communes of the 1960s, concluded that several hundred survived in one form or another.[1] A few have even grown and prospered like Twin Oaks in Virginia and Stephen Gaskin's Farm in Tennessee, which has added a retirement community named Rocinante.

As for those that vanished without a trace, the reason may have been as much in the utopians themselves as in the hostile social environment that surrounded them. There was a restless and footloose quality that permeated the period; the young were impatient and forever moving on with too little interest in putting down roots and working out the inevitable problems. Those who were on hand to launch a commune one day were on their way to Katmandu the next. Ultimately too many wanted a steady job and a family and the amenities of the modern world. Living hand-to-mouth, roughing it through the rest of their lives, was asking too much of themselves. In some cases, like Synanon in northern California, a drug-rehab facility that elaborated itself into an intentional community, a megalomaniac leader brought the whole enterprise crashing down. Other experiments had more to do with getting high than saving the world and quickly disappeared when the dope ran out; still others broke up over issues of who was sleeping with whom, or who had done what with the money, or who was going to make the big decisions. There were groups that shrank down to two or three couples, then one couple, then one angry guy grinding out manifestoes on the mimeo machine. Grand visions done in by petty bickering. Utopians are as human as the rest of us. Still, Timothy Miller, who helped organize the '60s Communes Project, believes the experience, even if short-lived for many, left a

positive mark. He discovered, in interviewing former commu-
nards, that many believed this was a *pivotal* moment in their
lives. Not many went on to become high-earning entrepreneurs;
rather they became socially committed teachers, organic farm-
ers, social workers, or artists.

Altogether, there is plenty of material here for satire. There
must be thousands of boomers who once spent a year, a month,
a week in one or another of these intentional communities. I suspect that those who bother to look back see that phase in their
lives as very quaint and very foolish. It was certainly ephemeral.
Sustaining a divergent way of life outside the mainstream is ex-
tremely hard, especially in the absence of some binding religious tradition and a great deal of workaday competence — all
the more so when you are young and unformed and at war with
the prevailing order. The temptation was always to be moving
on. If the parents of that period were afflicted with powerlessness, the children suffered from a sort of existential hyperac-
tivity: the on-the-road disease. I remember the refrain I heard
countless times from young friends and students. "There's this
group I heard about in Oregon…in Hawaii…in Patagonia…in
Costa Rica…They've got it all worked out." And off they would
go. But what interested me more than the durability of these efforts were the values they tried to honor. Some called their effort
voluntary primitivism or living lightly on the planet. All were
seeking a way out of the consumer economy and careerist rat
race; all were dedicated to the sort of simple living and natural
ways they found in Ernest Callenbach's *Ecotopia*; all preferred
the do-it-yourself techniques laid out in *The Whole Earth Catalog*; all represented a serious effort to achieve the human scale of
life that E. F. Schumacher described in *Small is Beautiful*. How
remarkable, I thought, that values so counter to urban industrialism should surface in the United States, worldwide defender
of the modern market economy. The discontent was healthy,
even if it lacked the competence to survive. Maybe these efforts

were no more than gestures, but they were commendable gestures.

As I look back over this checkered chronicle of utopian dreams, I suppose I could take satisfaction in knowing that the cautious and secure way of life I chose as a university professor proved to be more sustainable than most of the communes. But that is *not* what I feel. Those who gave years to such idealistic experiments were braver than I was. They had more to offer. I feel sad to recall that so few of those who tried to achieve these alternative designs for living could find a niche or a cranny where they could hold out against the consensus. Because what they returned to when they left utopia was the world of hit-and-miss happiness the rest of us settle for, where failed ambitions, alienation, divorce, depression, busted careers, dysfunctional families, corporate corruption, imperial wars, political scandals, conflicts, and pitfalls have become the norm. The world outside utopia does not necessarily work better; it just endures as the default condition of a confused and resigned public. I am reminded of the closing scene of the film version of James Hilton's *Lost Horizon*, the classic utopia of the 1930s. The hero, departing from Shangri-la, casts one backward glance at what he is leaving. His sorrow is obvious. Turning into the wind and the snow outside, he knows that nothing better awaits him. In fact, what awaits him is the world of 1938, 1939, 1940....

Even when they washed out after an unpromising start, these fragile communitarian efforts achieved something of value. *They found their way back to the root meaning of utopia.* Utopia, they discovered, is not about perfection. It is not Shangri-la, a wishful shelter from death and disease where virtue is guaranteed. Rather, the original goal of utopia was to create a community where personal autonomy, commonplace decency, and self-respect could be achieved. And what did that require? Sharing the wealth in ways that offered basic security and equal access to the good things of life. If that meaning can be recaptured in the boomers' later years, it may serve to inspire more mature and durable political initiatives in the years ahead. Utopia, properly understood as an exercise of the moral imagination, is the only hope we have for making the good society. Again to quote Paul Goodman, among the most provocative utopians of the boomer generation: "Our plea for community wakes up sleeping dogs and rebellious hopes; we mention ancient wisdom that everybody believes but has agreed to regard as irrelevant.... Naturally, we who are beguiled by the sirens of reason, animal joy, and lofty aims, fail to notice how far out into left field we sometimes stray; but we are most out of contact in naively believing that, given simple means and a desirable end, something can be *done*."

Three Practical Utopias

There was a time when words like that commanded attention and inspired action. But like so much else in history — cities, roads, monuments, whole civilizations — words, ideas, and visions get lost along the way, forgotten unless archaeologists manage to rescue them from oblivion. Sometimes ideas get lost in the dust because they are authentically defunct — like Ptolemaic astronomy — or because they were held by the losing side in a great historical struggle. That is what happened to Marxism. In the course of their lifetime, boomers have seen this once-prominent body of radical thought all but vanish in the wake of the Cold War. Marxism suffered from many flaws, as do all ambitious ideologies, but it did include a cry for social justice that hardly deserves to be labeled obsolete. Marx read as a Biblical prophet fulminating against those who grind down the poor is more persuasive than Marx read as an economist. More unfortunately still, Marxism took down with it whole categories of social thought that had only one "failing" in common: They were openly critical of free-market economics. That is a pity, because free-market economics is itself an ideology that contains a number of questionable, even superstitious, notions — such as its faith in an *invisible hand* that automatically provides the best solution to all economic problems. That is as dubious a principle as Marx's belief in historical dialectics.

The dominance of free-market ideas in politics, business, and the academic world has crowded out useful alternatives. The result has been a serious case of cultural amnesia that has left us with too few choices when it comes to solving the issues raised by the longevity revolution, a demographic shift that will prove to be as history-making as the rise of the urban proletariat. Let us try then to salvage a few of those utopian prospects from the premature burial to which market orthodoxy has consigned them. That project ought to appeal to boomers, for it brings with it a sense of discovery. Just as so many boomers in their youth found their way to Zen, Hinduism, yoga, the teachings of the Yaqui shaman Don Juan, and many other rich strains of exotic and antique wisdom, so they may enjoy the adventure of rediscovering the utopian insights that have been written off by the political and academic authorities that currently dominate policy making.

I have been arguing that the senior dominance that lies ahead of us will shift values throughout the industrial societies in ways that will encourage populations as a whole to demand the same entitlements that the elders of the society receive. For many, spreading the benefits of Social Security and Medicare to every citizen from the cradle to the grave may seem like a utopian proposal in the worst sense: an unaffordable pipe dream. We can be sure it will be ferociously resisted by the same forces that insist we cannot afford such benefits for seniors alone, let alone the rest of the population. But those who argue that point are in need of a history lesson that takes us back to the early years of the baby boom.

What follows is a small inventory of social alternatives salvaged from the youthful years of the baby-boom generation.

This is no mere remembrance of things past. These proposals, as well as others that might be gleaned from that period, are as relevant today as they were 30 and 40 years ago. If they have been forgotten, that is because of the amnesia of the public, not the impracticality of the ideas. At the very least, this brief sketch may serve to remind us how we once understood the great issues of security, justice, and decency. As unfamiliar as some of what I relate may seem to many, we deal here with what was once a lively public debate that filled the media with bright new possibilities. While boomers were making their way through nursery school, high school, and college, here is how some of the liveliest minds of the 1940s, 1950s, and 1960s were seeking to provide for their future. For those in the elder culture who still seek political relevance, here are some surviving countercultural possibilities.

1. Paul Goodman's Dual Economy

Among the thinkers who still speak eloquently to the issues of our postindustrial future is Paul Goodman. In 1947, in collaboration with his architect brother Percival, Goodman published an astonishingly precocious work of social analysis. Their book *Communitas*, subtitled *Means of Livelihood and Ways of Life*, predicted the Great Affluence that was to dominate social policy in America for the next 30 years — predicted it, praised it, and artfully skewered it.

Communitas is among our earliest examples of post-scarcity economic thought. It takes the position that, since the end of World War II, the American people have been living in an economy so vastly empowered by "surplus technology" that it could put a permanent end to poverty. In Goodman's day, the United States stood alone in that status; it has since been joined by all the major industrial nations and perhaps in another generation by China and India. The secret of the plenty these societies enjoy lies in a remarkable possibility that anti-capitalist ideologies never sufficiently appreciated, namely that *surplus value* (to use the Marxist phrase) can be wrung from machines and from the skillful application of science to the forces and materials of nature. Proletarian sweat need not be our only source of wealth. We can have slaves of steel and electrical circuitry working for us.

Were our newfound abundance intelligently used, Goodman argued, it could eliminate the drudgery and alienated labor that have been with us since the advent of industrialism. "Intelligently," for Goodman, meant honoring Thomas More's basic distinction between necessities and luxuries. The economy created by World War II provided a unique opportunity to take charge of our lives. It had, Goodman believed, given us an "extraordinary flexibility and freedom of choice." The choice was between "still more mass-produced goods" on the one hand and "leisure and the artistic culture of the individual" on the other. But of course America's postwar abundance was not being intelligently used, as it still is not. Instead, the plenty that might provide a decent standard of living for everybody has been subordinated to a culture of compulsive consumption that lumps necessities and luxuries together, allowing us no opportunity to choose between the one and the other. It is as if we had mixed all the nutrients we need for a healthy diet into a vat of fat and sugar, so that the only way we might get *enough* to eat is by indiscriminately consuming everything we spoon out of the vat — in which case, we could not expect to be well nourished unless we risked obesity. (Come to think of it — that is not such an inaccurate description of the post–World War II eating habits of our increasingly weighty American public.)

At one point in *Communitas*, Goodman proposed a satiric alternative to our existing way of dealing with excess. He called it the "City of Efficient Consumption." The city in this fanciful proposal was a vast department store acres in size where residential neighborhoods, factories, offices, and shops exist under one great roof. There everything was stocked in abundance and could be bought on liberal credit. (Recall, Goodman is writing before the appearance of the first credit cards.) Periodically, when all the credit had been used up and nobody could fit one more piece of merchandise into their lives, the government declared a kind of Saturnalian romp. People ran riot destroying and wasting in all directions. All debts were forgiven in the merriment. "Next day, when the carnival is over…it can be seen that our city has suffered no loss. The shelves have been cleared for the springtime fashions; debtors have been given new heart to borrow again; and plenty of worn-out chattels have been cleared out of the closet and burnt."

In this amusing image, Goodman hit upon an important truth. As our economy is organized, if the market for stereos and automobiles is used up, the economy goes slack, investments are lost, entrepreneurs rush to cut their losses and move their capital, jobs vanish, communities wither. As Goodman put it, "Unless the machines are running at nearly full capacity, all wealth and subsistence are jeopardized…Unless *every* kind of goods is produced and sold, it is also impossible to produce bread." Thus, we cling to the belief that there must be indiscriminate and limitless growth (the GDP) simply to produce the necessities. Nothing is more astonishing than our willingness to continue accepting economic policies based on such an absurdity. But of course it is only by refusing to make judgments as between wants and needs, subsistence and luxury, that professional economists defend their status as scientists.

For some 40 years after the end of World War II, the military-industrial complex provided the continuity of profits that kept our war-born system working — of course at a shameful waste of skill, resources, capital, and with the constant risk of nuclear annihilation. Now, while military spending remains high (for no reason that relates to the public good), the military-industrial complex has changed the rules and distributes less and less of its profits. Instead, corporate employers, claiming to be under global competition, downsize ruthlessly, in effect fattening the profit margin by shortsightedly firing their customers. So workers must scuffle to hold jobs, perhaps more than one, and give up their hope for security.

But this is nonsense. No such scenario need transpire. The abundance that our amazing technology has given us is real; it need only be intelligently configured. Goodman was bold enough to propose such a configuration. He called it "the direct solution," a divided economy that would provide "planned security with minimum regulation."

> The direct solution, of course, would be to divide the economy and provide the subsistence directly, letting the rest complicate and fluctuate as it will. Let whatever is essential for life and security be considered by itself, and since this is a political need in an elementary sense, let political means be used to guarantee it. But the rest of the economy — providing wealth, power, luxury, emulation, convenience, interest and variety — has to do with varying human wishes and satisfactions, and there is no reason for government to intervene in it in any way.[2]

So we would have two economies running side by side, one sensibly proportioned to basic needs, the other run for profit and allowed to become as zany as it pleases. Let us call the first economy the *minimal economy*. It would be organized to provide the common necessities of life. Let *necessities* be generously defined to include wholesome food, serviceable clothing, modest but decent housing, efficient transport (perhaps including economy cars), basic communications (a cell phone, a modest television, a cheap computer), access to superior education, excellent health care, a modicum of low-cost entertainment, and maybe (alas!) an iPod. Meanwhile, the other economy — let us call it the *surplus economy* — would be left as a concession to entrepreneurial compulsives, spendthrifts, and conspicuous consumers, those who need richly rewarded careers, sumptuous meals prepared by celebrity chefs, high fashion, the home beautiful, prestige cars, trophy wives, expensive divorces, swank parties, the best booze, the finest cosmetic surgery, etc. As wacky and wasteful as it might become, that economy could be filled with an exhilarating effervescence. Perhaps it would from time to time invent something worthwhile. So let it run its merry way.

Goodman believed each economy would need its own workforce. The surplus economy would, of course, be supplied by avaricious hard-chargers pursuing lavish salaries and hungering for luxury. But where would the minimal economy find its labor? Here Goodman was somewhat troubled. He suggested (rather uneasily, writing in the wake of a war effort) that the labor might have to come from universal conscription and be managed "as a state monopoly like the post office or the army." His image here is rather like a mandatory Works Progress Administration under the New Deal. He imagined that a contract might be negotiated with the youth of the society: In return for a two- to four-year tour of duty in the fields, factories, and offices of the minimal economy, each would receive a guaranteed lifetime claim upon subsistence in that economy. Not a bad deal. This would make available to everyone the freedom that artists and contemplatives have always sought in order to get on with a creative or spiritual life. Of course, many people might need or want more than the subsistence an artist or contemplative finds sufficient. One might then freely drop in and out of the surplus economy as often as one wished, picking up extra earnings. The mix would be fascinatingly personal. There might be those who, after seeking God in the wilderness for some period of years, would return to the surplus economy to play the stock market. Or there might be others who, after a successful career as a computer programmer, would drop out to complete a slender volume of verse.

Goodman assumed that the minimal economy should be reserved for the young. He was writing long before longevity began to affect our demographics. Here, we must make a major revision in his design. We would now see a significant role in that economy for retired citizens who might find enough employment there to supplement their basic retirement. We begin to see that the utopian vision Goodman developed in *Communitas* may be far more relevant to boomers in their senior years than in their youth. It may provide one of the best insights we have into the entitlements debate, offering a clearer understanding of *necessities* and the cost of providing them. Though some of the labor in the basic economy — construction and field work — might be more than older workers could take on beyond a certain age, surely the advantages of automation would place many jobs within their reach. We might, therefore, want the basic economy to employ a mix of old and young: the retired and the unskilled youth of the nation. They would get to know one another on the job, the ideal place for eldering to be carried on.

Goodman's argument has the persuasiveness of plain common sense. It is neat and well targeted. Its basic principle could be applied to all welfare and subsidy programs we still carry on the books today. Define the program by need, not by population. It also has the refreshing quality of assessing the economy from the viewpoint not of economists and entrepreneurs, go-getters and workaholics, but all those who would settle for modest means, simple pleasures, and much leisure. But he was wrong on one score. He believed the surplus economy, being nonessential, could be allowed to run wild, with almost no government supervision, gyrating through the usual business cycles. Today, that permissiveness would have to be moderated for environmental considerations; the surplus economy could not be allowed to disrupt the planetary ecology. But within that limit, it could be given enormous latitude. While those content to live in the minimal economy might have little to do with the surplus economy, they might in one respect take great interest in its goings-on. Watching the conduct of those who caper in the economy of excess might provide all the entertainment those in the minimal economy need. Where would one find a greater display of human foibles and follies?

2. John Kenneth Galbraith's Cyclically Graduated Compensation

There is something to be learned about the era of the Great Affluence by comparing Paul Goodman and John Kenneth Galbraith simply as personalities. Goodman was a voice from the countercultural margins of our society, the somewhat screwy man of letters who wrote more about sex, art, and psychology than about economics and whose finest piece of writing (*Empire City*) was a novel, not a political treatise. He fancied himself a Socrates of the streets, more homoerotically at home with boys on the basketball court than with decision-makers in the corridors of power. It was just this maverick stance that allowed Goodman to cultivate an audience among young boomers of the 1960s. He offered himself to them in the school yards and on the campuses as a true elder. The fact that someone so offbeat could find a significant audience tells us much about the spirit of the times.

In contrast, Galbraith was every inch the professional economist and man of affairs, a Harvard professor who served as US ambassador to India. His style, lofty and elegantly mordant, dripped with respectability. Academically trained and practically oriented, he might, therefore, seem as remote from utopian philosophy as one can travel. It is all the more impressive, then, that so restrained a theorist shared so much common ground with Goodman. Both came to see that our high industrial economy had, in the aftermath of World War II, reached a point where the difference in degree — of output, profit, production, consumption — had become a difference in kind. The economy had not simply changed; it had mutated. Not only can we produce more, we can produce too much. Thinkers like these could recognize that even before the means of production had been automated.

In Goodman's case, the inspiration for redesigning industrialism derived from anarchist ancestors reaching back to Prince Kropotkin and William Morris; Galbraith, working out from Keynesian–New Deal liberalism, reached the same conclusions about the abundance of our postwar economy. Indeed, his 1958 book, *The Affluent Society*, helped name the period. Like Goodman, Galbraith wrote with a sense of astonishment and hope at what he saw before him. Surveying the American scene from the vantage point of the Eisenhower era, he was amazed at the productive potential he saw, wealth that might well spell the end of poverty. He was among the first of those in the intellectual-academic mainstream to recognize that America's expanding economy changed all the rules of the game.

Hitherto, he observed, economic thought had been based on "poverty, inequality, and economic peril." That was the world of yesterday. "Poverty," Galbraith reminded his readers, "was the all-pervasive fact of that world. Obviously it is not of ours.... So great has been the change that many of the desires of the individual are no longer even evident to him. They become so only as they are synthesized, elaborated, and nurtured by advertising and salesmanship.... Few people at the beginning of the nineteenth century needed an adman to tell them what they wanted."

Galbraith's study was an effort to accommodate the new affluence, but with minimal changes in the existing system. Even so, what he advocated was bound to seem extreme. He saw no chance that affluence could be enjoyed if the economic system, especially employment, was left wholly under the control of market forces — as even liberal, growth-oriented economists of that day believed it must. Market forces were, after all, committed to the production of more and more goods, all of which must be moved steadily out of the stores in order to keep the economy ticking. Like Goodman, Galbraith saw the link between paychecks and production as the key problem. What was needed, he argued, was "a reasonably satisfactory substitute for production as a source of income. This and this alone would break the present nexus between production and income."

Galbraith believed that the model for what was needed was as near at hand as unemployment insurance, which was, as of the 1950s, more generously available in the United States than in recent days. Galbraith's suggestion: Let unemployment insurance be an honorable alternative to work and let it be still more generous. In this way, the jobless could continue to fulfill their role in life as consumers. This might, of course, lead to "voluntary idleness," but in so productive an economy, Galbraith saw this as no great threat. Instead, he integrated it into his program. He proposed the creation of Cyclically Graduated Compensation. CGC was unemployment compensation that would increase in value as unemployment increased and decrease as full employment was approached. Galbraith's CGC would give us a population of income earners who did not have to work for their income. There is one point he might have mentioned in this context. The economy itself has been disemploying working men over the age of 65 since 1900. At the beginning of the 20th century, two out of three men over 65 were still on the payroll; by 1980, the number was one in five and many of them working part time. But only since the 1940s have the unemployed elderly had at least minimal Social Security to fall back on. As one sociologist puts it, "The old are forerunners of a future leisured society." Galbraith might have made the CGC permanent as a universal substitute for Social Security. As he saw it, CGC would not only relieve hardship, but it would balance out the business cycle. When the economy began to sag and unemployment rose, CGC would place greater purchasing power in the hands of the jobless to prime the pump. When the economy improved and boomed, CGC would decrease and so induce the unemployed to seek work. No doubt timing these transitions would be tricky.

Unlike Goodman's proposal for a dual economy, Galbraith chose to keep a single economy in operation. In this regard, Galbraith was less utopian than Goodman. While his point of departure was economic surplus, Galbraith did not, like Goodman, offer us another choice in life, a way to get off the treadmill of the consumer society. The very graduation of CGC was designed to pressure people back into the regular economy as the need for employment increases. His was a means to keep the high-consumption economy running more smoothly and more equitably. And like Goodman's *Communitas*, *The Affluent Society* was a pre-environmental study that did not take into account the pressure that high-industrial economies were placing on the biosphere — a significant failing.

Because he was seeking to rationalize high production, Galbraith thought of the public as a workforce that fluctuated in and out of jobs. Thus, he missed a promising possibility: withdrawing some people from the workforce once and for all. That is called *retirement*. While Galbraith touched here and there on Social Security as an aspect of public policy, it never occurred to him to nominate *subsidized retirement*, rather than subsidized unemployment, as a model for compensated joblessness. Again it was too early on to connect utopian philosophy with entitlements. Galbraith was on the far side of the demographic divide. The baby-boom generation was only beginning to appear on the horizon.

3. Robert Theobald's Guaranteed Annual Income
As early as the mid-1950s, Robert Theobald, an English economist then resident in the United States, was, like Goodman and Galbraith, convinced that the link between jobs and paychecks

was growing so tenuous that it ought to be cleanly and honestly sundered. But he introduced another, urgent consideration: automation. Theobald's fear was not that the job market was growing unpredictable, but that it might catastrophically collapse before anything took its place. As in the industrial past, technological unemployment was the threat — but on a scale far beyond anything created by the railroads or the assembly line. It was not until the early 1960s that the potential of computerized systems, originally called cybernetics or cybernation, became clear. Goodman might have assimilated the computer to his category of "surplus technology," which he assumed was destined to grow; he wrote from the viewpoint that conventional technology was already operating at the level of surplus. But then, how could one have envisioned the even greater influences of what we call *high tech*, the automation of more and more mental, administrative, service, and decision-making labor?

In 1962, a major liberal conference in Washington raised all these prospects. Titled the Ad Hoc Committee on the Triple Revolution, its leaders included economist Robert Heilbroner and physicist J. Robert Oppenheimer. The Triple Revolution quickly became a special project of the Center for the Study of Democratic Institutions, a Ford Foundation think tank run by the much-respected Robert Hutchins, former president of the University of Chicago. The Triple Revolutionaries met with a special new concern foremost in view. They sought to link the three issues of war, racial justice, and automation. They were among the first to focus concern on the labor-saving potential of high-tech systems. They concluded that the best way to make use of our promising high level of productivity would be to pay every citizen, employed or not, a guaranteed annual income. Some went further. The Center's extended deliberations on the proposal eventually turned up bizarre but imaginative variations — like that of the noted social psychologist Erich Fromm. Fromm seriously advocated the creation of government "free stores" where citizens could walk in and carry away the necessities of life, no questions asked, no cash required. His whimsical notion would be given a trial run on the streets of San Francisco during the 1967 Summer of Love. At least for a few months there was a free store where people could leave their furniture and appliances for others to use, and free food in the park begged off of local supermarkets. As brief as that countercultural improvisation was, it illustrated how much usable "waste" our society produces: good food thrown away, household goods scrapped before their time, wearable clothing that was simply not fashionable. Many might live off what others cast off. We are truly a society of excess, though we seem not to know it.

Theobald became the main advocate of the guaranteed annual income within the Triple Revolution movement of the mid-1960s. His interest was in breaking the jobs-income link, which he believed "harnesses man to the juggernaut of scientific and technological change and keeps us living within a whirling-dervish economy dependent on compulsive consumption." Theobald was clear that the guaranteed income must become a matter of legal right — an entitlement, as we would call it — lest it be abused by government agencies that might withhold payment as a means of social control. Unlike Galbraith, he saw Social Security as the best model to imitate for that purpose. "Basic economic security can be best regarded as an extension of the present Social Security system to a world in which job availability will steadily decline." Within that context, Theobald was able to work a few charming cultural embellishments, such as "consentives." A consentive was a "nonprofit-oriented productive organization whose members consent to work together" while receiving the guaranteed annual income. Theobald regarded this as an opportunity to create handicrafts or artistic works that might be sold on the open market to supplement income.

How realistic was Theobald's proposal? Let us sketch in a bit more historical background.

Imagine aiming a zoom lens at the America of the 1960s and using it to bring one notable episode into sharp focus, a forgotten moment in history that reveals what it once meant to be *the affluent society.*

We are focusing in on Washington, DC, in November 1966. We are looking at a large public event. No, not a rock concert, or a teach-in, or a Kool-Aid acid test. We are looking in on a conference of the United States Chamber of Commerce, the leading voice of the American business community. It is hosting a gathering titled "The National Symposium on Guaranteed Income."

That event has drawn together ranking economists of the day to discuss establishing a legal right to the necessities of life for all American citizens, whether they hold jobs or not.[3] In the course of the proceedings, several proposals are laid before the symposium — mainly by liberal economists, many still under the influence of the Roosevelt New Deal. The conservatives on hand prefer either family allowances or an adjustment in the income tax that provides for decent subsistence. But there is an overwhelming consensus that, whatever form it might take, the proposal is an idea whose time has come. This is America's version of the worldwide revolution of rising expectations. Those who question the idea do not raise doubts about its economic feasibility; their reservations are drawn from traditional ethics ("Those who do not work, neither shall they eat,") or based on conventional psychology (hunger is the only incentive that will drive many to work).[4] In the presence of the country's unprecedented abundance, however, few of those in attendance seemed to feel urgent about such moral reservations.

Given the sponsorship of the event, the ideas under discussion were obviously not seen as wild-eyed or left wing. In fact, by the mid-1960s, ambitious schemes for redistributing the wealth of the nation had a considerable history behind them. During World War II, English social reformers had begun advocating what they called a *social dividend* (and would later call the *welfare state*), a flat grant to every citizen that would then be balanced out by a wealth tax which would give the poor a subsistence income. The Canadians had been toying with the idea since the appearance of the Social Credit Movement in the 1930s. In the United States, the first mainstream proposal for such a guaranteed annual income appeared in 1946 in the solidly professional *American Economics Review*. In a highly technical discussion of full employment and minimum wage policy, the economist George Stigler concluded that "the principle of equity involves the granting of assistance to the poor with regard to their need... but without regard to their occupation." In other words, though they do not work, nevertheless they must be fed. What was the best way to go about achieving that goal? Stigler advocated "extending the personal income tax to the lowest income brackets with negative rates in these brackets. Such a scheme could achieve equality of treatment with what appears to be a... minimum of administrative machinery." Stigler had hit upon a formulation that was destined to appeal strongly to conservative tastes. After all, his proposal seemed to lead to the elimination of costly and intrusive bureaucracy. That was what the libertarian economist Milton Friedman liked about this approach when, a few years earlier in 1962, he came up with the notion of a *negative income tax*. The idea was seductively simple. Let the cost of a modest, working-class living be declared on one's income tax as a deduction. If an individual or family earns less than that, let the federal government send them a check to make up for the shortfall. This arrangement, Friedman believed, would serve to shake down numerous government programs. The Internal Revenue Service would be all the bureaucracy we needed, replacing aid to dependent children, farm price supports, public housing, and of course Social Security. Why bother dividing poverty into categories? The needy all have one overriding need: to survive. Send them the money to do that. Providing a safety net of that kind might actually diminish the greatest cost that poverty unloads on our society. Crime. For not only does crime cost us the loss of property and life, but when the wrongdoers are finally apprehended, it costs on average $40,000 a year to keep them in prison: food, clothing, shelter, health care, and supervision, not to mention the expense of courts, trials, legal fees, etc. If a check in the mail from the IRS eliminated that cost alone, it would be a bargain.

The idea was neat, fair, and, in Friedman's view, affordable. Once any society makes the basic, moral decision that it will not allow people to starve in the streets, it is going to pay for the poor one way or another. It may do so grudgingly; it may make them jump through bureaucratic hoops; it may find ways to humiliate them — but it will pay. Go that far and you have a clear choice. Either the nation strikes out toward a confused proliferation of expensive social programs that will surely grow in administrative cost — or one wraps all public assistance together into a single package and simply provides the money. As Friedman acknowledged, our existing "grabbag" of relief and welfare measures already constitutes "a governmentally guaranteed annual income in substance, though not in name."[5]

In 1964, with Milton Friedman serving as his campaign advisor, Barry Goldwater, the founding father of the American radical right, took up the negative income tax as a plank in his presidential campaign. Soon after that the Republican Party advocated cutting the work week to four days (without lowering wages) in order to make jobs available to the unemployed. The affluence of the time made such proposals seem like the sheerest good sense all across the political spectrum. Goldwater lost the election, but his rival Lyndon Johnson at once launched a War on Poverty that became the official centerpiece for new ideas about sharing the wealth. In 1966 Johnson summoned a National Commission on Guaranteed Incomes. The immediate impetus for Johnson was a meeting of civil rights and labor leaders that paralleled the Chamber of Commerce symposium.

The meeting drew up a "Freedom Budget" as a comprehensive solution to poverty in America. It included a guaranteed income as a replacement for the "patchwork" of public assistance programs. The Commission began a two-year series of hearings that finished by recommending "the adoption of a new program of income supplementation for all Americans in need."[6] Still another study at that time by the Brookings Institute reached the same conclusion.[7] By 1965, the University of Chicago School of Social Service Administration had began publishing a *Guaranteed Annual Income Newsletter*.

Before the decade was out, major American publications had run editorials and articles on the proposition, all of them addressing it as realistic if not inevitable. The radical political philosopher Dwight McDonald, addressing an upper-crust reading audience through the pages of *The New Yorker*, advocated the "principle that every citizen should be provided, at state expense, with a reasonable standard of living regardless of any other considerations.... The governmental obligation to provide, out of taxes, such a minimum living standard for all who need it should be taken as much for granted as free public schools have always been in our history." Pronouncements like these were but a few of many lively discussions of the period that laid a simple but astonishing new economic vision before the American public — namely, that there was more than enough to go around. Some experts estimated that industrialized technology, including its use in agriculture, now made it possible for a mere 10% of the population to feed, house, and clothe the remainder. Others wondered with some trepidation if work was not about to vanish from history. Even the conservative Richard Nixon was willing to include an Earned Income Credit in the tax laws, a modest version of the negative income tax and probably the most unadvertised of all government benefits.

What did all this amount to but across-the-board recognition that capitalism was a success? It had delivered the goods.

But now that the goods were at hand, how might they be used to sustain, nourish, and civilize? That was not a question to be answered from within the assumptions of the market economy. But there were others outside those assumptions — and not least of all the young boomers of that period — who saw in the abundance of the industrial world the opportunity to refashion society into something like Thomas More's *Utopia*. There were plenty of ideas, Theobald's proposal among the leading contenders for official policy.

Then, soon after 1970, all the proposals I list here dropped out of sight as if the Earth had opened up and swallowed them. As Theobald himself recognized, other matters were crowding utopia off the political landscape. In a second edition to his anthology *The Guaranteed Income*, published in 1970, he bemoaned the "collapse of liberal dominance" in the United States and the increasingly polarized character of our politics. "Today the society is fragmenting into many sub-cultures," he observed. In the relations between these sub-cultures, power was what mattered more than simple economic security. Some, especially youthful dissenters, seemed to care less and less about the high productivity on which the guaranteed annual income was based. Theobald believed that these dropped-out youth were cultivating a "new view of man" that saw "consumption as a means to an end rather than as an end in itself." He feared that where cultural values began to diverge so sharply, the guaranteed annual income could no longer be seen as the "next step in socioeconomic evolution." Less still could it be brought about by mere social engineering.

Theobald puts the matter cryptically, but what he had in view was the front-page news of the day. He was referring to the rising tide of anti-war protest and racial unrest of the mid-1970s. The affluent society was coming apart at the seams. As that happened, the cultural context that utopian planning requires began to splinter. Within the next decade, serious discussion of proposals like his — or Goodman's or Galbraith's — would fade. With radical dissent raging in the streets and on the campuses, those who controlled the wealth of the nation were not about to reward their countercultural critics with a constitutionally guaranteed paycheck.

"Hippies, LSD, and Free-Love Cults"

That is exactly the vindictive description we find in one of the most highly regarded books of the 1960s: *The Year 2000* by Herman Kahn and Anthony Wiener.[8] Published in 1967, it was the first in a series of studies by the richly funded Commission on the Year 2000. Given its provenance, the book offers a revealing glimpse into the mind-set that had come to dominate commanding heights.

Kahn and Wiener were haunted throughout the volume by one great concern: *work*. They fretted that "our high future standard of consumption" might bring an end to work as we have known it. In the age of automation, labor simply will not be needed, certainly not in the quantity we have become accustomed to and to which our powerful Protestant work ethic disposes us. In the affluent society, they ask, what will people do with themselves when they need not work more than a few hours a week? Here the authors detoured into the province of social psychology. "Freedom from necessity," Kahn and Wiener felt, might not be a blessing. Rather it might deprive people of their traditional purpose and give them no good substitute. The result would not be "more generous, public-spirited, and humane enterprises," but rather widespread alienation and depression. Among the fears they expressed most insistently was that a growing population of *hipsters* would emerge, brooding and dropped-out layabouts who might live off the abundance and infect others with their "effete attitudes." The result might then be that "hippies, LSD, and free-love cults" would begin to recruit the younger generation. In such an unruly future, "many would live indefinitely on the resources of friends and relatives and on opportunistic sources of income without doing any sustained work, or…would cloak themselves in pretensions of artistic creativity."

At no point in their exhausting survey did Kahn and Wiener raise the slightest doubt about the dazzling prospects for productivity and affluence. Indeed, their main goal was to announce the advent of "increasing affluence" and to explore the future it made possible. Within that optimistic context, their main concern was social control. They darkly predicted the possibility that "resort to drugs, otherworldly religions, delinquency, crime, and mental disease could increase significantly, requiring medical, social, and criminal sanctions to prevent or contain those forms of disturbance that are excessively dysfunctional for the social and political systems." That conclusion is telling evidence of how the military-industrial complex was coming to view the strange new society it had brought about. There was no doubt the economy could provide the goods, but in such a society, would it still be possible to control the public and enforce virtue? What would affluence do to our moral character in the long run?

Kahn and Wiener finished their discussion with a prophetical insight: "While few would now believe that the mere multiplication of productive powers is likely to bring mankind into Utopia, or into anything resembling it, it would be ironic (but not unprecedented) if this multiplication of resources were to create problems too serious for the solutions that those very resources should make feasible." Their words are a clear, if stilted, prediction of the problem that the rising counter culture of their day would soon pose. Free people of the yoke of necessity and they will become unruly. In the 1960s, unruliness was located among the young. But as mature boomers claim their entitlements, they will once again be in a position to grow unruly. We may be in sight of a surprising display of elder insurgency.

CHAPTER 7

The Doors of Perception

*LSD opened the road into the future as wide as the sky
and we were soaring! Acid blasted all the negativism and
fear out of our bodies and gave us a vision we needed to go
ahead, the rainbow vision which showed us how all people
could live together in harmony and peace just as we were
beginning to live with each other like that.*

— John Sinclair, *Guitar Nation*

Creating a society in which everyone will be entitled to long
life, good health, and basic security requires a dramatic
shift in our society's ethical consensus. That transformation lies
at the heart of the longevity revolution. It draws upon the simple
fact that industrial society is leaving behind the ethical impera-
tives that created it. The fascination with limitless productivity,
the passion for conquering and exploiting nature, the appetite
for unrestrained acquisition, the ethos of competitive individualism — seen from the viewpoint of an elder culture, all these,
the aggressive and acquisitive qualities that once made profit
and power the highest values in life, look more unbecoming by
the day. Changes of this magnitude do not arise from rational
analysis or ideological debate; they derive from seeing life in a
new way. They are grounded in consciousness.

Consciousness was the god-word of the 1960s, the term and
the pursuit that lent the protest movement its special distinction. "Changing your head" elevated you to a new, higher political level from which tired old issues took on a new meaning.

The arrogance of that claim probably did more to alienate many older lefties than any other aspect of the counter culture. In times past, the concept of consciousness played a significant but very different role in Marxist theory. For Marx, *class consciousness* — once it was instilled — heightened the proletariat's sense of victimization. Plays and novels of the period often focused on the hero's experience of finding his or her true class identity. Making workers sensitive to their exploitation and aware of their interests was understood to be basic to revolutionary action. *Consciousness raising*, in the view of Marxists, was the beginning of a sweeping cultural revision. It meant the end of all hierarchical social structures and social privileges. It also meant the rejection of ecclesiastical authority and the supernatural in favor of a strictly materialistic vision of life.

But in the 1960s, consciousness raising took off in a very different direction, one that the old-line left found utterly repulsive. The term began to acquire heavy psychological connotations, and finally unmistakably religious overtones. Young boomers reached the point of recognizing that consciousness is in the nature of a style which can, like any style, be changed — as it has often changed from culture to culture, from era to era. Indeed, unless we can make such a change, we will continue to be faced by problems that cannot be resolved. The state of consciousness in which we address great issues — the unarticulated and often inexplicable sensibility that spontaneously leads us to like or dislike, support or oppose, trust or reject, commit or hang back — has more relevance to moral action than the most soaring ideological rhetoric.

This sense that consciousness is a grand and boundless exploration that transcends the narrow political categories of the past became a serious bone of contention between radicals of the older and younger generations. Whatever else radicals of the past rejected about the capitalist status quo, they clung to the materialism and functional rationality that characterized modernity. Marx, after all, referred to his own philosophy as *scientific socialism*. For him and all his disciples the word, spoken or written, was the principal medium of politics. Hence the heavy tomes, pamphlets, manifestoes. What is the image we have of great political movements of the past? Somebody of commanding presence — almost always a man with a big voice — looking out over an audience or a mob, speechifying, ranting, reviling, spelling out the goals, calling for action, wielding language like a weapon. A soapbox orator might inculcate class consciousness on any street corner; facts, figures, and impassioned invective were enough to do the job. But in the 1960s, consciousness raising came to mean broadening the mind beyond intellect and the limitations of language. And where consciousness went, words might not be able to follow. The project might require rewiring the electrochemical foundations of the nervous system so that one might rise to the level of great ineffable truths. The goal was not ideological clarity but visionary flights and mystic epiphanies. Raising consciousness became expanding consciousness. And at last that meant dope.

Surrounding every stereotype we inherit from the 1960s and 1970s, there is the pungent aroma of dope. The signature imagery of the period offers us, alongside the angry faces of the revolutionary vanguard and Black Power, the blissful smile, the thousand-mile gaze of the beatnik, the hippy, the flower child. Protest well-laced with a sense of nirvana: no demonstration was complete without it. Worse than being wrong, deceptive, evil, the men in suits and uniforms who ran the world were lost in samsara. But, then, how could society, understood as a parade of illusions, become a meaningful object for revolutionary change? How could one escape the illusion and yet stay engaged with it — especially if dropping out meant joining a commune where dope would be plentifully available?

As the bard of the times proclaimed, "Everybody gotta get stoned." Throughout the period, psychedelic and narcotic fashions came and went with bullet-like rapidity — LSD, peyote, Ecstasy, Jimsonweed, speed, meth — each spawning a bewildering vocabulary of cryptic references. Lucy in the Sky with Diamonds…white rabbit…Puff the Magic Dragon. Before the era was out, there must have been 50 not-very-secret code words for marijuana alone. The jargon contributed to a mischievous sense of conspiratorial doings: the hip young undermining the stodgy old. The willingness to imbibe, smoke, or inject anything that somebody told somebody would turn you on became compulsive and frighteningly mindless. I remember cringing at some of the concoctions my students reported using. It seemed any weed, leaf, berry, fungus, or mold was worth trying. One student, already wasted by overuse, tried to interest me in his pet recipe for a cheap trip: well-rotted mushrooms gleaned from the garbage bins of the supermarket, a large admixture of baby aspirin, and just a soupçon of rat poison to give it the right kick. Did this person survive?

Yet, for all the zaniness that surrounded the drug culture of the time, dope was part of a new political agenda. It was the one element of mainstream culture that could be appropriated for revolutionary purposes — or at least its leading promoters so believed. LSD was, after all, an invention of the pharmaceutical industry, originally compounded by the Swiss company Sandoz, as a possible cure for migraine headaches. The purely recreational aspect of shooting up was there, of course; but that use was significantly paralleled by other intentions — most obviously, the growing fascination with lawbreaking. The fact that the sale and use of dope were illegal lent an aura of daring and defiance to getting high. If the authorities were out to suppress it, it automatically fell into the category of social revolution. No official authority deserved to be questioned more than the Federal Drug Administration. But there was more to it than that. Dope belonged to a deeply subversive query. *Is there more to the mind than we know in our normal state of awareness?* Wasn't that what William James had in mind when he concluded that "our normal waking consciousness, rational consciousness as we call it, is but one type of consciousness, while all about it, parted from it by the filmiest of screens, there lie potential forms of consciousness entirely different"? Wasn't that what Freud had taught us — the power and prevalence of the unconscious in all we do? And what if there was more to the unconscious than Freud ever discovered? Thanks to a handful of influential writers, dope took on the mystique of a grand cultural adventure. Aldous Huxley's *Doors of Perception*, William Burroughs's *Naked Lunch*, and Alan Watts's *Joyous Cosmology* turned consciousness alteration into the ultimate act of disaffiliation. They presented dope not simply as an act of political rebellion, but as an effort to outflank the reality principle on which modern life is based. The official definition of sanity and reality was being called into question.

In the hands of Huxley and Watts, and eventually a growing contingent of poets, novelists, and rock stars, dope — especially LSD — became the royal road to revolution. The phrase Huxley used for his title — *The Doors of Perception* — illustrates the widening front on which the counter culture was moving. When the Romantic poet William Blake spoke of "cleansing the doors of perception," he was seeking the spiritual transformation of society. His "mental fight" against the "mind forg'd manacles" of an increasingly materialistic and commercial society was a heavyweight match between two worldviews, that of the prophetic poet and that of the mechanistic scientist. The cleansing that Blake sought was a visionary enterprise. To "see eternity in a grain of sand" would restore the depleted soul of his society from the grinding materialism of the factory towns and the horrors of the marketplace. Huxley, the Vedantist sage, was after the same thing: a return to what he called *the perennial philosophy*, the path to mystical union with God. But Huxley, a many-sided mind, believed that western science was compatible with that goal. It had, in fact, discovered a faster, more accessible route to the godhead. Spiritual liberation, he believed, could be chemically induced through the use of mescaline — which, it is rumored, Huxley was using on his deathbed. The doors of perception had only to be "suddenly thrust open by a chemical substance such as mescaline or LSD," Huxley announced, and "the world would appear in a new light." The rock star Jim Morrison borrowed the name of his group, "The Doors," from Blake by way of Huxley and, along with other minstrels of the period, began retailing dope to a young audience of millions. Eventually, we reached the point at which hundreds at a time were being treated to the Kool-Aid acid test, novelist Ken Kesey's itinerant campaign to mass produce enlightenment. Among my friends there were those who were taking daily doses of LSD throughout the 1960s and 1970s as if it were a prescribed medicine for restricted consciousness. Dope had become an act of devotion, a pitting of the free spirit against an imprisoning secular culture.

All this is now a colorful and well-known chapter in the period. Did any of it have the transformative effect Huxley, Watts, Kesey, and others hoped for? Hardly. Paul McCartney may have believed that dosing the world's heads of state on LSD would "banish war, poverty, and famine," but in the years since, no political leader, radical spokesman, or social theorist has ever claimed that he or she took a significant cue in life from getting high. The one president who was willing to admit a passing acquaintance with pot swore he never inhaled. There were communal experiments where dope of one form or another was used ritually; some of these groups or their practices may survive. Timothy Leary, the leading proponent of turning on, spent his last years in a thickening science-fiction haze of metaphysical speculation. His one-time partner Ram Dass went on to become a wise and gentle spiritual counselor who may to some extent have drawn upon psychedelic experience. As his assumed name suggests, LSD at some point merged with more robust Asian traditions of meditation. That seems to be as far as it goes. We have certainly not seen a growing movement of psychedelic revolutionaries out to build the New Jerusalem. On the other hand, in my home town of Berkeley one can still count the casualties of this dogged search for the chemical paradise. They live on the streets, an increasingly senior population of hopelessly addicted derelicts panhandling for loose change. They are not an example of highly evolved humanity.

With the benefit of hindsight, the fascination with narcotics looks less daring than it once seemed. We are in truth a drug-obsessed culture, dependent on ever more medications to get through the day. The culture of drugs is a major industry, more lucrative today than ever. We have learned that the distinction between good drugs and bad drugs is little more than arbitrary. If Restoril, Lipitor, Ambien, or Prozac were to be illegalized, we would have the same result as with marijuana and cocaine: a criminal black market. Aging boomers are probably using more pharmaceuticals now than in their youth simply to keep body and soul together. But legally speaking, the distinctions we make among these substances can be horrendous. Today, narcotics — once indiscriminately touted by the countercultural young and indiscriminately condemned by their elders — have become an outlaw industry, a grubby, criminal enterprise that fills our inner cities with turf wars among small-change pushers for whom seriously toxic substances are simply a desperate way to make a fast dollar before they get arrested or gunned down. Those who retail speed, coke, crack, or hash may have a range of clients that stretches from hopeless junkies and thrill-seeking kids to hard-charging junior executives and media celebrities, but whether those users crave drugs for fun and games or addictive relief, there is nothing redeeming about shooting up these days. It has simply become a bad, expensive, and corrosive national habit. According to a 2007 government survey, the search for a chemical nirvana during the 1960s has left us with a sizeable population of overdosed boomers who will soon be burdening Medicare with addictions acquired in their distant youth.[1]

Worse, a generation that saw drugs as the gateway to a higher form of consciousness has, in its naiveté, made a major contribution to the organized crime that has become a deadly social virus of modern society. Liberals and conservatives have been allied in creating that sad legacy. In the mid-1970s Jimmy Carter, at the time a presidential candidate, was prepared to support the legalization of marijuana. That opened the door for Ronald Reagan's war on drugs which has been worth millions of votes to right-wing Republicans ever since. Trapped between an impractical permissiveness and a witless "Just say no!" resistance, the United States has become the narcotics industry's richest market. Everything that was ever wrong about prohibition in the roaring 1920s is wrong with the war on drugs today. But as with booze in the era of Al Capone, illegality is the price-support system of the drug trade. And with organized crime doing all it can to keep its commodities illegal, the only realistic and humane solution — decriminalization — remains out of reach.

Adventures in Consciousness: Episode Two

Does this mean that the politics of consciousness alteration has proven to be a false start? Not at all. Probing the irrational depths that underlie political action has yielded some of the richest insights of our time. We have learned that politics is one of the most psychopathic activities of human society, the breeding ground of madness in its most virulent form. No other human activity leads to so much bloodshed. The lies that are used to hide the true motivations of political leaders are often no better than psychotic cover stories; they cry out to be stripped away. The greatest egomaniacs have carried out the worst crimes with professions of justice and humanity on their lips. The opening scene of the 1964 movie *Dr. Strangelove* shows us two airplanes coupling in mid-air, a gigantic phallic shaft being inserted to fuel a bomber carrying thermonuclear bombs powerful enough to destroy millions. In the background, the music is "Try a little tenderness." The image tells us more about the compulsive masculinity of war than we could ever expect the Pentagon to confess. Similarly, in race relations, we needed to plumb the psychic depths of black-white antagonism as Eldridge Cleaver did in *Soul on Ice* and James Baldwin in all his novels to be aware of the full meaning of racism. Politics is freighted with age-old phobias and anxieties that underlie the high ideals we are so quick to expound. We need some way to tear ourselves free of these hidden compulsions. But drugs are not the way to do that.

Searching for a quick, push-button, chemically induced technique to achieve enlightenment was surely naive. Even if there are instances of beneficial transformations, there have been too many bad, even destructive, trips. Powerful psychotropics are hard to control and erratic in their effect. That is especially so given the massive drug dependency of our culture. Ever since the introduction of caffeine — in the form of coffee, tea, and chocolate in the early industrial period — our society has been relying on drugs of one kind or another to prop up its overworked population. We still — most of us — start the day with coffee and keep dosing on it until the workday is over and happy hour arrives. Starbucks is the psychotropic adjunct of modern society. Every urban industrial society uses a repertory of permissible drugs to stay awake, fall asleep, relieve tension, aid digestion, stave off depression, have reasonably satisfying sex. Who can say how these substances mix in the organism with cocaine or speed or pot? I was first offered LSD when I was on heavy doses of asthma medications — mainly steroids — that were driving my physiology at a worrisome clip. What risk would I have been running to load more drugs into my system without any medical supervision? Whose judgment would I trust about the quality and safety of anything I might use?

Is there, then, a more effective means of cleansing the doors of perception than playing chemical roulette with one's nervous system? Of course there is. Any powerful emotional jolt, something that tears you up by the roots, can make a different person of you. Near-death experiences can do that, or severe loss. The evangelical churches are rooted in the jarring effect of the born-again experience. They draw on time-tested methods to bring their members the sense of ecstatic transformation. They offer music, song, shouts and howls, gyrations, hand waving, and swooning. Such deep emotional turbulence accompanied by the reassuring support of the group and the guidance of the all-knowing man in the pulpit offers everything boomers ever found at a Grateful Dead concert — minus the dope. These traditional techniques work now as in times past and have a more enduring effect than any psychedelic drug. If religion is the opiate of the masses, it is proving as popular as ever. Born-again Christianity is surely the most potent form of consciousness alteration on the contemporary scene, and not only in the United States. How ironic that through the 1960s and 1970s, while the drug culture was at its zenith among boomers, the Jesus freaks were working at the same goal by other means — and having far more success. The old-time religion had more of a future than the new psychedelics.

But effective as evangelical consciousness alteration may be, it has a major liability. With few exceptions, the churches that offer the experience do not seek to enlarge the mind, but to narrow it. Their claim to know the absolute truth closes them, as do all ideologies, to taking delight in human diversity. Evangelicals see the devil at work in everything that diverges from what kids learn in Sunday school; indeed, it regards all that differs from a narrow Christian orthodoxy as temptation. Offered a cultural experience that lies outside the tight boundaries of scripture and doctrine, they are obliged to cry, "Get thee behind me,

Satan!" and run for shelter. That is the vision of life the evangelicals hold — exactly the opposite of the counter culture I have in mind. Grounded in dogma — and in fundamentalist dogma at that — born-again Christianity diminishes the critical faculties and closes itself to multicultural insight. Worse, it sunders the bonds of fellowship, for there can be no greater gap between people than the gulf that separates the saved from the damned. It is beholden to a religion of the book — of *one* book and of only one way to read that book. Its spirit is adversarial, punitive, and ultimately coercive. How else to characterize the threat of hell and damnation? Those who admire Jesus for his compassion and universality find little of that in a faith that is so exclusive it regards even other forms of Christianity as apostasy. Perhaps there was a moment, a crossroads, where the evangelical ethos might have sided with the wretched of the Earth, but instead it has dovetailed neatly into the conservative backlash of the 1980s. It is willing to tolerate social injustice if it can impose its witless orthodoxies on the nation.

Fortunately, there is another form of consciousness alteration that is neither chemically induced nor dogmatically delimited. It is the perfectly natural process of aging. Nothing changes consciousness more effectively than growing older, especially when we reach the last few decades of life. We arrive there with years of hard knocks behind us, with the illusions of youth dissipated, with the careerist aspirations of mid-life left behind. With age, we learn the realities of love and family and worldly achievement. Is this not what all of us who have made it to those later years experience when we hear the young carrying on about romance, success, fame, and fortune? We may indulge their fantasies, even try to share them for a time, but we know how it will end for them. The voice within us that whispers *Alas! Alas!* is the voice of wisdom. In his classic work on the varieties of religious experience, William James spoke of potential forms of

consciousness that lie all about our normal state. He was thinking of ecstatic and transcendent states of awareness that might
qualify as religious. What he left out was a change of consciousness that lies *ahead* in life — in *everybody's* life — but possessing
the subtlety of the ordinary and universal. It is that state we recognize only when we reflect — if we can find the candor — on
how foolish, how naive, how shallow we have been. Clearly, having the ability to say that means we have changed.

Not that we arrive at that condition automatically. Wisdom
is the result of *examined* experience. If there was ever a need in
our lives for Socratic dialogue, it comes with age. That is when
we have a mountain of experience to look back upon; that is
when we begin writing the epilogue to our story. I have never
met anyone who did not believe they had learned from experience, though often the lessons have brought bitterness and depression. This is not to say everybody who reaches the age of
60 or 70 is a wise, old soul. Age is often wasted on the old. But
if they turn out foolish, narrow, and intolerant at the age of 70,
were they any wiser at the age of 25?

Aging changes consciousness more surely than any narcotic;
it does so gradually and organically. It digests the experience of
a lifetime and makes us different people — sometimes so different that we are amazed, embarrassed, or even ashamed at the
person we once were. Pious people often claim that religion offered them the chance to be born again. But, curiously enough,
growing old can also lead to rebirth, a chance to leave old values,
old obsessions, old fears, and old loves behind. Aging grants
permission. It allows us to get beyond the assumptions and ambitions that imprisoned us in youth and middle age. That can be
a liberating realization. Perhaps there is a biological impulse behind that possibility, a driving desire to find meaning in our existence that grows stronger as we approach death. It may even
lead to rebellion, if one has the time and energy to undertake
the act.

The Dirtiest Four-Letter Word

It is impossible to generalize about the way aging will change a population of millions — except in one respect. Everybody who makes it into deep old age needs help. That fact comes built in with the passage of time. There are those who can still cope and even hold jobs in their advanced years; some draw the attention of the media — the accountant still reporting for work at 93, the librarian still coming in daily at 102, the film star who wins an Oscar with some great final role. But all of us who live on into deep age finally reach what some physicians have called "the ragged fringe," where self-reliance gives out. At that point we need help, whether physical assistance or emotional support. And we need more of it as time passes. We have outlived the illusion of self-reliance. *Help*, the dirtiest four-letter word in the individualist's vocabulary, becomes imperative. We turn to family and companionship and beyond that to professional help. We may one day face laws that prohibit the elderly from driving. At that point, senior transportation will become a growth industry. But there will be other needs reporting in — cooking, cleaning, and every kind of heavy lifting, and above all, sympathetic companionship.

The economic implications of an elder culture are already coming to be recognized. What needs more attention is the philosophical meaning behind those needs. They are a return to our true nature as convivial animals. We are born needing help, and we finish life needing help. Indeed, we need help throughout life. But we tend to lose touch with that paramount fact during the adolescent and middle years — especially in the United States where the ethos of self-reliance bulks so large. Americans take pride in standing on their own two feet. "I never asked anything from anyone," "I never took a handout," "I've always looked after my own needs." How often, especially in the wake of disasters, do we hear people saying they deplore taking charity or signing up for government programs — as if

seeking help were a shameful act? All part of the Social-Darwinist ethic.

The illusion of self-reliance has deep roots in our culture. It
conjures up images of brave pioneers, daring gunslingers, self-
made millionaires. But it is, at last, sad self-deception. Nobody
makes it through life on their own. We may find ways to ignore
the help we get in the course of a lifetime from friends, teachers,
and family, from the subtle network of mutual aid that perme-
ates our lives, but the help is there. The independence we all seek
to achieve in becoming adult is tightly circumscribed by countless forms of help. Hard-charging business types are especially
prone to claim they are self-made, brushing aside the support
they receive from partners, a wife, secretaries, and coworkers.
Even rugged individualists need help to build a business empire. At some level, we all know this; everybody who wins a public award responds by thanking all those who helped. We expect
them to do so. But instead of integrating this into our social
ethic, we keep reverting to phony images of autonomy, insisting
that needing help is a sign of weakness or incompetence. Conservatives especially tend to configure public debate about social
programs as if taking welfare from the government is a disgrace
and a shame. That was the way right-wingers characterized Social Security when it was introduced. "No one will work," a Republican editorialist of that day announced. "No one will have
to provide for old age or widowhood. There will be moral de-
cay, financial bankruptcy, and the collapse of the United States
government." They do not see social programs as mutual aid
that benefits the entire society; rather, they condemn the taxes
that fund such programs as a burden unfairly laid on the shoulders of hard-working, self-reliant citizens for the benefit of freeloaders, welfare queens, and other social parasites. Only when a
growing number of elders assume power in our society will we
see a willingness to agree that *help* is not a dirty word.

Near Death, Return to Life

The trials of aging have always been a schooling in the meaning of life. But in our time, we have happened upon a new, consciousness-expanding experience that makes it all the more likely that the elder culture will have a deeper appreciation of the spiritual meaning of aging than any previous generation.

Until the 1970s, most of the statistics about the health and intelligence of the elderly were collected from the residents of nursing homes and poorhouses. Surveys of aging then focused almost exclusively on a population that was impoverished, seriously disadvantaged, often quite ill, and usually demoralized, men and women who had been warehoused and had little to live for. Very little in the culture reflected their needs or values. If you gave them any sort of intelligence test, why should they even try to do well? While there are still institutions for the elderly that are substandard and even abusive, geriatric medicine no longer treats the elderly as a population of decrepit dolts. Indeed, many gerontologists have fought to redeem the qualities of elders and to defend their interests. Doctors — and society generally — have learned that lumping all the elderly into one category labeled *senile* is as valid and as fair as classifying all blond women as *bimbos*. And yet there is a certain truth in the familiar belief that age brings unremitting decline. Today we have a growing population that remains fit enough long enough to participate in the senior Olympics; nevertheless, those who reach old age do at some point give out, some by way of catastrophic illness, most more gradually. That is how people have faced their senior years since time out of mind. They entered old age moving rapidly or gradually along a smooth continuum, losing a little here, a little there, and finally succumbing. It was a lot like the steady deterioration of a piece of machinery.

No wonder, then, that few books on aging leave out Shakespeare's well-known lines from *As You Like It*, the passage that finishes with "sans teeth, sans eyes, sans taste, sans everything." For generations this famous lament has been the melancholy conventional wisdom. Growing old has been seen as an inexorable stream of losses — and not simply in the popular culture. An acquaintance of mine — a gerontologist — once told me that this quotation from Shakespeare might serve as a summary of geriatric medicine as she learned it no more than a generation ago. "Every textbook you could find was filled with depressing charts and graphs," she told me, "all of them pointing down, down, down. The body, the mind, the emotions, sex, memory, alertness — all of them were shown in steady decline. After 50 or 60, it was all downhill. Of course, there were notable exceptions, but even they reached a limit. We were all destined to run down like an old car and finally to die of old age — as if old age were a disease without a cure."

The mechanistic image of aging has been enshrined in actuarial thinking since the early 19th century when Benjamin Gompertz, an English population theorist, invented the concept of the "mortality slope." Based on the best statistics of the time, as well as pure common sense, Gompertz concluded that the force of mortality increases exponentially with age with each passing year after adolescence. Young children are at risk for many diseases; but at puberty human beings reach their prime. Generally speaking, they will never be healthier or more robust. From there deterioration sets in, placing an absolute limit on survival. As recently as 1980, prominent demographers took 85 to be the absolute limit for life expectancy. Only within the last few decades has the longevity revolution produced a different and highly surprising view of mortality. We now know that at age 70 people take on a sort of late-onset vitality that makes their chance of reaching 100 greater, not less, as Gompertz would have predicted at a time when there were few 80-year-olds to study. Demographers now know that mortality decelerates after 70, reaching a ceiling at about 100.

This leads to speculation that, with a few key breakthroughs in medical science that allow for such possibilities as organ regeneration, age deceleration may be improved to a far later age. For actuaries, this long-standing underestimation of the life span has come as a jolt, implying that all calculations about the costs of aging are significantly out of kilter. Aging is no longer what it once was. It may be lengthened and delayed indefinitely.

With the boomer generation, an increasing number of people will enter their elder years in a far more dramatic, if not traumatic, way. Rather than via a smooth or perhaps precipitous downward slope, many will approach old age by way of a wrenching ordeal, perhaps more than one. As the Hemingway-esque cliché would have it, they will find themselves facing that "moment of truth" the toreador confronts in the ring at the end of an exhausting battle with a beast that might kill him. That moment may be frightening, but it may have as much to teach us as other great moments: being born, finding our first love, greeting our first child.

As medical science increases its inventory of lifesaving techniques, more and more people will survive into old age by passing through at least one life-threatening medical crisis. They will come home from a visit to the doctor shaken to their core by *bad news*. Or they will be rushed to the hospital, taken into surgery, or dosed on a wonder drug. One way or the other, they will find themselves under the care of physicians for some extended interval during which their habits of life will be radically altered. Everything else — job and family, obligations and responsibilities — will be placed on hold. And in case after case they will survive an illness that would have killed their parents. They will in ever greater numbers recover to live another year, another decade, another 30 or 40 years. Indeed, they may actually be healthier after receiving those attentions than they were for years before the crisis. Whether it is by way of heart bypass surgery or a medication that manages diabetes or arrests cancer, ever more people are already being saved from death by some heroic medical intervention. They are diagnosed with something serious, maybe they very nearly die, and then they are brought back from the brink. The experience is so commonplace that gerontologists have a name for it. They call it the near-death-return-to-life experience. An episode such as this medical crisis jars and batters — but it has no spiritual meaning — at least not yet. It is simply a close call. When we emerge, we are in a different stage of life.

In times past, one might have thought of life as a children's slide. We start at the top and move steadily down. But thanks to modern medicine the course of our lives is now more like a roller coaster. Yes, we move down, but along the way there are sudden surprising upward sweeps. And each is a moment of anxiety and then thrilling relief, assuring us that we did not crash or run off the rails. Moments like this are rites of passage, experiences that shake us out of our accustomed routine and raise us to a higher level of awareness. In traditional societies, these rites are highly structured occasions that mark the great transitions of life. They usher us into a new phase of existence as we move from childhood into adolescence, from adolescence into maturity, from maturity into old age, and finally from old age into death. In this respect more than any other, primary peoples have proven themselves wiser than us: They take the course of life seriously, seeing it as an educational progression. Where rites of passage fade from the cultural repertory, as they have in the modern western world, maturing into a true elder becomes all the more difficult.

In many rites of passage, episodes of great fear are designed to capture the full sense of crisis that faces us at the main turning points in life. Sometimes death is mimicked, as if one were dying to one's old self and being reborn into new life. Young boys in some tribal societies are put through the moment of their own death and taken into the terrors of the underworld — and then ushered back. Outside of religious communities, we have few rites of passage that retain the dignity and depth of these traditional practices. Prom night, wedding receptions, and marriage anniversaries are lightweight in comparison and almost always wrapped in commercial fluff. To that degree, we have cheapened the quality of life. Perhaps that has something to do with the cult of youth that still holds sway over our popular culture. We cling to youthfulness with no desire to move on, even though the effort to hold back is futile. Nobody is better suited to the task of detaching us from our infatuation with youth than those who belong to the generation that created the cult in the first place.

A close call — that is how I recall thinking about the medical crises I have passed through. There have been two; the first, and most telling, came in my late fifties. When, after emergency surgery that came close to costing me my life, I returned to my senses, I woke feeling as if I had hit rock bottom: feeble, dazed, unable to eat, drink, or move. I learned I had lain in the intensive-care unit hallucinating for hours at a stretch. My body felt shattered to pieces — as I have heard that shamanic apprentices feel after they have been through one of their vision quests. But for them the experience is one of transcendence. For me it was nothing but numbness and confusion. I wanted desperately to take hold of a friendly hand as if that would keep me in one piece. Slowly, I came to realize I had dodged a bullet. But I knew I had been through far more than that. Or at least I felt I *should* make something more of it than a lucky break. I *wanted* this to count for more. But it was up to me to supply everything the hospital and doctor could not. I almost felt cheated. After suffering all this, I should have become wiser. My life should have been turned around, but I saw no way that was going to happen. The doctors came to check me out; nurses came to take my vital signs. I was in the hands of caring experts; I was grateful. But nobody came to minister to my soul.

With the best intentions, medical professionals often take it to be their duty to return those they have saved to their *normal* life — that is, to the routine they had before. In their view, medical crisis is a bad patch in the road; the sooner you get over it and put it behind you, the better. Their goal is to make us as good as new. If patients can resume their job and their family responsibilities, that is seen as ideal. The upshot of the exercise is to gloss over the terror and anguish of the crisis. Nothing could be further from the purpose of a rite of passage, which is to stand as a landmark along the way. In some tribal societies, the body is marked during the rite; blood is taken, a scar is left, or a part cut away to serve as a reminder. Our medical rites of passage often seek to eliminate any reminder of that kind. If possible, the body is left whole and unmarked, or perhaps repaired by cosmetic surgery later on. In my case, it was not. The scar, an ugly one, remains as a chapter in my life etched upon my flesh. Every time I see it I remember: *That was the day you might have died. But here you are. And what are you going to make of that?*

Making the Most of It

As traumatic as it may be, medical crisis offers an opportunity of the greatest value. Sanctioned by an air of emergency, it is a deviation from all normal routines. Work and family responsibilities are postponed; bills wait to be paid; appointments are canceled. Bedridden and largely incapacitated, patients are left with time on their hands, perhaps the first time in years they have the chance to take stock. If they are given nothing better to do, they while away the time watching television. But that need not be the way the occasion is used. It is, after all, a situation where social conventions are put on hold as if to clear a space. One's food is prescribed, like it or not; everybody under care dons the same ridiculously awkward and revealing gowns; nurses, who will take no nonsense, appear with bedpans, esoteric equipment, and medications at all hours of the day and night. They expect their patients to do as they are told, eat what they are served, and undress and be washed with no great show of modesty. Of course it is an ordeal; one comes to deplore it. And the healthier one becomes, the more agonizing it all is. But this is exactly what many rites of passage are designed to be: a suspension of the ordinary, a time of tribulation when one's fate is entrusted to the judgment of others who know what is best.

In the years ahead, more and more of us are going to be leaving hospitals after a brush with death that subjects us to a crisis like this. We will have a story to tell; but if all it comes down to is the excitement of a hairsbreadth escape, the story will soon wear thin. My experience led to an odd result. Though I am a writer and teacher somewhat skilled in words, I discovered with some embarrassment that there was not much I had to say — at least nothing that sounded earthshaking. One cannot expect others to make much of phrases like "glad to be alive;" they do no justice to the event. Yet that was what I felt. That was all I felt. For me, it was a discovery that yearned for expression. Perhaps this is what religious people find at church testimonials: the chance to stand up and say what everybody has heard a hundred times: "Praise the Lord! I am saved." The words are a formula; one utters them knowing that everybody present will be able to fill in the full feeling behind them.

The modern world provides some techniques for articulating ineffable moments in life. Support groups are created for that purpose. As a therapeutic invention, the support group dates back to the creation of Alcoholics Anonymous in the 1930s, a self-help movement based on local associations of people who shared the suffering of a common condition. Those who gather at AA meetings do not come expecting to hear eloquent declarations. They listen for the emotional subtext from which they judge the authenticity of what is said. A perceptive therapist might see the possibility of using the medical crisis in somewhat the same way, as an occasion for building the kind of camaraderie that keeps the experience alive. As the elder culture takes shape, we will need therapists who know the value of deepening the medical rite of passage. They will want to work with that moment, not as a trauma to be talked away but as the beginning of a quest. Very little current therapy has that skill or intention. Most therapists, after all, take their degrees in "childhood, marriage, and family," relationships that belong to early and midlife. Death transcends those relationships; it reaches out for the solitude that lies beyond society. A therapist I know once told me she often finds herself at a loss dealing with clients old enough to be her parents or grandparents. They have left behind so much of what she was trained to keep at the center of the therapy. Among her older clients, marriage tends to take on very different parameters. Companionship, gentleness, and patience come to outweigh sexual gratification. The trials of chronic illness, physical decline, and caregiving replace issues of child rearing or domestic decision-making. Thoughts turn to asking, "What will I do when I'm the one left on my own?" The near-death medical crisis throws all these questions into high relief. At that point, what people may need more than conventional therapy is a heavy application of philosophy. The medical rite of passage cries out for the sort of *support* that only great minds and great hearts can offer. If we move with the grain of that need, we may discover wonders lying in wait.

Three Going on Four

Young...middle-aged...old. The image of our lives playing out in three acts is so commonplace that it is almost impossible to think around it. It seems to make perfect sense. Or at least it did until boomers took possession of elderhood. As this big, assertive generation moves into its senior years, we are apt to identify distinct stages within what we now still think of as *old age*. As one might expect, boomers, seeking to avoid being old for as long as possible, have been taking advantage of our lengthening life expectancy by extending middle age to 60 or 70. "Sixty is the new 40." And many of them have done a remarkably successful job. When I look at photos of my grandparents, I see people who were *old* at the age of 50. They were clearly out of shape physically; their clothes were frumpy, their general appearance tired and sad. (Of course one of those grandparents lived to 104, so she must have been basically resilient. Even so, she also looked old at 50, and then older and older.) Today I see far fewer people who look old at 50 — or even 60. Fitness has made a difference, as has better diet — though too many Americans are now eating themselves into an obesity that will shave years off their lives. Above all, there is the awareness that at 50 and 60 they have a couple more decades ahead of them. That does wonders for morale. Imagine how differently your life would have been shaped if, at the age of 20, you had seen little more than another 20 years ahead of you.

And still — *defying age*, as one of the cosmetic advertisements invites us to do, is clearly a losing proposition. A middle age that extends from 30 to 70 is an unwieldy period that overlooks too many significant changes. It also precludes what may be the most intriguing possibility of the longevity revolution. Instead of envisioning each stage of life as simply stretching out longer, like the sections of a rubber band, suppose there is *another* stage to come, as different from *old* as adolescence is from childhood. Suppose there is something new coming along that has yet to be explored — an unexplored region of the life span. In that case, the next generation of elders may see *le troisième âge* (as the French call it) leading on to a fourth age, a stage of life we have failed to notice. Why? Because so few have lived that long enjoying decent health and a degree of independence, so few who have seemed to merit much attention from the busy and preoccupied younger generation that had no reason to give their burdensome elders more than occasional attention.

Once we get around to reconfiguring the later years, I suspect we will recognize that there is indeed an *old age* on the other side of midlife, a time to slow down and detach, to relinquish and retire. But it will not be an end; it will be a transition. There will be something more, a period of growth and deep maturity for which we may want to redefine the word *elder*.

A fourth age. That was what George Bernard Shaw proposed in *Back to Methuselah*, his most eccentric and most thought-provoking play. Shaw is the only thinker who ever sought to build a philosophy on the aging process. Combining themes from Henri Bergson's *Creative Evolution* and from Nietzsche's philosophy of the superman, he took up the possibility that if we could live longer — very much longer — and stay healthy, we might, as it were, unlock the door leading into another undiscovered wing in the house of life. And there all the counsels of perfection we inherit from the best and wisest minds would be achieved before death cut off the search. So he imagines a race of sexless, ascetic, contemplative *ancients* — people a lot like himself — who live hundreds of years and at last discover the meaning of life.

Biologists would have us believe that reproduction is the purpose of life. Therefore, when reproduction has been achieved — and the more the better — there is no need for old animals to continue living. But Shaw turned the conventional biological wisdom upside down. He contended that *enlightenment* was the purpose of life, a goal that required more study, thought, and experience than could be crammed into a life span of 70 to 100 years. This was Shaw's way of castigating the immaturity of his fellow humans. The only way human beings now had of pursuing the highest levels of wisdom was by producing new generations. But that, in turn, burdens us with all the nonsense surrounding courtship and marriage and child rearing — a major distraction that subtracts decades from the life of the mind. Far from being the goal of life, sex was, in Shaw's view, an obstacle. So in the future he anticipated something like test-tube fertilization to keep the human race going in minimal numbers. With sex out of the way, we might then devote all our time to higher purposes. Only someone as old as Shaw was when he wrote *Back to Methuselah* and as odd as he was in general could come up with so jarring an idea.

Still he leads us to wonder: Would the stage of superlongevity he anticipated not already have been discovered by those who made it into deep old age? One should not preclude the possibility that this age-based minority has indeed arrived at a radically different view of life and a very much wiser one than the society they are leaving behind. They had something to say, but they were too fragile and demoralized to speak up, or perhaps there were too few willing to listen to them. Shaw tried to will himself into an extra-long life that would take him into the realm of the oldest old, still with a clear, quick wit. But too few centenarians retain that mental clarity or the desire to stay in touch with the rest of us to judge the philosophical value of their extraordinary experience. Still, there has been a Verdi, a Frank Lloyd Wright, a Michelangelo, a Georgia O'Keefe — all doing their finest work in deep old age. Were they the exceptional few, or harbingers of a potentiality yet to be discovered? We may soon find out. Centenarians are now the fastest growing part of our population. As of 2000 there were 65,000 Americans over the age of 100; there are estimates that predict anywhere between one million and four million by 2050. If they stay healthy and assertive enough, who knows what influence they may one day exert?

The Spiritual Meaning of Aging

As the bridge between life and death, the elder years should not be left in the hands of physicians and gerontologists, much less retirement advisors, cruiseship vendors, spa owners, or fitness trainers. Age, if we are to get the most out of it, cries out for a greater spiritual investment. While the powers of modern medicine will always be a welcome and life-enhancing part of our lives, the result of its achievements needs to assume philosophical depth. This should be the season of life for confronting the teachings we inherit from spiritual masters. The final decades of life need to be seen not as an extension of the middle years and still less as a time of elderly resignation, but as a distinctly new stage of life. Boomers, I believe, are well suited to that task for some of the very reasons for which they have been ridiculed. Social critics have called them the *me generation*, given to the sort of narcissism one expects from spoiled children — a sweeping generalization that overlooks the possibility that what looks like self-indulgence from the outside may, on the inside, be a search for self-knowledge. The resort to psychotherapy that has become so common over the last generation may express the same need to take every aspect of experience seriously.

There is one more quality that has generally characterized boomers — a fascination with the varieties of religious experience. The youthful disaffiliation of the 1960s and 1970s was not limited to politics; it extended to the religious life of modern society. Not since the Romantic movement have we seen such a desire to sample the varied spiritual insights of the world. A generation brought up on existential angst and death-of-god theology set about finding food for the soul in every tradition it could uncover. At its deepest level, the counter culture sought to address the most wounding price we have paid to build an urban-industrial society: the loss of the sacred. Quite spontaneously, the young of that period sought out gurus — wise old souls who might have something better to teach them than their professors. The result was a flowering of traditional lore that flowed into the western world from every exotic source on Earth. Swamis, shamans, Zen masters, and *brujos* were suddenly in demand. Native American lore, like the teachings of the Sioux medicine man Black Elk, became, for the first time in the nation's history, part of our popular culture. At the time, I wondered how much of this wisdom literature and these arcane teachings could take significant effect among people in their teens and twenties. For some, I'm sure the encounter with spiritual insight was life-transforming. But clearly a great many more did little more than sample and move on — for look at how little the mainstream has changed. Still, if the appetite for spiritual sustenance was there in youth, why should it not return when time and experience have prepared more fertile ground — and, above all, when mortality is that much nearer?

A Declaration of Interdependence

The elder culture is a quiet revolution, but it brings with it a powerful transformation of consciousness. It may one day find expression in a Declaration of Interdependence that reads something like this:

> Self-reliance is a lie. We are all born into dependency — and not simply the dependency of infancy or childhood, but the dependency that is lifelong, our need for one another's respect and support. Dependency doesn't end when we get out of diapers. It just becomes less obvious, if not invisible. Maybe that invisibility begins when parents first encourage their babies to toddle on their own. The baby toddles, but the parents stay close and watch to make sure the child doesn't take a bad fall. The baby may not know it's still being watched over; it may think it's on its own. But it isn't. It's entering another stage of dependency. Perhaps that's when people begin developing the illusion of self-reliance: when parents try to encourage kids to believe they can do this or that all by themselves. And we do learn to do this or that on our own: crawl, walk, hold the spoon, go to the toilet, read a book. Call those the little tasks of life. Parents use the little tasks to convince us we can do everything on our own. They go so far in that direction that they distort the reality that will be with us for the rest of our lives.

The fact is, dependency never goes away, it just becomes more subtle and systemic. Without someone to feed us, change our diapers, carry us from place to place, we would never survive to grow up. Later, all these forms of help recede into the background. They no longer look like mommy and daddy putting the spoon in our mouths. They look like the supermarket, the restaurant, the sewer system, the electrical grid, running water, the emergency room. Help becomes endemic, pervasive, and invisible. But it's still there. For every one thing we think we have done on our own, there are a dozen things that had to be provided for us by others. We live in a dense fabric of mutual aid. That's what makes us a social species. Even when we go out to compete in the world for money and acclaim, we never achieve on our own. We build upon parents, relatives, friends, teachers, and neighbors who helped along the way. Help is to each of us as water is to the fish.

At its highest stage, civilization returns to a truth that was obvious to our prehistoric ancestors: There is no such thing as the stand-alone individual. We are family, clan, tribe, city, society, nation, world. Help is the invisible web that makes us members one of another. It's time to tell the truth. Let's stop shaming those who have no way to disguise their need for help. Let's proclaim a declaration of mutual dependence:

We hold these truths to be self-evident: that all human beings are created in equal need of help and endowed by their creator with certain inalienable rights, that among these are full access to the good things of life, a decent chance to achieve their potential, pride in who they are and what they can do. And that whenever any society fails to provide those rights, it is the right, it is the duty, of the disadvantaged to make a revolution.

CHAPTER 8

Aging and the Alpha Male

Nuncle,... Thou shouldst not have been old
Till thou hadst been wise.

— Shakespeare, *King Lear*

But if interdependence is indeed the age-old truth about the human condition, where does the illusion of self-reliance come from, and who keeps it alive?

Self-reliance is a recent ideological construction that has become a nearly universal psychological delusion. As it is most prominently practiced in our society by alpha-male business types, self-reliance was spawned by the marketplace. Like white supremacy and male dominance, it serves as a way of justifying selfishness and repression. Self-reliance, rugged individualism, the survival of the fittest — all these are rhetorical masks used to hide the fact that nobody makes it on his own. And the *his* means what it says: male, masculine, macho. We are dealing here with a male-ego thing that gets drummed into boys in their early years. Boys are raised with a craving need to stand on their own two feet and fight the world. Their fathers, and maybe their mothers too, teach them to be autonomous. Most mothers play along to keep their boys from looking like sissies, but they know better than to believe anybody is truly self-reliant. Boys grow up into men who have blinded themselves to the way others have helped. They marry women who keep mothering them in all the daily details of life. They go out to fight the world, but somebody back home does the laundry, washes the dishes, cleans and sweeps, raises the kids — either an underpaid nanny or servant or an unpaid wife. Macho men exploit secretaries, co-workers, partners, and friends to become boss-big-shot. Above all, they bully those that work under them to create the impression that they stand alone and rule the roost. But others pull food out of the ground to put on our tables, others keep the water and power coming, others keep the streets reasonably safe and clean, and others deliver the goods and cart away the garbage; others do the shit work without which, if it wasn't done, the bosses wouldn't get to the office in the first place.

I remember the first time I had to ask for help loading my suitcase into the overhead rack on a plane. Blocking the aisle as the airplane loaded, I wanted to find another male passenger who might give me a hand, but the first person to catch my eye was a young woman flight attendant. As if she had been trained to come to the aid of the old and infirm, she hefted my bag and slid it into place. I started to explain that I was on steroids for asthma, that the steroids had weakened my tendons and had led to an injury of the rotator cuff, that…it would have been a long excuse. The flight attendant had no time for all that. She smiled and moved on. What was there to explain? In her mind, it came down to a simple rule: *Old guy, needs help*. And she was right. The injured shoulder wasn't the problem. Weakness and bad joints were. That was what troubled me most. I realized that an episode like this was the beginning of a phase in my life. From now on, I would be asking people — younger, stronger people, including women — to lift and carry pretty regularly.

A trivial episode, I admit. But it is something I'm sure every man confronts the first time he registers physical frailty or inca-pacity: the first time he cannot change a flat tire, the first time he cannot make it up a ladder or a steep flight of stairs, the first time he cannot carry his groceries out to the car. He is failing at something expected of him, something he expects of himself. Some men find ways to put that moment off until they are well along in years. They work out, they muscle up. But these male expectations go beyond physicality. What about holding a job, earning a living, paying the bills? After a certain point, if he survives into his retirement, all these responsibilities which he was trained to shoulder from childhood pass out of a man's life. How is he to face that fact? I suspect few women realize how shaming it is for a man to admit to frailty.

If there is one style of consciousness that will surely have to change radically in the elder culture, it is that of the alpha male. Deeply rooted in our biology, the alpha-male syndrome lies close to the primitive core of human personality, a feature we might have hoped to leave far behind us in the evolutionary story, but have not. Many mammalian groups, especially the primates, live under the dominance of a tough, old male who monopolizes the females and stands as a target for eager young males who must prove their selective advantage by overthrowing him. Freud had something like this in mind when he invented his fanciful notion of the *primal horde*. He imagined there were once human males who ruled by taking all the women into their harem and castrating any son who challenged them. Resorting to dramatic license, as he often did, Freud thought this was the prehistoric origin of the famous Oedipus complex.

Whatever its anthropological validity, Freud's image of the despotic elder has shown up prominently in our popular culture. We see it in the careers of numerous male movie stars. When he was in mid-forties, John Wayne had aged beyond playing conventional romantic leads. He was ready to turn to character roles. But then, in the 1948 film *Red River*, Wayne was cast as a ruthless cattle baron, a distinctly senior figure who was nonetheless a domineering stud possessed of potent sexuality and capable of intimidating younger males. It was a role he would play for the next 30 years, never once relinquishing his claim to power, dominance, or women. At roughly the same time, the slightly older French matinee idol Jean Gabin was staking out a similar film persona for the remainder of his career: the lonely, hard-bitten, older male, the survivor of a dead wife or a hard divorce, perhaps a kingpin criminal who carries on with as much erotic power as ever, feared by the men around him, pursued by lovely younger women.

Sexual attraction is the key ingredient in the alpha-male syndrome, the litmus test of virility. Since it is the body that most obviously ages, it is the body that must prove itself stronger than time and especially in the one kind of performance that notoriously becomes most demanding with the passing years. As Henry Kissinger once said, "Power is the ultimate aphrodisiac." The successful sixty-something CEO with a twenty-something trophy wife on his arm (and perhaps a well-advertised mistress or two) is the human counterpart of the alpha-male chimp who must constantly display sexual prowess to his adolescent rivals in the pack. Many other senior stars have followed in John Wayne's footsteps: Clint Eastwood, Sean Connery, Paul Newman, Anthony Quinn, and perhaps most tellingly Clark Gable, who went to his grave playing the indomitable stud opposite an adoring Marilyn Monroe in *The Misfits*. Nobody in the movie is as much of a misfit as Gable — the actor, even more so than the antiquated cowpoke he plays. Cast as a macho guy, he is more pathetic than heroic. Reportedly, he brought on the heart attack that killed him trying to wrangle wild horses as the script required his character to do, rather than having a stunt man do it for him. Macho to the last.

Needless to say, few men in their fifties and sixties, not even the great Gable, have what it takes to be alpha males — namely, a professional makeup artist; all the right camera angles; a stunt man to take over the running, jumping, and fighting; a director to call "Cut!" when your toupee slips; and a million-dollar publicity department. Nevertheless, all men to some degree feel the weight of that image. It stands over them like the looming threat of failure — as failure is judged by a cruelly unrealistic standard. After adolescence, obsolescence.

The Separative Self

At the outset of this book, I observed that the modern world is rapidly gravitating toward gerontocracy, and I found that good. Perhaps that struck a curious note for some readers who might wonder if the world has not been under gerontocratic rule for as long as anyone can remember. Haven't there been old men like King Lear running things since the river valley civilizations — pharaohs, kings, emperors, dictators, gray-haired politicians? True enough. The superstar movie stud is patterned on the real-life prominence of dominant older males. As age-denying as our culture is, senior men continue to wield great power in politics and the marketplace. We see them in the news of the day giving speeches, attending VIP conferences, making deals, announcing policy, getting richer. As heads of state and as high corporate chieftains, they do embody a certain kind of gerontocracy — the *wrong* kind. They are the boss, the big shot, the bully, the brute. As such, they are, paradoxically enough, the worst impediment to the making of a true elder culture, men who dominate by force rather than by wisdom, men who live in egotistical isolation and the fear of rivals.

In Alex Gibney's 2005 book, *Enron: The Smartest Guys in the Room* (and in the documentary film by Gibney based on the book), we have a rare insight into the faux eldering that plagues the experience of aging in many societies, and none more so than the United States. Here is a study of our corporate culture that makes clear how little-boyish the men who earn billions can be. Enron's CEO Jeffrey Skilling took pride in instituting a harsh Social Darwinist regimen on the company: relentless, high-pressure competition among traders to achieve ever-higher profits, with *losers* terminated in large numbers. The men of the company augmented the macho ethos in which they worked every day, gaming the nation's energy supply, with daring dirt-bike excursions to the Baja California wilderness and trips to stripper clubs. It was a mischievous frat-boy ambience overseen by the company's senior executives and by bankers, brokers, and accountants who were, in effect, encouraging the greatest fraud in the history of American business.

This is probably the way warrior elites have been hardening their apprentices since the days of Ashurbanipal: conquer, loot, rape, and move on to the next battle without remorse. Instead of the older male drawing the younger up to his level of experience, here we have supposed elders gleefully stalled in their boyish ad-olescence. The memos and recorded phone calls collected in the wake of the company's collapse reveal an utterly conscienceless delight in dirty dealing on the part of young traders who were whipped into a money-mad frenzy by bosses who had trained them in predatory ways. They giggled and made foul-mouthed jokes about scamming the *grandmas* of California, even as the largest state in the nation was being driven into bankruptcy by their manipulation of the energy market. It should not go un-mentioned that none of this would have been possible if re-sponsible federal authorities at the Federal Energy Regulating Commission had intervened to stop the pillaging. But the Bush administration refused to do so, declaring — in one tough-guy response from the president — that the free market must be left to solve the problem. So the hemorrhaging continued.

False elders are, in the area of age, what token women are in government or corporate life. Women, in order to qualify for positions of leadership in the political and corporate world, must often become honorary men. Why? Because the positions women must win in order to hold power are saturated with stereotypic masculine qualities. That is commonly recognized now, a major barrier to full female equality. But what often goes unnoticed is that the male values which permeate institutions and social roles are *young* masculine qualities — very young. Like ambitious women, old men who cling to power must also become *one of the boys.* Betty Friedan made the point in her study of gender relations among the aging: "In the debate about women and men, sex roles and sex, over the last 30 years, it is never pointed out that all our assumptions and definitions of masculinity are based on *young men.*"[1]

That truth is at the heart of David Gutmann's groundbreaking psychological study of older men. Gutmann makes an insightful comparison of the alpha male in industrial society and elders in Native American cultures.

> The elder rulers of "advanced" societies are only older versions of successful young men, those who have laid down the bases for their economic and political power early in life. They receive little honor, title, or credit on the basis of their age alone. For the rest, for the majority of undistinguished older males who have not laid up power and riches in their early years, personal and social prospects can be bleak, making for a striking and disheartening contrast with the typical older man of the folk-traditional assemblage.[2]

Older men may often run the show in human affairs, but they do not qualify in Gutmann's eyes as true elders. They are essentially enacting the part of adolescents. In the corridors of power, the king-of-the-mountain game-playing that every boy learns in the schoolyard remains the rule. Old men in the power elite continue to compete for supremacy as if to prove that they are not really old. Worse, they set the standard and pose the target for young men coming along and bucking for dominance.

Alpha males live by their own calculus of success and have managed to convince the rest of us that we must respect that measurement. They appropriate all the social wealth they can, not because they enjoy it but to display it as the criterion of achievement. In times past, the royal elite garbed themselves in gold and jewels, they moved in the world of crowns, gowns, and thrones. These days the corporate elite prefer raw money; it is so conveniently quantifiable, and so a much keener measure. *Forbes* magazine once ran a box score indicating that even Bill Gates of Microsoft, though not old enough at the time to qualify as an alpha male but well on his way, might be in danger of falling behind in the money race. "Asian Billionaires Gaining on Gates," cried the headline. There followed a list of the pursuers who might soon "dethrone" him, the "poorest" of whom had a personal fortune of $10.5 billion. Only one woman was listed, the usual token, identified as "heiress" to a cosmetics empire and thus not a self-made man. In any case, she lagged well behind the pack with a mere $5 billion.[3] What is the meaning of money like this? It is more than a man can spend and enjoy, more than his family needs to remain affluent for centuries to come. Money in these obscene amounts is an abstract score, the alpha-male version of computer games like *Mortal Kombat*, meaningless points that simply tell the public who the lords of the universe are.

Feminist psychology has done much to illuminate the structure of the *separative self*, the typically stunted psyche of the alpha male. The separative self is the man that every little boy is encouraged to become as he breaks free of maternal influence. In the life of the male, the separative self is wholly nonrelational, a thing-in-itself; it never becomes a person-in-relation that would lack identity outside of relationship. As Jean Baker Miller, one of the founders of feminist psychology, described it, "the concept of a 'self' as it has come down to us has encouraged a complex series of processes leading to a sense of psychological separation from others. From this there would follow a quest for power over others and over natural forces, including one's own body…. Our tradition [has] made it difficult to conceive of the possibility that freedom and maximum use of our resources — our initiative, our intellect, our powers — can occur within a context that requires simultaneous responsibility for the care and growth of others and of the natural world." [4]

As the women's movement discovered early on, gender stereotypes have more than social consequences. They determine our relationship with the Earth itself. Real women groan beneath the power of the alpha-male human, but so too, the woman called Mother Nature. The ecological psychologist Paul Shepard once raised the key question in environmental ethics: "Why do men persist in destroying their environment?" And he did mean *men*, for his answer was that men are "ontogenetically crippled" by childish fantasies of power. "The West," he believed, "is a vast testimony to childhood botched to serve its own purposes, where history, masquerading as myth, authorizes men of action to alter the world to match their regressive moods of omnipotence and insecurity." [5]

In reaction to feminist pressure, a spirited men's movement has grown up since the late 1970s, seeking to meet the need many beleaguered males feel for a new identity. But these efforts are too often based on outmoded images of the warrior and hunter, roles freighted with excess historical baggage, all of it having to do with some repertory of supposedly exclusive masculine traits. Typically, the literature of men's groups touches not at all on aging but emphasizes ways to maintain a youthful virility. Sometimes compassion is mentioned, but there is always much histrionic rhetoric about experiencing wildness and fire in the belly; the manliness they seek remains youth- and midlife-biased and therefore will not last out a full lifetime. Age bias cuts deeper than gender bias because it ties men to an essentially adolescent phase of life when their main psychological project was to differentiate from the mother — and from all that is identified as feminine. But as the lives of women come to include more social space, what is the point of that task?

Alpha males, struggling and thrusting to prove their warrior virtues long after any true grown-up would care about such nonsense, are the old guys who make age obnoxious to the young. They may grow old, but they are not elders. They are geriatric boys. They do not lead by virtue of wisdom, but by cunning and intimidation. They may take pride in holding their own with the young bloods, but in truth, clutching at power until it is torn from one's grip makes for an unbecoming end to life. If these old boys were as wise and brave as their years should make them, they would long since have put the strenuous pursuit of salaries, status, and sexual dominance behind them and moved on to other, better things. As we enter the longevity revolution, it is essential for elders to assume a greater role in our affairs. That role ought not to be a mere extension of midlife getting and spending. Far more challenging is the task of remaining involved and responsible, but in a new key, one that sounds a note of gentleness and ethical responsibility.

Among counselors and therapists, there is a clear professional consensus that the role of the alpha male has become a burden that more and more men need to unload and want to unload. It is plain unhealthy for men, encouraging them to drive their aging bodies to keep up with a handful of wealthy business tycoons or with movie images of compulsive masculinity. If the pace and strain of the macho lifestyle does not kill them, depression and despair will. Men can be so good at hiding their emotions that they conceal even suicidal intentions from professional counselors. And unlike women, for whom attempted suicide can be a cry for help, when men elect to kill themselves, they use the means most likely to do the job: guns, hanging, or car accidents. "Men," as Royda Crose observed, "are more at risk of early death because they are taught to ignore weakness, illness, and health concerns.... They not only don't listen to their bodies, but they are applauded for the denial of pain and discomfort."[6]

The search for a way out of this lethal trap has produced the quaint concept of male menopause. Technically speaking, there may be no such thing as a male menopause that fully corresponds to a woman's later-life transformation, but emotionally, as a psychological stage of life, there is something very like it. Since menopause is not as decisively announced by the male body as it is for women, men have been able in the past to override the crisis. No longer. "Putting the men back in menopause," as one therapist cutely put it, is now a well-developed psychological and cultural project among boomers. At its heart lies the search for intimacy, a word that always requires another to be intimate *with*. That other is usually understood to be a lover, in most cases female. But liberating the male capacity for intimacy may also awaken another male potentiality, one that has to do with other men — younger men. Becoming intimate in love may be the gateway to becoming an elder to one's children and to one's society.

Erik Erikson was among the first psychologists to see aging as "a stage in the growth of the healthy personality." In his study of the human life cycle, he coined the word *generativity* to refer to the eldering project of an elder's later years: "the interest in establishing and guiding the next generation," as he defined it. When that important task is left unattended, "regression from generativity to an obsessive need for pseudo-intimacy takes place, often with a pervading sense of stagnation and interpersonal impoverishment."[7] Erikson, however, saw generativity as primarily a parental responsibility toward one's children; he gave little attention to the collective responsibility of the whole senior generation in society.

That is precisely the orientation that Daniel Levinson sought to provide in his broader study of male developmental psychology. Referring to eldering as *mentoring*, Levinson took this defining responsibility out into the society at large, where men must deal with one another in school or the workplace. It is a complex role, combining the function of teacher, sponsor, guide, exemplar, and counselor. "The mentor represents a mixture of parent and peer; he must be both and not purely either one." Significantly, Levinson regarded mentoring as a social task that had best take place outside the parent-child relationship. Parents, he felt, are "too tied to their offspring's pre-adult development (in both his mind and theirs) to be primary mentor figures." At his most challenging, Levinson identified mentoring as "a form of love relationship." But love between men, so long shadowed in our society by fears of homoeroticism, is a difficult emotion to cultivate, especially for the alpha male. Some cultures, like the Greeks in the time of Socrates, saw no problem. Ours does. The alpha male is compulsively heterosexual, needing what he hopes will be a yielding woman to validate his sexual domination.

Levinson believed the ideal age differential for mentoring is about a half generation; but he added "a person twenty or even fifty years older may, if he is in good touch with his own and the other's youthful Dreams, function as a significant mentor."[8] In Levinson's work, *dream* has a special, technical meaning. It is the self-chosen life task that ushers the adolescent into the world as a man or a woman. Not all young people form a dream; not all are allowed to have one of their own. But the job of the mentor is to connect with the passion of the dream and help make it real. In his eldering work, the poet Robert Bly has pursued much the same thesis, defining the "true adult" as "one who has been able to preserve his or her intensities…so that he or she has something with which to meet the intensities of the adolescent." Both Levinson and Bly remind us that cynicism and despair make for the worst kind of old age; such negativity leaves us unable to nourish the lively aspirations of the young. The essence of youth is *beginning*. If those who have lived longest cannot resonate with the adventure of beginning, what will the young want to learn from them? Bly concluded that the rampant wildness of young men, their difficulty with commitment and responsibility, has only one cure: Older men must show the way. "The fundamental problem in the continuation of a decent life everywhere in the world," he insists, "is this question of the socialization of young males.... It is not women's job to socialize young males. That is the job of the older men." But, he wisely feared, "we are losing our ability to mature.... We are always under commercial pressure to slide backward, toward adolescence, toward childhood. With no effective rituals of initiation,...young men in our culture go round in circles.... Observers describe many contemporaries as children with children of their own."[9]

Eldering, as Bly and Levinson defined it, is nearly impossible to carry out in a culture that takes the alpha male as its model for social leadership. There is simply too much social luggage to that role: The inherent cynicism and ruthlessness of the marketplace, its deceptive strategies, bullying habits, and conscienceless opportunism cripple the capacity for effective mentoring. Entrepreneurs have nothing to do with gentleness or compassion; the role does not encourage men to be mentors, only winners. The commercial pressures Bly cited as an obstacle to maturity are the creation of world-beating entrepreneurs whose goal is running up a score measured in dollars. Where values of that order are in play, it takes more courage to stand *against* the alpha male than to *be* the alpha male.

Hair

The very fact that I can raise these issues out of the depths of the psyche tells us that things have changed — if only a little and too slowly. The countercultural young played a key role in challenging our infatuation with patriarchal power, but even they, so quick to indict the misuse of power at all social levels, did not see the issue immediately. Man-woman relations are among the most convoluted episodes of the 1960s. There was a period when every liberated woman was a "chick" — or told she should be — and expected to advertise her liberation by being sexually promiscuous. In an essay dealing with the issue, Beth Bailey reminds us of the "macho posturing" that characterized the early counter culture. She recalled that, in the underground press, "the graphic representation of freedom was a naked woman."[10] Sad to recall that in its first male approximation, sexual freedom gave us slogans like "Say hello to a chick by grabbin' her ass." In 1969 Robin Morgan addressed a widely quoted essay to "friends, brothers, lovers in the counterfeit male-dominated Left," as well as to her sisters who betrayed feminist values as part of a "desperate grab at male approval." She angrily bade "good-bye to hip culture and the so-called sexual revolution." In her view, the counter culture "functioned toward women's freedom as did Reconstruction toward former slaves" — namely, it "reconstituted oppression by another name." That was what Morgan saw behind the "Stanley Kowalski image and theory" of "sex on demand for males."[11]

Ironically, at the same time that countercultural men were enjoying a sexual field day among the liberated females of their generation, they were themselves tasting something of the misogyny of their society. Oddly enough, it had to do with hair, one of those *little* issues of the time that managed to make for huge animosity. Men who adopted the long-haired hippy hair style were universally mocked for their femininity. This was, after all, the era of the organization-man crew cut, a distinctly military tonsure. In the context of a military-industrial economy, long hair, not at all remarkable for men in centuries past, looked plain queer. Even gunslinger moustaches and a healthy growth of beard did not offset the jarring quality of a womanish hair style. Long-haired males quickly became a public hallmark of dissent and a target for ridicule. Hence, the signature "tribal love-rock musical" of the period was an exuberant celebration of…hair. "Hair, hair, hair, hair, hair," the show's hero sings shortly before the cast stripped naked, "Flow it, show it/Long as

God can grow it." And the song finishes, "Hair like Jesus wore it/ Hallelujah I adore it/Mary loved her son/Why don't my mother love me?" Chauvinistic as they might be with the women in their lives, countercultural men were, in spite of themselves, picking a fight with alpha-male values. Thus, in the film *Easy Rider*, when the two long-haired hippies walk into a redneck lunch counter, it is their hair that draws the most derision and hostility — and will finally mark them out for assassination. "Why do they hate us so much?" asks one of the hippy bikers. The answer: "They don't hate you. They're afraid of you. That's what makes them dangerous."

The elder culture, predicated on the need for help and compassion, will have far more consequential grounds on which to draw an indictment of alpha-male dominance. The need for physical and emotional help that comes with age is a vivid reminder of our interdependency. And, as it grows, that need draws more and more people into the ranks of the caregivers. As the longevity revolution runs its course, there will be an increasing population unashamedly asserting their need for help and an increasing number of people offering help, a spreading network of mutual aid. If altering consciousness was ever meant to make people more compassionate and convivial, more willing to share and support, I cannot think of anything that is more apt to make that happen than the simple and inevitable process of aging.

How do we change a state of consciousness as deeply rooted in our heritage as the alpha-male syndrome? Even in the dissenting 1960s, when so much was being called into question, compulsive masculinity distorted man-woman relations among the countercultural young. Though much has changed since then, the war lords and the corporados are still with us, throwing their weight around. Women who would challenge them still feel compelled to assert their toughness. Like England's Margaret Thatcher, they must be *iron ladies* (or, as she was also called, Attila the Hen). But it may be that, once again, longevity will have a part to play in shifting the values that shape our lives. As a matter of biological necessity, aging brings with it forces that are distinctly transformative, usually darkening the mind with longing or regret, the bitter wisdom of Ecclesiastes or Rembrandt's final self-portraits. No hallucinatory substance can ever have the power of a truth revealed. And no truth can have the power of mortality.

Love, Loyalty,
and the End of Sex

*The novelists never told us that in love, as in other mat-
ters, the young are just beginners and that the art of loving matures with age and experience.... The only hope of
mankind is love in its various forms and manifestations —
the source of them all being love of life, which, as we know,
increases and ripens with the years.*

— Isaac Bashevis Singer, *Old Love*

The year was 1985, the mid-point of the great conservative
backlash. Boomers, many of them now middle-aged parents (usually mothers returning to repair a busted education),
were beginning to appear more frequently in my classes. They
stood out as those who had the most to contribute to discussions — especially of Vietnam and the protest movement. This
old stuff interested freshmen in the room about as much as
the Spanish-American War might once have interested me.
The past has a shrinking shelf life in our time. One of my students, a woman in her late thirties, came up after a lecture that
had included a passing reference to the Summer of Love. She
requested an office hour. I could see when she arrived that she
was sincerely puzzled. "The Summer of Love," she mused. "I was
there, on the streets, in the park. It was non-stop sex. Free hash
and non-stop sex." I could tell she was not remembering the
time fondly. At last she added, "I've got a 12-year-old daughter.
She's becoming a problem." How so? "I've tried not to raise her

the way I was, thinking sex is taboo. She spent a few years with me on a collective where we were pretty frank about nudity and making love." With a big, troubled sigh she admitted, "Now I wonder if I did the right thing. Because I don't really want her running wild the way I did in my teens. Out all night, getting high, having sex round the clock. That doesn't feel like libera- tion to me any more. I think it messes up your life. This kid's got no father, she's got no sense of moral limits. And damn it! If she behaves the way I did, she's not going to survive. I mean this is a matter of life and death."

We both knew what she meant. The party was over. AIDS hovered like a vulture over every casual sexual encounter.

There were others who came to me with the same question about that time. I always begged off giving advice, but I could feel their anguish. It is one thing to rebel against an outmoded prudishness; it is another to teach intelligent restraint to children burning with the fires of adolescence. In the 1960s, a cause that had long enlisted keen minds — the long, hard struggle against a defunct Puritan ethic — had neatly coincided with what all teenagers have on their mind. It was a time when sexual need could dress itself in the principled language of free thinkers, feminists, libertarians, novelists, playwrights, even hygienists. Making love was the alternative to making war. But carry that cause to an extreme, make it the core of every relationship and the focus of every political gathering, and how do you then re- treat from so exposed a position? What language do you use to cool the hormones of the young once you have removed the fear of pregnancy and undermined authority — including your own parental prerogatives?

There is one group that has come forward with an answer, a belated, told-you-so riposte to the beatniks and hippies. The Jesus people, who began to emerge in the 1970s with a demand for total abstinence among the unmarried young, have given new life to the old-time religion. Back to Jesus, back to shame and terror, back to hell and damnation. And millions have opted for their way. The hypocrisy that has always surrounded religious authority especially in sexual matters is still there; the evangelicals have had their scandals over the years, but there are parents of the boomer generation who are willing to run that risk to keep their kids under control and alive. Myself, I believe the Puritanism of the evangelicals is more the distant historical cause of our sexual hang-ups than a cure. These are the people who once pilloried sinners for fornication and forced women to wear the scarlet letter. They surrounded sex with guilt and fear, and that made it more tempting and less gratifying for millions.

While their parents dither, the young, whether disciples of Jesus or not, seem to have worked out a serviceable improvisation. Oral sex — which many teenagers may feel is not really sex at all, but a kind of fooling around like the necking and petting of previous generations. When Bill Clinton, under pressure of impeachment, claimed he had not had "sexual relations with that woman," adults scoffed. But the adolescents of the day probably understood what he was saying. Fellation and cunnilingus have become a strange kind of sexless sex that I suspect many parents are willing to settle for, no questions asked, as the safest kind of intercourse they can realistically expect. Boomer parents and their adult children are, after all, up against terrific odds. In the wake of the 1960s, the sexual climate of the modern world has heated up in ways that make it all but impossible to keep children as repressed and ignorant as in times past. Frankness to the point of vulgarity dominates the media; movies, rock music, and the Internet flood our lives with references and images that go beyond the borders of obscenity. Even evangelical Christians now publish materials on sex whose frankness would have shocked their pious grandparents. (One pamphlet I picked up along the way goes into nauseating detail about gonorrhea of the throat — a warning about the dangers of oral sex.) Thanks to no-holds-barred marketing, our popular culture is now so saturated with sexuality that it is nearly impossible to pass a day that is not filled from morning to night with hormonal stimulants. The market is what America is all about, and sex rules the market. The media are currently campaigning to convince us that children of seven and eight are ready for sexier dolls, fashions, games, videos. The only psychology behind such an effort is to establish an early reflexive connection between sex and consumerism, a button that can be pushed again and again for the next 50 years of the kid's life. The pendulum of permissiveness has swung so far from the Puritanical extreme that we run the risk of turning sex into a reflex that has no sensation, no meaning, no purpose behind it. I have the feeling that sex — seeking it, getting it, talking about it — has become the default meaning of life for everybody below the age of 60, the one unquestioned way to pass that perplexing period of time called *being alive*.

Nobody doubts that the domineering force behind sex is rooted in an evolutionary imperative. Animals driven to reproduce at any cost have a distinct evolutionary advantage. They've got to have it. And the more they have, the more progeny they put out there in the world. Passion may inspire love lyrics, but far from being a cultural ornament, sex is part of our reproductive instinct. And what could be more important? Answer: survival, which, in the case of our species, may now be more endangered by fertility than sterility. We have reached the point at which we can smother under our own numbers. Population control is now an imperative. And we do see population growth abating, even in China, where many urban couples, especially young professionals, now welcome the single-child policy. A few societies, worried about a *birth dearth*, have brainstormed pronatalist policies to encourage childbearing, but it is doubtful they will ever persuade ambitious, upwardly mobile, young couples to have babies for the good of the nation.

What we may very well see in the future is parents choosing quality over quantity. In the highly developed economies, those who do seek a baby or two are slowly turning to something better than hit-or-miss fertilization. Parents are being offered the possibility of designing their children and having them started in the safety of a laboratory — and finally delivered on schedule by way of Caesarean section scheduled for maximum convenience. (Thirty percent of American births now are completed with an elective C-section.) As we will see in Chapter 10, this possibility is already having a powerful effect upon the ecology of the high-industrial societies. Here, we may simply note that whatever sexual relations couples may continue to have, they are apt to have steadily less to do with reproduction. Instead, they will become a separate activity based on a still undefined set of expectations. Making babies may one day soon become the province of experts who can (so we assume) do the job better. Can it be the case that sexual passion, so important in the past when it was tightly linked to reproduction, has been left spinning in the void, a surging biological drive without a sensible application? Has our species reached a boundary condition where the problem before us is too many rather than too few? So sex grows more and more distant from its original purpose. And because it is thwarted in that direction, it becomes obsessive even as it becomes less necessary. Perhaps some physiological signal that would once have lowered or turned off the drive is failing to register, and so the drive increases in strength until it becomes an abstract craving that intrudes itself into everything. If so, post-boomer generations may be facing a dilemma of evolutionary proportions. What will the purpose of sex be when it has left behind its eons-long biological purpose? Can the force that once drove young lovers into one another's arms be transferred to another use?

For Better or Worse

I watch the two of them, struggling past my car as I wait for the light to change, trying to make it across the street. They are well over 60, solemn faced and deeply fatigued. He is a very large man in a wheelchair holding two bulging shopping bags; she is half his size, pushing for all she is worth to reach the curb. It looks almost comic, but of course it isn't. It is sad and touching — this little woman trying to maneuver her weighty husband (I assume they are a couple) through traffic. It is not all that unusual a sight, one person helping another, often pushing a wheelchair or holding the arm of a companion using a cane or a walker. But this couple embodies something about the elder culture that needs greater understanding, especially for the premier generation of the sexual revolution. At least in this momentary view I have of them, these two represent love's end game, the stage of life when a shoulder to lean on is as precious as lips for kissing once were.

Love between the sexes has played a central role in western culture — in art and song and storytelling — since the days of the troubadours. During the Romantic movement, it became the preeminent theme of fiction, poetry, opera, and painting. But throughout those centuries, love was surrounded by protocols and inhibitions that derived from the fear of pregnancy and the subjugation of women. Love had more to do with gestures, social codes, manners, and contrived displays than with the physical act of sex. Before the 20th century, simply getting a lady out of her cumbersome clothes was a daunting exercise. In contrast, for those who came to adulthood in the 1960s and 1970s, sex became more blatant, more shameless, and more domineering than ever before. It was stripped of its refinements as well as its hypocrisies. From the invention of the contraceptive pill in the early 1950s to the outbreak of AIDS in the mid-1980s, boomers enjoyed unprecedented sexual freedom, a window of erotic opportunity the world may never see again. They are the only generation in history to have known risk-free, care-free, responsibility-free sexuality. No aspect of inherited morality came in for more ridicule by young boomers than the prudishness that once surrounded sex. Nothing parted them more from their parents than the guiltlessness and sexual promiscuity of their teens and twenties — even if promiscuity was more a possibility than a reality for many. In the post–World War II era, for the first time anywhere, confessing to virginity became an embarrassment.

This shift in public morality has been especially jarring for those of us who have some basis for comparison — meaning those who came of age in the 1930s and 1940s. I grew up in a world where the words *virgin, pregnant, abortion,* and *homosexual* were literally unmentionable, where married couples in the movies had to use separate beds, where condoms were sold under the counter like contraband. Not only was the F-word forbidden, but there was no word like *F-word* to refer to the F-word. The nuns who taught me my religious instruction scolded kids who asked them what *adultery* meant in the ten commandments; priests regarded masturbation as a sin that must be confessed for absolution and which might produce insanity. Now all this seems like life on some distant planet. Whenever I turn on cable television or go to the movies, I find myself facing a blizzard of profanity and graphic coupling. Most surprising of all, now that all the iron rules of middle-class sexual propriety have been scrapped, the sky has not fallen. So what was it all about — all those centuries when the sex life of people was being so tightly patrolled by church and state?

It was inevitable that the generation that pioneered our new permissive sexual code should wind up clinging to sex as one of life's great adventures. In recollection, perhaps the thrill of it all, the time when you could have sex on demand anywhere anytime, becomes magnified. But even without exaggeration, it was an intoxicating era, not least of all because sex became entangled with the high ideals of the day. In Berkeley, after one of the big, day-long, night-long demonstrations in the long hot summer of 1968, the campus, the streets, and the parks were filled with boisterous revellers, many stoned, many unclothed in the warmth of the day, many preparing to bed down for a wild night. Having said *no* to making war, it was time to make love. The same was true of youthful protest everywhere — in England, in France, in eastern Europe. Nuclear disarmament marches, rock concerts, university rallies, and anti-war demonstrations were likely to end in shared sleeping bags and love beneath the stars. Sex was charged with politics, politics was laced with sex. And so now we have boomers determined to keep their sexual juices flowing well into the retirement years. On the Internet and in bookstores everywhere, the beat goes on. Never too old for sex, never too *seasoned* for another fling — though perhaps with a bit of pharmaceutical help. Robert Butler, a founder of geriatric medicine and the country's leading gerontologist, has, with his co-author Myrna Lewis, tracked the love life of elders over age 60 since the 1970s, offering sage advice about possibilities and limits, but the steadily rising erotic temperature of our commercial culture makes slowing down sexually seem like shameful surrender.[1] Butler's eminently sensible book is shelved in my local bookstore between titles like *Great Sex, Incredible Orgasms*, and *Letters to Penthouse* — and all but crowded out of sight. Perhaps there will come a time when boomers will reach the point of passing out medals for sexual activity over the age of 60, 70, 80 — with oak-leaf clusters for the number of times. Sex has ceased being a youthful sprint; it has become a lifelong marathon.

Love comes in many modes, or at least the word has taken on many nuances — perhaps too many. Romantic love, brotherly love, parental love, and love of God, of country, of mankind. We have stretched the meaning of the word *love* to cover any relationship that is gentle, warm, generous, supportive — but also clinging, possessive, needy, domineering, or submissive. Love has become the overlay for many other emotions, the sine qua non of all forms of intimacy. There is a wealth of literature that seeks to discriminate among these modes, but the word is never completely free of its sexual connotation. In any context, it resonates with carnality, the experience that happens between lovers, the usage most associated with courtship and marriage. Is this a lower form of love — or its highest expression? Plato would arrive at one conclusion, Percy Shelley and D. H. Lawrence at another. In a treatise widely read among evangelicals, C. S. Lewis distinguishes four kinds of love: eros, friendship, affection, and charity. In his view, sex for the physical pleasure of the act, the sort of love D. H. Lawrence celebrated at least on the printed page, is vastly inferior to eros — a disgraceful waste. That kind of love, so Lewis believed, especially outside of marriage, is like chewing the flavor out of meat and then spitting it out. Like most Christians, Lewis would have us believe that God is the reservoir of all true love, its highest source and expression. But of course this is the same God who reserves the right to condemn his erring children to eternal damnation — as an act of love. Go figure.

For my own part, I have come to believe that there is another emotion that is often mistaken for love but which deserves to be appreciated in its own right. I will call it *loyalty*, a bond between people that may lack the heat of sexual love but which has a power and a durability that transcends the erotic — *transcends* in the sense that it rises above a love that depends on the comeliness of the beloved. No love poem can do without praising the lover's beauty — even if the beauty is primarily in the eye of the beholder. Love in this sense cannot be wholly parted from reproduction, from a subliminal evaluation of the beloved's physical attributes. Beauty is the bait of erotic love, the love that reaches out to youth, health, vitality — the qualities that breed sturdy children. But loyalty looks beyond the pleasing surface to the more essential self that lies within, the self that is there when biological need has waned. It inherits from love when passions cool. Loyalty is of the person. It says of the person that remains when youth and beauty are gone, "I have known you for many years, though now more vividly than ever. And I will be your companion through all that follows." Though they may not know it, young lovers — those who join in some version of Christian matrimony, including courthouse vows — are being called to loyalty by the words of the traditional marriage ceremony. The promises made — that the couple are pledged to stay together for better or worse, for richer or poorer, in sickness and in health — have more to do with loyalty than love. So, too, St. Paul's paean to charity — the bond he believed would hold the early Christian congregations together: "Charity beareth all things, believeth all things, hopeth all things, endureth all things." The troubadours sang of love and celebrated the act of love, the union of the flesh, but Paul's charity is another thing entirely. Once again, as in the case of caregiving, we are dealing with a capacity that has to do with the final stages of life. Every marriage is built on risk, a gamble people take with one another. By the later years of life the major part of that risk becomes health. We marry into a game of genetic roulette, and until the biotechnicians find a way to read the genome down to its last detail, that risk will remain. If fidelity has any moral significance, it is more a matter of loyalty than love. It is a pledge that I will stay with you when others — more youthful, more sexually appealing — might tempt me away.

We inherit a vast body of romantic literature, but loyalty is not easy to depict in literary terms. When it does appear, critics are often quick to read sexual undertones into the story. Huck and Jim wordlessly pledged to one another through one close shave after another, Lenny and George in *Of Mice and Men* are all but universally understood to be involved in homoerotic relationships. But that is clearly not what Mark Twain or John Steinbeck intended, any more than Don Quixote and Sancho Panza were intended to be a couple of gay caballeros. Cervantes instinctively recognized that the loyalty Sancho feels for the Don would touch his comic tale with a deeper pathos. In other works — Longfellow's *Evangeline*, Mrs. Gaskell's *Ruth* — it is clear that the authors want us to look beyond romance to a bond that endures after love has faded. Or sometimes we are left to wonder: Is it finally sex that ties Jane Eyre to the blind and battered William Rochester at the end of the story? "Reader, I married him," she declared curtly as if checking an item off on an agenda. But why? Is it because she had committed herself to him "for better or worse, in sickness and in health" long before they married?

Loyalty lacks the emotional juice of *desire, lust, passion, sensuality*. Literature and art depict the many phases of love ranging from bliss to betrayal — powerful emotions that have to do with possession or loss. *Loyalty* most often appears in a political context. We speak of being *loyal* to a nation, a cause, a flag, and less often to a person. That gives the word an abstract quality that comes rather close to duty. Once again, sex has so permeated our relationships that it may be difficult to appreciate an impassioned bond between people, especially between two people who come together to share their lives and perhaps raise a family, that is grounded in the ethical rather than the erotic. But that is the essence of loyalty. It is a moral, not an amorous, pleasure. When we thank somebody for *being there* for us, we are dealing more with loyalty than love.

In speaking of *the end of sex*, I am playing with words. I am using *end* in the sense of a goal, rather than a finish. Of course, often for reasons of health or declining libido, many of the elderly do sign off on sex, some sadly, some gladly. Falstaff bemoaned how strange it is "that desire should so many years outlive performance." But as the years accumulate, it becomes easier and easier to regard sex as a need that has more to do with relief than ecstasy, an itch that needs to be scratched. Certainly the trouble some people now go to in order to remain sexually functional — everything from cosmetic surgery to couples' workshops — looks a lot more like hard work than pleasure.

Perhaps the work would make more sense if we knew there is an end toward which our years of sexuality, with all the anxiety and frustration and the heartache they include, finally lead. In this sense, I suggest that the goal toward which sexual partnering leads (if we are lucky) is not some kind of score in a hard-fought game. It is loyalty, the willingness to be there for one another when little remains of the beauty, vitality, or excitement of our youthful encounters.

We are dealing here with an insight that is distinctly of our time. In the past, when life expectancy was 45 or less, most people died in the middle of their sexually active years, still caught up in married life or still pursuing courtship. In a sense, they did not get to the *end* of sex — to it and beyond it. The elderly who were fortunate enough to survive past 60 were by and large a used-up and burned-out population who were more concerned about bare survival than sexual satisfaction. In the poorhouses of that period, husbands and wives, if they arrived together, might be assigned separate quarters as if their life together was over. That image of seniors as asexual is now being left in the dust as boomers keep at it. The media are filling up with older characters, older stars who treat 60 as the new 40. Boomers are proving that seniors can remain sexually active a great deal longer than anyone ever expected. But as our society moves deeper into old age in ever greater numbers, perhaps it is time to ask if the fourth age, as we have called it, has more to offer in the way of relationship than a simple extension of middle age. Indeed, giving loyalty its proper value may be one of the signal features of entering the fourth age.

In That Moment

I have had many warm and moving encounters in my lifetime, but the moment that taught me most about loyalty came in the depths of a medical crisis. I had just been through heavy-duty surgery for a life-threatening condition. When I finally came around in my hospital room, my strongest feeling was that I was shattered. It was as if my arms, legs, and torso were scattered across the room with no identity, no coherence. I was too weak to move my limbs, too cloudy to know exactly where I was. There were doctors and nurses on hand, working over me, doing their job, but I was in complete despair. And then my wife was allowed to come in. I saw her, I reached for her, she took my hand — and in that moment I began to become whole. The hand I held was infusing me with strength. I gripped hard, muttering, "Don't go away, don't go away." She said, "No, I won't." Later I remembered that holding her hand had once been, 30 years before, our first, tentative act of intimacy. I reached across the front seat of the car and felt privileged when she left her hand in mine. That was the beginning, the first step along the road that would one day lead us to this hospital room, this dark moment when touching hands would have a very different meaning.

Love begins with courting — such a quaint term. But in one way or another the young get together — the moonlight walk, the front-porch swing, the church social, the school dance. I grew up in an era when the drive-in movie was often the beginning of sex. Across the country, on weekend evenings, cars with steamed-over windows filled the parking space in front of gargantuan movie screens; nobody below the age of 18 was watching. These days things move along a great deal faster than the measured pace of earlier generations. So many inhibitions have broken down, so many taboos have vanished. But as swiftly as hookups unfold at a club or a house party, this is still the preening and pretending of courtship, the rites that usher couples into their years of sex, marriage, and family, often with erotic expectations of one another that will soon cool down. In those years, when people are seeking to remain attractive to each other, it is impossible to look beyond to the time when sex will fade. As boomers survive into many more post-erotic years, there are still those in the media and marketing world who are working hard to keep the hormones flowing. Pleasure cruises, workshops, singles bars, tango and salsa classes — all are meant to recapture as much of age 20 as possible. But beyond the reproductive years there will always be something awkward about courting, a custom that does not quite fit, because at a certain point it is loyalty people are seeking in the guise of love. And for loyalty we do not have the words, gestures, or rituals that poets and artists have given us to declare desire. There is nothing romantic about asking someone simply to be there, to stand by, to help and comfort. And that is just the point. This is not a request for romance, but for something that comes after and later.

Once when my wife lay asleep recovering from bypass surgery, I sat beside her in a darkened hospital room grateful to see that she was breathing steadily, regaining her strength. And I thought of all this person meant to me, the many bonds of joy and sorrow and strife that made up our relationship. It was as if, looking at her as she slept, I could see the woman I had been with for all these years, face after face after face — all the many phases of our life together finally culminating in who we were now in this room, in this hour of need. I thought of all I knew of her — and all I still did not know, wishes, desires, aspirations that I may have unknowingly done more to thwart than further. However awkwardly, our lives were braided together and pledged to one another in ways that made the task of bringing her through this crisis — as she had brought me through my own dark hours — more important than any few moments of sexual rapture.

When the distractions of an oversexed media finally lose their power to obscure the greater meaning of life, I suspect boomers will find their way to loyalty as, if not the highest then at least the final, stage of love. And they will no doubt make much of the discovery. But it will not be easy to teach the value of loyalty. Unlike sex, it cannot be captured in an eye-catching image; unlike romance, it cannot happen at first sight. It is rather a quality that must grow over the years, the result of a tested companionship, though not always of a smooth, stress-free relationship. Loyalty grows between people who know one another, the best and the worst. It is what survives hard words, emotional bruising, and many disappointments. Such trials are like a testing to see if loyalty is there. And if not, that might be the best justification for parting company. If love begins by idealizing the beloved, loyalty sees the other for what the other truly is — flawed and imperfect, but still there at one's side.

It is now eight centuries since the troubadours of medieval Europe began singing the praises of high romance, tales of swooning ladies and devoted knights, forbidden trysts and ecstatic heights. They sang of a passion that ended, as with Tristan and Isolde, in a blissful union of bodies, the most sublime of all experiences. Well, what else was there to hope for when the life expectancy of the society was not much over 30? And so, down to the present day, our popular culture remains filled with songs of amorous longing and plaintive heartbreak, seduction and surrender. In the clubs and singles bars, at high-school proms and on the websites designed for teens and twenty-somethings, that will continue to be the beat. But there will be ever more of us who have outlived that transient exhilaration and need relationships that endure to the end. As yet, though loyalty has no music to celebrate its consolations, I would not be surprised if boomers, always so self-aware and self-congratulatory, get around to launching such a tradition.

Ecology and Longevity

Elders are not "senior citizens" who get gold watches at retirement, move to Sunbelt states, and play cards, shuffleboard, and bingo ad nauseam. They are wisdom-keepers who have an ongoing responsibility for maintaining society's well-being and safeguarding the health of our ailing planet Earth.

— Zalman Schachter-Shalomi and
Ronald S. Miller, *From Age-ing to Sage-ing:
A Profound New Vision of Growing Older*

As deeply personal as the trials and joys of longevity may seem — matters of private inner contemplation and spiritual transformation — for society at large the elder culture has profound implications for the future of the planetary ecology. This is not apparent at first sight. It is indeed a factor that can easily get lost among the demographic and political details of policies and programs. Yet the longevity revolution may be the solution to what now sometimes seem intractable, eco-cidal trends.

When I was growing up, kids used to amuse themselves eating colored candy and then showing off their brightly dyed tongues — red, blue, green, purple. In novelty shops, you could buy jitter beans to play with: little plastic capsules that contained a drop of mercury, which, inevitably, we would squeeze out and accumulate into large puddles that we then ran through our fingers. Remarkable stuff, mercury. It even has an interesting taste.

In shoe stores, you could use an X-ray machine to see if your shoes fit — and keep the bones of your feet on view for as long as you liked. The food products you brought home from the grocery carried no list of ingredients. Smoking, as advertised by men in white coats, was understood to be good for you. It was assumed that all toxins and pollutants vanished when poured into the nearest river or lake. Automobile exhaust vanished into thin air. Asbestos was promoted at the 1939 New York World's Fair as the *miracle material*. I often wonder: How have I managed to survive this long?

Boomers can be credited with launching an environmental movement that has made us acutely aware of how hazardous the everyday industrial world can be — and not only to humans. When Lawrence Ferlinghetti and his friends published the first edition of the *Journal for the Protection of All Beings* in 1961, whether they knew it or not, they were announcing the agenda of ecological politics to come. As Gary Snyder put it in language no politician of that era (nor perhaps of our own) could understand, "The conditions of the Cold War have turned all modern society, Soviet included, into hopeless brain-stainers, creating populations of 'preta' — hungry ghosts — with giant appetites and throats no bigger than needles. The soil and the forests and all animal life are being wrecked to feed these cancerous mechanisms."[1] Thus, we have issues before us today that are of an unprecedented character: endangered species, global warming, acid rain, and problems that link us to the whales, the rain forests, the plankton of the seas, and melting glaciers few of us have ever seen. Only a generation that could at least imagine a world beyond the city limits of our culture could invent the first political movement to include the nonhuman environment. But as much as boomers achieved in seeking to rein in the excesses of industrial society by way of research and political action, their most important contribution is yet to come. And that has to do with the simple act of passing the years and at last becoming elders. Their unique demographic is the best gift they have to give the planet.

To start with a benchmark that will tell us how far we have come: By the time of the first Earth Day in 1971, a solid consensus was forming among environmentalists. At the core of our dire ecological condition was population. There were simply too many people. The list of environmentally destructive practices might be pages long, but most of these transgressions could be absorbed and put right by the natural recycling processes of the Earth — *if there were not so many of us.* A bit of pollution here, some deforestation there, some loss of top soil or clean water — the Earth had suffered such insults in the past and had managed to repair the damage. But now our growing numbers multiplied every bad environmental habit to the point of irreparable disaster. In short, Malthus had been right: We were victims of our own swinish drive to procreate.

This was surely a remarkable tribute for environmentalists to pay someone who had lived a century and a half in the past, a man who knew no science, who had studied not a single habitat or species, whose grasp of statistics was faulty in the extreme — a man who might easily qualify as a total ignoramus. But environmentalists were not alone in attributing so much authority to Thomas Malthus. Any list of the ten most important books of modern times would be sure to include his 1798 treatise *Essay on Population.* This slender volume, only 100 pages long, was hailed in its own time as a brilliant, if sobering, contribution to economic theory. Later, as it passed through the mind of the young Charles Darwin, Malthus's conclusions about population growth would eventually generate the theory of evolution by natural selection. Moreover, as the first serious effort to connect a species to its environment in a dynamic and reciprocal way, it has come to be appreciated as a founding document in environmental science. Malthus is one of that stellar few whose influence has been preserved by updating; just as there are neo-Marxists, and neo-Freudians, so there are neo-Malthusians — most of them leading figures in the environmental movement.

Malthus's achievement is all the more remarkable when one realizes that he was neither an economist nor a biologist. He was a vicar, working from nothing more than bleak Augustinian assumptions about human nature and a deep-seated distaste for the radical politics of his day. He was especially perturbed by the work of the radical legal philosopher William Godwin (Mary Shelley's father), who blamed all the evils of society on the way children were distorted in their upbringing. The clash between Malthus and Godwin is a classic debate on human nature: Are we born good or bad? More than anything else, Malthus was determined to refute the revolutionaries of his day who were seeking to create a new, more humane social order. In the bloody streets of Paris people were battling for a society where the pursuit of happiness would be the birthright of everyone. *Nonsense!* Malthus replied. Believing he had discovered a crucial relationship between people and their food supply, he set about attacking the optimism of those who thought society might be rebuilt on altruistic values. Nature itself, in Malthus's view, made altruism impossible. Why? Because people, sinners that they are, will fornicate and reproduce without limit; they are no better than rutting animals. There can therefore never be enough food to provide for all. His conclusion that fertility must always outstrip sustenance was, he believed, a "fixed law of nature." Thus, there must always be a "struggle of existence." Kindness, good-heartedness, compassion — all these are no more than "mere feathers that float on the surface."

In discussing "the constant tendency in all animated life to increase beyond the nourishment prepared for it," Malthus seemed to be citing matters of obvious fact. Not so. He was working from pure reason without a scrap of research. Take his famous dictum that the food supply can only increase "arithmetically." What does that mean? If it means the food supply can only increase slowly and modestly, he need only have looked around him and he would have seen an agricultural revolution in process in his own country. In his time, the English were enormously enhancing food production, a revolution that has continued into our own day. Malthus knew little about this. He was far more interested in making censorious judgments about people and their vices. In effect, he was laying the groundwork for one of the most hard-hearted philosophies the world has known, a worldview based on selfishness, greed, and brutality that would one day be called Social Darwinism. This was the view of life that Charles Dickens would attribute to Ebenezer Scrooge and all the other money-obsessed men who serve as the villains of his tales. Asked what he would do about the starving paupers who would not endure the discipline of the workhouse, Scrooge answers, "If they would rather die, they had better do it, and decrease the surplus population." They are, in other words, useless old people, those who are past it, out of it, and completely dependent.

We rarely hear such crude contempt for the elderly voiced in the modern west, but the worldview of Thomas Malthus can still be found in the newer industrial societies, where elders, powerless to defend themselves, are once again seen as parasitic remnants of the old order. In India, where economic priorities are fiercely oriented toward rapid development, elder abuse is more and more common. There, as the once-domineering extended family rapidly shrinks to nuclear size, the older generation, accounting for no more than 4% of the population and having no national pension plan to fall back on, finds itself facing abandonment and poverty. Until the currently young become the inevitably old and begin to experience the fate they have visited on their parents, elders who cannot keep up with the pace of modern life will face the miseries of Malthusian social policy.

As the long-lived pioneers of a longevity revolution, how willing will boomers be to see themselves as a *surplus population*? Will they agree that the senior dominance they bring with them is defying the laws of nature? There may not be many doctrinaire Malthusians left, but there are environmentalists who come close to the sullen vicar's point of view. What answer can they be given? Once, when I found myself in an argument about the ecological significance of longevity, the editor of a prominent environmental magazine burst out with impatience. "You should be recommending ecological suicide," he growled. "We need more Baby Boomers offing themselves for the good of the planet." Not that he was volunteering to lead the way. Another prominent environmental editor refused to consider any demographic statistics I had to offer about the declining birth rate. "We are," she reminded me sternly, "committed to population alarmism." Being ideological means never having to change your mind.

We now know that Malthus, despite his enormous impact on social philosophy, was wrong. In thinking about human beings the way one might more properly think about rabbits, he overlooked a basic cultural factor: Industrial societies become more cunning as they grow in numbers. The same scientific and technological genius that creates overpopulated industrial cities can be used to find solutions to overpopulation. As the last few centuries have shown, we have found myriad ways to increase food production and limit reproduction. But Malthus overlooked another factor, certainly among the most crucial when it comes to our long-term demographic destiny. He never touched upon longevity as an environmentally imperative phase in the history of modern society. Less still was he aware of the revolutionary changes longevity brings with it in ethics and economics. Yet just as rivers will carve out their own channel of least resistance and rainforests flourish in a tropical climate, so, by the logic of progress, industrial societies age and, as they age, alter their ecological footprint. That is what makes the conservative campaign against entitlements so ludicrously misguided: It fails to grasp the magnitude of the phenomenon it seeks to alter. Our society *must* age, and so it *must* pay the cost.

Something vast and irreversible is happening in the demographics of the modern world, a reproductive pattern that permanently affects our relations with the Earth as a whole. But in contrast to other developments such as acid rain or global warming, which threaten to diminish the quality of life, longevity is — potentially — the best thing that has happened since the advent of industrial cities. With all the force of a "fixed law," longevity confronts us with an ultimate limit to economic growth based upon the changing values of a mature industrial society. If we might fancifully imagine the biosphere thinking about the antics of its troublesome human children, the thought that may loom largest in its mind at the beginning of the 21st century is, "More people are living longer... *Good!* About time they grew up." Not only was Malthus wrong about population, he was *radically* wrong. Unable to foresee the longevity revolution, he was ignorant of the single most important social factor in our future. There is no guarantee that the baby-boom generation will achieve environmental enlightenment, but the longevity revolution is the next best thing: a pressing cultural transformation that makes enlightenment all but obligatory.

I once had a conversation with a Sierra Club activist who despaired for the environmental future of urban-industrial society society. His fears made up the usual list. Population will grow, and as it does, consumption will increase, nonrenewable resources will be depleted, pollution will worsen, species will perish — all as the result of human greed to which he could see no limit. He was, in short, a Malthusian. "There is only one solution," he concluded with sad resignation. "We have to import a new human species that has some sense of eternal values."

Boomers in their senior years may be that population — or as close to it as we are likely to come.

Cultural Demographics

By a nice coincidence, at about the time the first boomers were finishing high school, America elected a very young man to be president in 1960, an event that John F. Kennedy himself called a "passing of the torch" from the old to the young. Kennedy, only 42 years old, came to the presidency with a vitality and ambition that enhanced the youthful ethos of the decade to come. Whatever his failings, he embodied the exuberance of the period, and never more so than when he rallied the nation to spend billions of dollars to land a man on the moon. A dramatic way to begin the decade of the 1960s. But today it is likely that boomers who, in their youth, cheered Kennedy for his bold decision are preoccupied with less spectacular goals than colonizing outer space. They are apt to be far more worried about keeping their jobs in an unsettled economy or paying off the sub-prime loan on their home. Not much further down on their list of priorities might be a nagging anxiety about finding affordable medical insurance and providing for a secure retirement. Same public, but 40 years later. Those who may be facing upwards of $50,000 a year (as of 2005) to pay nursing home costs for their aging parents may wonder, as they make each monthly payment, where their children will one day find the money to afford as much for them. Concerns like these are not limited to elders; they implicate whole families and finally whole societies as matters of public policy.

Viewing the political and economic behavior of people in this way might be called cultural demographics — a head count that does not leave out the hearts and minds of the population. That is actually the way marketing analysts use the term *demographics* when they are positioning a product in the marketplace. Raw numbers matter, but a refined evaluation of preferences, income, gender, ethnicity, and class is even more important. The intention is frankly commercial; it concentrates on obvious money questions. What will any particular public buy? How much will it buy? At what price? How can we get their attention and induce them to spend?

Environmentalists usually regard this approach to markets and audiences as the enemy's way of thinking, a technique for increasing consumption and wasting resources. But there is something they might learn from the hucksters. It is as simple as recognizing that, in its relations with the natural environment, a human population cannot be dealt with in the same way as other species. Leave out tastes, values, ideals, sensibilities, and the numbers tell very little about the use that population will make of its space and resources — surely not enough to make sensible predictions or intelligent policy. How much pressure will a human population place upon its habitat? Is it not obvious that the answer has everything to do with whether the population in question is a community of medieval monks living a life of fasting and prayer or a population of high-consumption suburbanites composed primarily of young families who spend most of their leisure time at the mall?

Cultural demographics assumes that age is among the factors that most decisively shape people's collective environmental relations — even when the people themselves may have other things on their mind. Thus, for cultural demographics it is a matter of importance that many members of the baby-boom generation are beginning to register the fact that they have provided poorly for their retirement years. Survey after survey concludes that the vast majority of middle-aged, middle-class Americans have given little realistic thought to the cost of a lengthy retirement; many are only just waking up to what awaits them. In the 1990s, a great many wishfully, almost desperately, placed their faith in the stock market, only to see the dot-com bubble burst and take their savings with it. Some retirement counselors are now warning boomers on the brink of retirement that they will have to save up more than a million dollars to guarantee a comfortable retirement. Whatever the truth of such intimidating estimates (and the financial services industry has every interest in practicing scare tactics), they make for cautious choices.

Those choices can begin to influence values as early as midlife — about the time people begin to fear that losing their job or coming down sick could spell disaster. The fear is well-founded. If they find themselves in dire straits, what will they have to fall back on? Welfare has ceased to be an entitlement; it has been stripped to the bone, and the unemployed are now identified (in the eyes of conservative leaders) as little better than a public nuisance. To go for any length of time without a job, a retirement plan, or medical insurance is to be performing without a net. All these fears mount as one ages out of the workforce. At the age of 60, one is too old to scramble, especially if there is nothing to scramble for but part-time jobs flipping hamburgers. Multiply personal hopes and fears like these by tens of millions and the result is a force that cannot help but change the economic agenda.

There is a workshop practice used by some environmental activists. It asks people to *think like a mountain*. There is another more difficult exercise worth trying. *Think like a marketing analyst*. Ask yourself how maturity alters habits of consumption. What every marketing expert knows is that the senior market has rotten demographics. True, the numbers and the dollars are there, but so too is a sales resistance that advertisers find formidable. On the other hand, the 18-to-20-something demographics has the most important quality in the business: gullibility. This is the public that believes advertising. It is hard to sell grown-up people on the basis of hot copy and glossy imagery alone — and all the more so if that population has other things on its mind, like a heart condition, an ailing spouse, failing joints, the cost of supporting live-in children, or a far greater interest in courses at the university extension than in a dynamite new car. If you run ads showing a shiny BMW draped over with gorgeous females, you may catch the eye of young men who wish they could afford that car and those women, but nobody over the age of 50 is going to believe that the females come with the car — least of all older women who control most of our discretionary income. For that very reason, the cultural demographics of seniors ought to look promising to environmentalists. The analysis of senior values may begin with simple statistics, but it will finally have to integrate the ideas and ideals that people take with them into their later years. Within such a perspective, matters that are often treated purely statistically can assume a very different force.

Death, for example. The death rate normally appears in demographic charts as a simple calculation: so many deaths per thousand. But in living experience, death is not a statistic; it is as profoundly personal as anything can be. How people deal with mortality as it closes in upon them has everything to do with their habits in life. Simpler creatures ask no questions of their ultimate fate. Humans do. For cultural demographics that is a significant point, because the answers we find prescribe meaning. And the meaning we find for our lives becomes a part of our greater ecology.

How to Count a Population

The maturing of the boomers confronts us with a new population problem, one that belongs to the industrial societies more so than to the majority world. Heretofore, the image that has come to mind when we think of *overpopulation* is the back alleys of Calcutta or Kinshasa, filled with starving, jobless people — hungry, powerless masses whom the rich have seen fit to treat as invisible.

Population alarmists, viewing the plight of these impoverished societies, have urged aggressive population policies, but more than that, they have raised an impassioned moral appeal.

In addition to achieving population control in the nations of the majority world, they have called for consumption control in the affluent societies. They incorporate per-capita resource use into their analysis, arguing that the citizens of First World nations consume far more than their share of energy and resources. In the words of Paul and Anne Ehrlich, "Americans are super-consumers and use rather inefficient technologies to service their consumption.... America's total environmental impact is roughly six times that of the 900 million people of India."[2] In this sense, the Ehrlichs see the United States as the "most over-populated nation in the world."

The images that population alarmists have of high-industrial consumption are the gas-guzzling automobile and expensive beef—luxuries that can be easily targeted for ethical condemnation. Suppose, however, there were another population in the industrial world that was large and growing, but whose need was not for luxury goods. Suppose this was a retired population willing to settle for a reasonable provision of food, clothing, shelter, and medical care. And what if that population, unlike the propertyless and disempowered millions of the majority world, possessed rights that could not be ignored? What if it had the power to elect governments and demand the necessities of life? That would give us a new politics of population, one that could arise only in the developed economies. That is exactly what we see happening in the urban-industrial societies today, where active millions are living out a second life that frequently stretches 20 and 30 years beyond retirement, and where millions more, who are highly dependent on costly medical services, now fill hospitals and nursing homes.

Environmentalists, many of them still under the influence of the cult of youth that was so much a part of the boomers' lives, have given no attention whatever to age as an ecological factor. Clearly, we need a new demographics calculus to deal with longevity. We must ask what the age range of the population is and what effective claim its older members have upon care and sustenance. Life expectancy and life span must be added in. And more than that. Along with those purely quantitative factors, we must take into account the changing quality of life that comes with an aging society. In the advanced industrial societies, the economic impact of all population statistics must now be calculated as life expectancy multiplied by the cost of the social services and medical care that are likely to be necessary at each age. In the United States, this would be the cost of entitlements plus other forms of senior care, including private family care that may remove a husband or wife from paid labor outside the home.

Thus, when demographers predict that the population of the United States will stabilize at 320-some million by the year 2040, it is important to add that more than ¼ of that number will be seniors over 60 and on their way out of the workforce — many into volunteer services, higher education, and political activism, and some into intensive, long-term nursing care. Among the latter will be a small nation of some 14 million Americans suffering from Alzheimer's disease. With less than half that number stricken by the disease as of 2000, the annual cost of advanced Alzheimer's care is $100 billion. One estimate places the cost of the Alzheimer's population in the year 2050 at $1 trillion.

The new demographic calculus should also include the future shape of the population: namely, that it will continue trending toward age and away from youth for the indefinite future. That fact — especially if we take into account the mature ethical values associated with age — has everything to do with social policy and fiscal planning. For example, cultural demographics includes the growing use that retired citizens are making of educational resources and what they may be learning that makes a political difference. They may, after all, be reading a great deal of ecological literature with a view to becoming good environmental citizens.

The Bomb that Fizzled

If, at any point over the past 30 years, one came upon a news story titled "Population Bombshell," the phrase could have meant only one thing: overpopulation. Ever since Paul Ehrlich wrote *The Population Bomb* in 1968, a Malthusian nightmare has haunted the environmental movement. Fear of overpopulation was a defining feature of the 1960s and 1970s. It came to be so deeply engraved on the mind of the times that it is still difficult for people to understand that population can shrink as rapidly as it can grow. That is in fact what we see happening. In the course of the final quarter of the 20th century, the demographic doom the Ehrlichs foresaw from the heights of the baby boom has dramatically receded in the industrial societies. The phrase "population bombshell" as used by *New Scientist* magazine as of 1998 refers to the surprising *decline* in population that the United Nations had discovered in its most recent studies. "With the world's population doubling in 40 years, disaster seemed inevitable," *New Scientist* reported. "Yet now the population is beginning to stabilize or even fall in many parts of the world. So has the population explosion turned into a whimper?"[3] In light of this *baby bust,* the latest population projections by the United Nations now include a best-case scenario predicting that the world may number only 3.5 billion people in the year 2150. That is the most optimistic projection we have had for world population in over a century.

It would seem that environmentalists have achieved a victory they may never have expected. As of the year 2000, some 70 nations, including all the major industrial powers, are reproducing below the replacement rate, and some far below. Italy and Spain, Catholic countries where environmentalists never expected to make their voices heard against the authority of a Catholic church that still condemns contraception, are running fertility rates that are half of replacement, which means they are shrinking rapidly. Italy, it is predicted, will drop from a population of

57 million as of 2000 to 40 million by 2050; Germany will fall from 82 million to 73 million. In the European Union as a whole, it is expected that population will decrease steadily unless the numbers are made up by immigration. There are governments today that have greater fear of a *birth dearth* than of overpopulation. They worry that their workforce will grow too small to maintain economic growth.

But now that we have at least the hint of a more hopeful demographic future, conservative economists are hardly cheered by what they see ahead. They are gloomier than ever. In their eyes, the birth dearth has begun to loom as a major political threat to the global economy. Thus, in a front cover story on "The Global Aging Crisis" for March 1, 1999, *U.S. News and World Report* warned that "with the elderly population exploding, the social and economic costs could be staggering for all of us." Similarly, Ben Wattenberg of the hyperconservative American Enterprise Institute called global aging "the real population bomb." As he put it, "I am not a catastrophe-monger, but it is a hell of a lot bigger problem than too many people."[4] Why? Because like the conservative commentators who have been telling us since the 1980s that the United States cannot afford entitlements, Wattenberg sees fiscal catastrophe awaiting all the industrial nations that will have to pay for their growing senior numbers.

If fears like this prevail, we may see fiscally worried governments overreacting to the cost of the birth dearth as the Japanese, Czechs, and Germans have done by instituting programs to encourage population growth. In Germany, the birth rate has become a matter of acute political concern. As of the early 1990s, it fell to 9.3 births per thousand people. As a result, Germany is among the few countries that have adopted pronatalist policies aimed at turning back the demographic tide. The state of Brandenburg has undertaken to promote larger families by offering a cash subsidy for each new baby. The reward is in addition to other state benefits, including *Kindergeld*, substantial monthly payments to offset childrearing expenses. As the government sees it, unless Germans can be bribed into higher rates of reproduction, by 2030 there will be nine German retirees "living off" every ten German workers. In the Czech Republic, where births have fallen well below the replacement rate, the government has run anti-contraception ads advising couples to "stop taking care." Billboard ads show Johann Sebastian Bach as 20 naked clones. Workers at the Bandai Corporation in Tokyo are now being offered a million yen bonus (roughly $10,000 American) for every baby after the family's second child. The Japanese government encourages such programs. It fears that, at current levels of population replacement, it will not be able to afford the generous social programs that now support the elderly. Over the next decade, the number of young Japanese workers below the age of 30 will drop by 25%. Some analysts wonder if Japan may not soon have to import young people to prop up their aging economy. What Bandai and other employers are offering is now supplemented by official educational and child care subsidies aimed at boosting the size of families.

Will such pronatalist inducements work? The problem of persuading women to raise their reproductive rate is proving to be intractable, not because it is up against a clear desire to have fewer children, but because it must face the decision more women are making in the developed societies to delay having their first child so that they can go to school, hold a job, or wait to marry. The average age for first-time mothering in Europe and the United States has now reached 28. Wait that long, and it is harder to choose a second or third pregnancy. Baby booms depend on starting families early. Even if such policies worked, would they make any economic sense? Would the cost of bribing young couples to produce families of three, four, or five be any savings over entitlements? Or would this simply be exchanging one group of dependents for another? Where did we get the idea that raising more children is more beneficial than taking population pressure off the environment? Fewer people use fewer resources. They consume less, they waste less.

Those who fret over the birth dearth may be up against another, greater obstacle. There is reason to believe that the longevity revolution is grounded in a limit that is the exact reverse of Malthus. Fertility and life expectancy may be linked in ways that make it biologically and sociologically impossible to expect a baby boom from long-lived societies. If that is so, then the longevity revolution has brought us a new law of population. And as with most of what we know about population, the study begins with fruit flies.

As early as the 1970s, population geneticists began to notice a peculiar characteristic among *Drosophila*, the fast-breeding fruit fly on which so much of our genetic knowledge is based. They recognized that flies that reproduce late in life and have fewer young tend to live longer. This finding gave rise to a hypothesis called the *disposable soma theory*. The theory argues that there is a trade-off between fecundity and longevity. Animals that invest heavily in reproduction divert physical energy and resources from the maintenance and repair of cells and so age more rapidly. As one commentator put it, using the economic metaphors that now dominate genetics, "It is as if our genes are unscrupulous factory owners, skimping on quality control and exploiting their workforce to earn the profits needed to spread their empires."[5] Or, in more technical terms, "the mechanisms underlying the increase in life span involved greater investments in somatic durability." It would seem to follow, then, that the less energy a fruit fly puts into reproduction, the more it can devote to cellular repair and maintenance.

Do these mechanisms have anything to do with human beings? They do. It may seem a long reach from fruit flies to the lords and ladies of Great Britain, but a 1998 study focusing on the English aristocracy over a thousand years of history indicates the same demographic pattern we find in *Drosophila*. English aristocratic families can be traced back to the eighth century; that makes them one of the few groups for whom reasonably reliable long-term vital statistics can be found. The study, published in *Nature*, showed that parents who were barren or produced the fewest progeny lived longer than more prolific members of their class.[6] This corroborated a 1997 study indicating that American women who waited until they were in their forties to have their first and usually their only child had a far better chance of reaching the age of 100.[7]

The striking aspect about this longevity-fertility trade-off is that it applies to males as well as females. Fathers among the barren aristocrats shared their wives' longer life expectancy. Why should this be? Recent studies of male fertility now confirm that fecundity (meaning the ability to produce offspring within a given period of time) is governed in men as well as women by a biological clock. Men may remain fertile indefinitely, but from about age 24 on, a man's real chance of impregnating a woman drops by 3% each year. There is also a correlation between miscarriages and the father's age: the older the father, the more likely a miscarriage is to happen. Thus, the longer any couple waits to reproduce by natural means, the less likely they are to have young. But meanwhile, the maintenance functions of their bodies are free to keep their immune systems in better repair and so make their somas that much less disposable.

Is it possible, then, that *fertility is inversely correlated to life expectancy*? In fruit flies, the disposable soma may be the whole explanation for that astonishing fact. But in humans, there is another sociological factor at work: women's liberation, one of the counter culture's most enduring achievements.

When overpopulation was first identified as an environmental threat, the women's movement had not yet achieved its full impact even in the highly developed societies. Those were the baby-boom years when American women were running a record fertility rate and supposedly aspiring to little more than full-time homemaking. As soon as women began to rethink their role in life, their fertility rate slumped, reaching 1.7 by 1976 and staying somewhere between there and bare replacement level ever since. In a very real sense, Betty Friedan's *The Feminine Mystique* provided the solution population alarmists once thought could only be achieved by rigorously enforced contraception.

Environmentalists have been reluctant to admit it, but altering the psychology of women does more than all the scare tactics and coercive public policy in the world to change reproductive habits. What could be more obvious? Societies that educate girls raise female expectations. As their skills improve, young women want full access to the good things of modern life. Inevitably, they grow up to marry and start families late. As their earning power and personal independence increases, they find less and less resistance to their views from the men in their lives. As a survey by the National Marriage Project at Rutgers University discovered, American men and women in their twenties are steadily shying away from matrimony, instead choosing casual sex over courtship and marriage. Or, if they do marry, young wives and their husbands increasingly opt for an upscale lifestyle, preferring to remain childfree: *families of two*, as Laura Carroll calls them in her study of "happily married couples without children by choice."

Just as the old choose to live longer, the young choose to have smaller families. Boomers were the first to make that choice a matter of political principle; their children have followed in their footsteps. The longevity revolution is hardly a geriatric conspiracy. It is the result of intergenerational choice, the combination of longer life expectancy and lower fertility. Young and old, we are all in this together. When the media report that Japanese leaders are *desperate* about the growing imbalance between young and old, we should remember that this is not the result of life expectancy alone, but the choices being made by young Japanese women. Between the ages of 15 and 49, 30% of Japan's women are unmarried; one in seven is expected to stay that way. Similarly in the United States, *Time* magazine reported that, as of August 2000, 43 million adult women — 40% of adult females — are now single, many of them digging into an unmarried lifestyle that involves buying their own home and having fewer, if any, children. If the young choose to reproduce less, then they must necessarily have more elders to support. Entitlements are the long-term cost of the lifestyle for which youth is spontaneously opting everywhere, even in some of the poorest countries. In 1965 Mexican women were on average producing seven children. In 2001 that figure dropped to 2.4, mainly because so many women were working out of the home or attending school. When, in another 30 or 40 years, those mothers become part of their country's largest senior generation, no doubt there will be warnings that there are not enough children to support them. The familiar lament will be sounded again: too many old, too few young. But then, why leave out of account the fact that the long life enjoyed by the old, far from being some permanent class advantage, will one day belong to their own children?

There is another factor that may soon figure significantly in the demographics of the world's industrial societies: the promise of designing better babies. Biotechnology is bidding to take over the management of pregnancy, with a view to safeguarding the health of the newborn. Geneticists are already pursuing research that might eliminate the risks of Down's Syndrome and sickle-cell anemia. In 2007 researchers discovered a genetic marker that predisposes people to heart disease. Their ultimate goal is now to find some way to eliminate that risk *in utero*, along with any other diseases that can be located in the genome. Those who can afford these benefits will hardly forego the chance. In the meantime, until these techniques of genetic enhancement are perfected, parents can have recourse to embryo selection, which allows them to screen for defects and then choose the fertilized egg that comes closest to their ideal. Whatever the method, designer babies do not come cheap and will never be the basis for large families — especially if parents want to provide their offspring with the best possible education. Genetic improvements plus an expensive university education make for costly childrearing. At the same time, babies who come into the world engineered to be disease-free will certainly live longer and eventually claim more entitlements in their senior years. By virtue of this one act — the decision to make healthier babies — parents will be choosing smaller families and producing more longevous children. Though they are not aware of the result, they are contributing to the senior domination of our society.

Too Fertile — or Not Fertile Enough?

As younger couples register the increasing cost of entitlements or are forced to assume responsibility for aging parents, they are apt at some point to respond by seeking to reduce domestic expenses. The cost of elder health care is not the only pressure on them; they also need to provide for their own and their children's medical needs. That will grow more expensive, regardless of any change in health insurance. By the late 1990s, it became clear that managed care, once thought to guarantee cheaper medical services, had saved as much money as it could by imposing unaccustomed austerity on doctors and patients alike. The public's response to managed care, and especially that of retirees under Medicare, grows ever more critical. In response to public pressure, state after state has passed some form of a medical bill of rights that undermines frugality. Forced to spend more on their clients, HMOs see their profits falling and their stocks losing value. Their response is to raise premiums across the board for old and young alike, but the young, lacking Medicare, feel the pinch more acutely.

It is difficult to imagine what the effect will be upon younger people in the industrial world who find themselves on the trailing edge of the longevity revolution. The situation is without precedent. At some point, they may resent being born into the senior dominance, but they also know that, without entitlements programs, they would become fully responsible for aged parents — a less financially appealing choice. One result of this situation might be a high degree of demoralization among younger citizens. They may see less and less promise for their own lives in a society beholden to the values of an elder culture. They may feel increasingly less inclined to participate in the political process or even to vote — a decision that would lessen their power still more. One by one, they will in time age out of these feelings as they themselves join the elder culture. But meanwhile, the consumer demand associated with younger people is apt to become less effective as the youth market diminishes. In general, the daring, energetic entrepreneurial values that might win their support may begin to lose their influence.

While superior medical care is the most obvious force behind the shifting ratio of young on the job to elders in retirement, other factors are at work, some of them connected with features of modern society that are intended to make our lives safer, more efficient, and convenient. There is now an impressive body of evidence that suggests we are filling our environment with "a cocktail of pollutants," sometimes called "endocrine disrupters," that reduce the sperm count or cause testicular cancer.[8] Among the possible toxic culprits are chemicals widely used in ordinary detergent, floor polishes, plastic tubing, and food wrapping. If this is so, then a maturing industrial economy may *naturally* fluctuate toward lower reproductive rates as it increases the distribution of cheap, synthetic materials, many of which are valued for their convenience and seen as enhancing the standard of living. One might almost believe there is an inherent restraint that connects affluence with diminishing fertility, as if the ecology of the planet uses our own synthetic chemicals against us, hitting us where it hurts.

Many women experience diminished fertility as liberating, an opportunity to spend more of their lives exploring careers, traveling, and learning. As medical science progresses, women need not feel desperate about delaying motherhood into their late middle age; they can afford to wait until even age 45 — or, in at least a few highly publicized cases, until age 60. It is even possible for younger women to store ova so that they can be fertilized at any point in their lives by the sperm of their choice. The biological clock has very nearly been put out of commission. But by the time they reach 40 or 50, many women who decided to wait to have their first child may choose to forego childbearing, simply because of the physical demands.

The option this creates is still in need of fine-tuning when it comes to planning parenthood within the limits of population control. Older women tend to produce more twins, especially if they are using fertility medications. In the course of 1990s the number of twins born to American mothers, many of whom waited into their forties to conceive, increased by 50% and the number of triplets by over 400% , not to mention record-breaking deliveries of six, seven, and eight babies, all of which resulted from fertility drugs. The American College of Pediatrics now recommends that fertility clinics monitor their clients more closely to eliminate the risk of multiple births that may produce more babies than women want. If the advice gets through, we may see many more single-child families, settling for the number of young that parents really planned to have.

This changing pattern in reproduction began to appear in the United States in the 1970s. In that decade, the number of childless women in their twenties doubled, followed, in the next decade, by a tripling of births for women between age 30 and 35 — the largest increased birth rate for any age group in the society. Most of the late-age mothers were working women who would have preferred fewer babies, often no more than one. The change corresponded to a new vision of life. As one feminist friend of mine observed, "Most of today's women are not interested in going from the classroom to the diaper pail without having some time to achieve a certain amount of self-knowledge. The phrase 'giving birth to myself before I give birth to a baby' is one that more and more women are using to describe their approach to having children."

These new reproductive habits are creating a social order that once might have seemed unimaginable. In the United States at the turn of 21st century, the percentage of households that contain married couples with children has shriveled to just 26%, down from 45% in the 1970s. These figures reflect the growing number of people who are waiting to have babies. Singles and domestic partners living together out of wedlock may never produce families at all. Twenty-six percent of boomer women have elected to remain childless. Even more striking, 40% of baby-boom women between the ages of 36 and 54 have been sterilized.[9] Remaining childless by choice is becoming a far from unusual married condition, one that is less and less viewed as *unnatural*. There are, in fact, support groups at work on the matter. They seek to change the image of those who are childless by choice so that they will pass as *normal*.

Some analysts have flippantly, but perhaps accurately, characterized these preferences as a matter of parents having a refrigerator instead of having a baby. The assumption is that young working couples at some point choose to substitute consumer durables for extra children. Can the same transition to a stable population be expected in other countries? That is an open question until we know what demographic changes industrialization will bring about in major test cases like China, India, and Indonesia. China has been especially aggressive in enforcing its one-child family policy. In the 1990s, female sterilization surged forward to cut the national fertility rate to two births per woman. Ironically, the Chinese prejudice in favor of boy babies has produced a gender imbalance (roughly 114 boys for every 100 girls as of 2000) that will eventually work to lower the birth rate more: fewer females, fewer mothers, fewer babies.

Another factor affecting family size may be the growing acceptance in high-industrial societies of homosexual households, single-parent households, and unmarried cohabitation. When the classic Victorian family — the breadwinner father, the full-time mother at home with the children — prevailed, it was possible for women to specialize in pregnancy and homemaking, provided they did not die in childbirth along the way. And if they did, the husband could easily find another wife and carry on procreating — hence, the prolific middle-class households of the 19th century. If that domestic arrangement were still with us, there would be no need to bemoan the declining ratio of young to old; we would have baby boom upon baby boom.

If that is indeed what conservatives want when they speak of *family values*, then there is an ironic twist to the story of the waning classic family. Those on the political right may despair over the cost of entitlements and prefer to transfer that expense from the welfare state to families. But they have actually contributed to the very situation that makes that responsibility unaffordable for most people. The leaders of corporate America have behaved as one would expect them to behave. They have disempowered unions and depressed wages, placing American labor in competition with desperate workers in distant lands. That harsh reality has forced more and more women out of the home and into the workforce. Many of the new jobs celebrated on the financial pages are part-time, low-paid second jobs for working mothers who are racing to stay ahead of the family's credit card debt. But even with two paychecks, such costs as nursing home care for aged parents are well beyond the reach of working-class families. If something has to give in the grip of the tightening household budget, it is apt to be the number of children couples choose to have.

It would, of course, be a mistake to assume that family planning is always a rational matter, but insofar as it is, life in the longevous society is apt to reinforce all these influences. As younger couples try to stay afloat in the sea of consumer choices, they are likely to register the increasing demand of entitlements upon their paychecks and respond to it by trying to reduce domestic expenses. But as the working population is taxed more heavily to pay for senior programs, it will tend to cut back further on reproduction in order to maintain a standard of living that advertising imagery insidiously insists we must have. These factors make each successive younger generation smaller relative to the older, and that, in turn, diminishes the ratio of young to old. The result is a demographic circle from which it is difficult to see any way out. Or can we imagine rebellious young marrieds deciding to produce another baby boom, even though they will be forced to live poorer? A 2007 Pew Research Center poll reflected a sharp change in the meaning of marriage that helps explain the diminishing size of families. Fewer couples than ever — less than half — believed children are the best way to make a happy marriage. Having a family counts for less in their eyes than a harmonious relationship between husband and wife that includes adequate income and good sex. As one family-policy expert interpreted the findings, couples now seek "fulfilling the X-rated fantasies and desires of adults…. Child-rearing values…seem stale and musty by comparison."[10]

In such unforeseen ways, it seems that industrial economies find it harder to keep their numbers growing, except perhaps by immigration. But in time, as immigrant families adapt to the prevailing values of the urban-industrial mainstream — and thanks to the omnipresent media, that happens within two generations — their demographics fall into the same pattern.

The third generation of Hispanic migrants living in Los Angeles does not continue the lifestyle of a poor, newly arrived family of five or six from central Mexico. Immigrating turns into a form of long-term population control.

I return to what may seem like a quaint idea: namely, that the planet we live on possesses mysterious ecological constraints we have not yet fathomed — and those constraints include us in body, mind, and spirit. Far from being a frail damsel in distress, Dame Nature is a vast and robust system of life-enhancing controls, powers as mysterious as the way animals seem able to sense the approach of natural disasters. One of these has to do with subtle means of limiting the potentially eco-cidal behavior of human beings. Within that context, women's liberation and the longevity revolution become allied forces for diminishing population growth and frenetic consumption. Those constraints may not operate as swiftly as environmentalists wish, but they are there and available to us. Of course it helps for enlightened people to join in on that effort, offering their brains and their good intentions as part of a worldwide environmental movement. All I suggest is that our species may not be alone in that enterprise.

CHAPTER 11

Welcome to Eldertown

One of the main problems of urban culture today is to increase the digestive capacity of the container without letting the physical structure become a colossal, clotted, self-defeating mass. Renewal of the inner metropolitan core is impossible without a far greater transformation on a regional and interregional scale.

— Lewis Mumford, *The City in History*, 1961

In 2003 a man driving through a shopping mall in Santa Monica, California mistook his gas pedal for his brake, gunned his car, and slammed into a crowd of shoppers. Before he could bring the runaway vehicle to a stop, he had killed ten people. In court he was strangely remorseless and showed signs of being confused about what had happened and what his responsibility might be. Traffic accidents on the city streets and freeways happen every day, but the incident in Santa Monica was special, and not simply because of the extraordinary death toll. In this case, the driver was 89 years old and clearly lacking in the alertness and agility needed to drive safely. Universally, those who reported the story and those who judged his case were certain he was too old to be behind the wheel of a car. Other voices recommended that there should be stringent tests for elderly drivers; others recommended outright delicensing for drivers over a certain age. But what age? 70? 80? 90?

Are the elderly our worst drivers? Perhaps not. Just a few days before I began this chapter, a survey noted the high level of accidents on the part of teenage drivers who are often distracted by audio equipment, cell phones, or the antics of friends in the car. The report also lamented the number of young drivers who binge drink. As of 2006, there were 6,000 automobile fatalities among teenagers and another 300,000 injuries. When the call goes out to raise the legal age for a driver's license or for more rigorous safety standards for teenagers, adults are not apt to think of that as a serious issue, because we know cars are not essential to most kids, who use them mainly for pleasure driving — and will, in any case, soon grow into adulthood and qualify for a license.

Suggesting that elderly drivers should be delicensed will always be a controversial issue, because so many older drivers are dependent on their cars for the necessities of life. But they are also old. And at some point that makes a difference. No question but that the right to drive should be based on competence, but ask what the main elements of competence are, and we are back in the middle of the controversy. Good eyesight by day and night, good hearing, good judgment about speed and space, good coordination, agility, clear focus. Are these not exactly the capacities that diminish with age — if not for everybody, then for most? Delicensing senior drivers will be a hot-button proposal for years to come, but one day soon, when the roads are filled with impaired elders and their accident rate begins to mount, there will be no way around facing up to the fact that fast cars and freeways were never intended for the elderly. We already wonder if airplane pilots above a certain age — 65? 70? — should be retired. The pilots of one airline — American — have conceded the point and have agreed to step down at 60. Automobiles are not in the same category as planes, but the same issue arises. Does there come an age when the elderly should be taken off the roads? If public authorities take no action, insurance companies will. Long before it becomes illegal for elders to drive, it may become unaffordable.

The question is important in itself as a matter of public safety, but I raise it here within a larger, rather ironic context: the ecological future of the automobile in the world's most automotive society. Boomers have a peculiar connection with that society. They were born into an era when the automotive economy dominated our lives. What electronic gadgets like the iPod and the cell phone have become to the current adolescent generation, automobiles were to their parents in the years following World War II — a consumer fascination that all but defined modernity. The consequences were enormous. The automobile, steeped in illusions of speed, success, and convenience, inevitably led to urban sprawl; people chose to live farther from their workplace because they believed the car could all but eliminate the miles between. So why not move the family to a big house in a pristine new tract with some charmingly bucolic name — Thousand Oaks or Old Peach Grove — and have the best of both worlds, the city and the suburbs? Boomers in their babyhood were among the main reasons the automotive economy became the centerpiece of the postwar economy. As their numbers grew with the Great Affluence, parents — mainly white, middle-class parents — began to forsake the congestion, crime, and dirt of the city in favor of multibedroom split-level homes in safe, clean dormitory subdivisions. At a time when many European families were still living in cramped quarters in bombed-out cities, "Go to your room!" became a mantra of Dr. Spock parenting.

With considerable encouragement from automobile manufacturers and the oil industry, public transport was manically scrapped in favor of one-to-a-car private transportation. Fathers became commuters, needing ever faster access to their jobs. So too mothers, driving second cars, needed access to shopping and schools. The solution was more cars, more freeways, more parking structures. These days, the computer makers seem out to create a world where nobody ever needs to leave home. The style of the 1950s and 1960s was based on never leaving the car.

Everything then was *drive-in*: hamburger joints, banks, movies, even churches. The drive-in movie became the sex-education classroom of choice for postwar teenagers, more and more of whom had cars of their own that functioned as a boudoir on wheels. And when families were ready to trade their cars in, these sleek machines were consigned to the automobile cemetery that stood outside every city, mountains of rusting steel that stood like monuments raised to the gods of affluence.

In the world where boomers grew up, *inner city* became a euphemism for *ghetto*, as white flight left the impoverished *other America* behind in neighborhoods that lacked the tax base for public services. By the 1960s the car and the superhighway were no longer a convenience; they had become necessities. That in turn committed industrial society to ever greater oil dependence; it also laid the foundation for serious air pollution. The private automobile brought with it a foreign policy and an environmental cost that are only now reporting in as the nightmares we call *the war on terror* and *global warming*. One might almost say those who live by the automobile may have to die by the automobile.

That is the irony of the matter. Boomers — the generation that grew up believing the automobile was the emblem of freedom, progress, and success — have lived to see cars become a blight upon our lives. What started as a convenience that made a larger, more mobile urban lifestyle possible has become an unsustainable burden. Every city in the industrial world is strangling on traffic, struggling to afford the costly extensions, alternatives, and rebuilding that their transportation infrastructure now requires. The situation is so dire that some cities are outlawing private cars in their central sectors. Simply to park a car while on the job has become a major budgetary item. Cities everywhere have reached the outer limit of practical commuting, which can amount to as much as a two-hour drive each way to work and home. Economists estimate the amount of time wasted simply waiting or creeping in traffic runs as high as $40 billion a year. In her study of America's car culture, Jane Holtz Kay estimated that each of us may be paying over $10,000 a year to keep this foolish, extravagant system going. As for all the attendant costs — insurance, law enforcement, accident casualties, maintenance, and repair — these easily amount to trillions.

The problem is so vast, so expensive, that it might seem hopeless. We have all seen ghastly images of Asian cities blanketed in smog they have not even begun to control. Chinese leaders regard asthma as a symptom of progress. Is this the future we have before us? Many developers think so. They continue to clear land farther out for subdivisions along superhighways where they can build bigger, air-conditioned homes with lawns and pools and ever more electrical gadgetry. Some of the them, the McMansions, are several times larger than the suburban homes boomers grew up in. Developers continue to believe they can sell such ersatz luxury even to single women buyers or empty-nest couples simply on the basis of cultural momentum. But is it possible that, as with other ecological dilemmas, a solution may come from an unexpected source? If fast cars and superhighways were not meant for the elderly, then what will their future be in a world dominated by an aging population? What will become of the automotive city when we get around to building the city of elders?

Someplace Closer In

It is hardly likely that the industrial societies will give up on the private automobile altogether. But a great many older drivers may delicense themselves in the years to come as cars lose both their utility and their charm. They may begin to do so even before their qualification to drive becomes a public issue. My own experience bears out these changing values. As a teenager, I was caught up in the mystique of the automobile. I regarded learning to drive and making use of the family car as a rite of passage.

From that point forward, driving became as natural as breathing, a clear necessity that was still capable of being pleasurable. When my wife and I first settled in northern California in the 1950s, we used to visit San Francisco frequently to take advantage of its theaters, museums, restaurants — or simply to walk the streets of colorful neighborhoods. It was a quick drive of some 40 miles. But in the course of the last few decades, getting into and out of the city has become steadily more arduous. The bridges are often congested, the roads packed with drivers who seem to be starting the rush hour earlier and earlier, turning the hours from 2:00 to 7:00 PM into a traffic nightmare. We now creep along freeways where we once used to hit 60 or 70 miles per hour. The problem is not restricted to San Francisco. Every city in the country now struggles with traffic. The other city I know best — supremely automotive Los Angeles, which was created for cars rather than people — has become a round-the-clock horror for drivers. Even in my small university town of Berkeley, parking has become a maddening problem. I stopped enjoying driving years ago; now I wonder how much longer I will be able to trust myself behind the wheel. The day may come when access to public or shared transportation will force us to relocate.

What, then, would we be seeking? Someplace *closer in*. Closer to what? Everything that makes urban life interesting. But if *close in* means in the city itself, the cost of either renting or buying is prohibitive for all but the richest — many of whom do elect to live in luxurious condos or town houses. I would expect to see those who can afford the cost to make that move and begin treating a flat in town as the true measure of luxury. As for those who cannot pay the price, there are alternatives on the horizon, most obviously retirement communities where transportation by bus or van is a service rather than a piece of four-wheeled property. These days it is a common sight at concerts or the theater in San Francisco to see the street filled with buses from surrounding retirement communities. Choices like these are bound to cut back on use of the private, gasoline-driven automobile. So, too, the willingness of older drivers to use slower, more fuel-efficient vehicles. A major part of my driving these days could be done in little more than an electric golf cart. As the next generation of private and institutional retirement architecture makes its appearance, planners are already expecting senior residents to demand more green space than asphalt and concrete.[1]

Every sprawling city in the world hides within itself urban centers that have historic or commercial appeal, interesting, pedestrian-friendly places to be — or simply open green spaces. Such areas need to be singled out and densified. Housing in these areas needs to be built higher and more compact to share the charm of the place with more people who can find the transport they need close at hand — or perhaps do without it in favor of walking to the stores, movies, bookshops, coffeehouses, saloons, community centers they need. Add the possibility of rooftop or community gardening and the need to travel for food is diminished still more. Farming the cities remains a practical option, an opportunity for healthy work raising wholesome food. In my childhood, during World War II, every neighborhood in the nation planted *victory gardens* on its open lots or in its backyards. Few people now realize how richly productive these gardens were. At their peak in 1943, there were over 20 million home gardens in the United States growing millions of tons of produce. Claiming an open lot as a sort of community commons was the patriotic thing to do; it also built a sense of community and contributed good fresh food to the table. Some communities raised chickens and rabbits to supplement the diet. Then, when the war ended, the Agriculture Department in Washington made a deliberate effort to call off this experiment in urban gardening in favor of the supermarket industry. The result was to make American cities the least fertile in history. Vegetable gardens were replaced by sterile lawns that required more water and pesticides than ever before. Relying on trips to the supermarket became part of the busy boomers' way of life; raising your own fruit and vegetables seemed and still seems far too demanding. Easier to cart the food home by the bagfull in the station wagon or the SUV. Why grow your own organic, safe-to-eat beans and lettuce when you can buy it from Mexico or Chile or the Philippines by way of Costco or Safeway? But why not? Because food shipped from distant lands is loaded with pesticides, often lacking basic inspection, and dependent on fossil fuels for its transportation.

The novelist Barbara Kingsolver and her family have lately undertaken an experiment in returning to home gardening. In her 2007 book *Animal, Vegetable, Miracle: A Year of Food Life*, she recounts the same results the country found as a whole during that distant wartime effort: high yields of fresh food, good nutrition, and rewarding work. I suspect few of our overworked urban and suburban families, lacking the time available to a professional writer, would be able to follow her example. But a retired population could easily find the time and would value the sense of community. Why aren't retirement communities growing their own fruits and vegetables? Perhaps the next wave of boomer retirees will take up the idea. In my home town of Berkeley during the 1960s there were neighborhoods where the younger population tore down fences and merged backyards to create an arable commons. They were part of a *food conspiracy* aimed at better nutrition and lower prices. The spirit of that experiment has not died. A widespread *underground food collective* has spread across the country, uniting urban gardeners, artisan bakers and brewers, and small-scale local growers who have opted out of the global food economy. If they can connect with the nation's retirees, especially those who reside in retirement communities that now use their space for lawns and putting greens, they could become a new cottage industry that produced safer, healthier food at a cheaper cost.[2]

In their effort to limit suburbanization, some planners have taken the ideal of urban compaction to an absurd extreme. Paolo Soleri, creator of the Arcosanti experiment in Arizona, sought to house cities with populations of millions in single megastructures that have more the look of prisons. Even if his vision has a fanatical feel to it, Soleri has tried to answer a key question: How much land and resources do people need to meet their needs? By taking his megastructures to the extreme, he gave us a baseline. A city of a million might be reduced to a footprint of a few hundred acres and meet all its energy requirements by solar power and the recycling of waste. Short of his extreme, the environmental movement has inspired many imaginative new designs for quasi-urban living, holding out the prospect that where there were once sprawling suburbs, we may one day have relatively self-sufficient small cities or clusters of towns that draw culture and commerce to themselves. The town planners Michael and Judy Corbett have raised an attractive standard for sustainable community living. Their Village Homes suburb outside of Davis, California, is small (only 240 living units) but ecologically planned right down to its edible landscape. With the resources of a major university nearby, this might be an ideal place to retire while living lightly on the planet.[3] Richard Register, founder of Ecocity Builders, believes compact small cities would be an ideal sustainable human habitat. His principles include "access by proximity."

> If enough diversity is close enough, you don't need to travel a lot for life's basics: residence, job, school. The idea is to design maximum access right into the city structure.... Proximity access policies could also include local hiring practices, renting apartments to people who don't own cars and who work nearby, making bank loans

available in the neighborhoods from which the savings come (very often low-income urban areas have accumulated savings in great excess of the loans made in those same areas, while suburban developers use those funds for anti-ecological construction). Another proximity policy: ordinances permitting increased residential construction in activity centers and prohibiting it in farther-out areas. Land trusts and public bond issues, as in Stockholm, could purchase structures in car-dependent areas and convert suburbia back to nature, agriculture, or ecologically stable villages.[4]

As utopian proposals, Register's list of urban reforms may seem unrealistic. But think of his recommendations in another context. Suppose we see these mixed-zoning and financial standards as changes brought about in cities, not purely by the force of ecological idealism, but by the practical demands of an aging population for condos and rentals and live-work facilities in greater proximity to their daily physical, cultural, and medical needs — a rising demand that real-estate interests would be foolish to ignore. Does this not look like the direction in which we may soon be moving, most likely by fits and starts, as the elder population seeks an alternative to automotive sprawl? At some point, developers and civic leaders must realize that these are the needs of a reasonably affluent, highly empowered electorate. At that point, can we not imagine a sort of phase transition in our social life that gives us a new pattern for living? After all, if we think back to 1939, who would have predicted that in less than a generation the United States would be the suburbanized, automotive economy it had become by the mid-1950s?

When the Oil Gives Out

One way to evaluate the prospects of Eldertown might be to start from the viewpoint of one of the more apocalyptic environmental groups. The peak oil movement focuses tightly on the issue of energy, the Achilles heel of industrial society. Convinced that global oil production will soon peak — or perhaps already has — the peak oilers predict a horrendous cascade of disasters in our near future. Cars, lacking fuel, will vanish from our lives. Suburbs dependent on commuting will have to be abandoned. Big-box stores will be empty as both the goods and the money for consumption disappear. Big homes, too expensive to heat or cool, will stand untenanted. At the extreme, this is of course an unlivable world. But short of that, if one looks at the lifestyle such radical changes demand, are we not dealing with choices that elders are far more apt to make than a younger population? Smaller homes or condos in more densely populated centers. Less driving or no driving at all in private cars. Lower consumption. To be sure, environmentalists, who have never given any attention to aging, are apt to feel none of this will happen soon enough, but it is of some importance surely that one is working with rather than against a powerful demographic trend.

In the near future, as a growing retirement population fans out across the land seeking a new phase of life, we can expect a plethora of schemes for small-town restoration, efforts to turn the backwater into communities of character, many of them health-care-based. However it comes about, the private automobile may one day become an industrial relic, part of a pattern of life that belonged to the world that came before the longevity revolution. The challenge for city planning will be to transform what started out among seniors as culturally barren Sun City retirement communities ("glorified playpens for seniors," as Maggie Kuhn called them) into the sort of vital, decentralized cosmopolitan nodes many boomers will prefer. That opportunity is at hand. Culture once available only in metropolitan centers now comes our way via road companies and traveling exhibitions. The rest can arrive by satellite, phone line, mail order, and broadband. Lewis Mumford, our premier historian of cities, recognized this possibility soon after World War II when he predicted the "etherialization" of cities. The result might be an "invisible city…penetrated by invisible rays and emanations.… If a remote village can see the same motion picture or listen to the same radio program as the most swollen center, no one need live in that center or visit it."

Today Mumford would have included the enormous potential of broadband transmission via the World Wide Web among those "rays and emanations." Here is a sector of our economy that is more than ready for the elder culture. Just as a restless, perpetually ambient, post–World War II generation aspired to a highly mobile, drive-in lifestyle, our digitalized, networked society today aspires to an online way of life. Stay put, find what you need on the Web. To an absurd degree, the computer makers and home-entertainment entrepreneurs seem out to keep us confined to our own homes. At its extreme, I find that vision stultifying, as if the face-to-face convivial experience we all need and seek in gathering places — town squares, public parks, shopping malls, cafes, sporting events, coffeehouses — were not the very essence of city life. But there is no question that the Internet can be put to good use in the elder culture, especially for those who would give up on automobiles if they had a viable alternative. Once again, as in the way computers can be an aid to failing memory, the high-tech novelties we now associate with adolescents may have their greater future with the elders of the society.

Earlier on I mentioned *The Ghost Map*, Steven Johnson's study of early industrial London. As hellish as life was in the primitive factory towns, Johnson concluded that cities at last have matured into the most ecologically enlightened habitat for a world that numbers billions of human beings. Urban density compacts population and saves the land, its resources, natural beauties, and human lives. Cities are where ideas are exchanged most rapidly and where medical progress is made. Subtract the cars and freeways, condense the suburbs back into urban centers — some large, some small — mix in a good measure of social justice, and we have the best design for living in a world where over 50% of the human race now chooses to reside in cities. Eldertown makes all this more possible.

As I phrase the matter here, my words may sound overoptimistic. But it will not be words or ideas that draw people to Eldertown. It will be the body, not the mind, that spells the end of the automotive era. The last word will belong to diminishing stamina, declining coordination, aching joints, dimming eyesight, and a general need to get closer to quality medical care. On the small scale, these facts of life are already making a difference. The Japanese, who are reconciled to life in a *gray economy*, have turned longevity into the basis for lucrative investment. Instead of groaning over the size of their senior population, they have become the world leader in geriatric robotics and electronics — homes that give the elderly remarkable independence with security. Even in the United States, new forms of domestic architecture — so-called *universal design* — are becoming the rule in home building, a commitment to convenient access and functionality for residents of all ages and physical conditions. Elder-friendly domestic architecture is becoming commonplace: wider doorways, fewer stairs or none at all, ramps to connect different levels, drawers and cupboards that open at more accessible heights, step-down bathtubs and showers equipped with grab bars and non-skid surfaces. Boomers in their fifties now commonly demand such features in new homes so they can anticipate staying where they choose to live into their deep senior years. They are thinking about the walkers and wheelchairs in their future. When changes of this kind finally reach the level of city planning, we may see garages, parking lots, and city streets that were once filled with expensive SUVs numbering far more electrically powered go-carts, hybrid flex-cars, and jitneys. Perhaps at that point boomers, who were born to drive,

will look back to the world of suburbs and freeways in bewilderment, asking *What was that all about?*

The industrial city, the source of so many of the worst environmental ills over the past two centuries, still has a promising
future — but not as the entrepreneurial arena for competitive
self-interest it has been for the past few centuries. Nor for the
frivolous fun and games that appeal to the young and well-off.
As it becomes the place where a growing population of elders
turns for care, security, and tranquility, it will become an expression of what is best in us, the substance of our deepest ethical and religious values. Utopian literature has never explored
the possibilities of Eldertown. It will take time to get used to its
unhurried pace, its serenity, and its frugality, and to see that as
the goal toward which industrial power has been moving. But
will we get there soon enough to escape the environmental horrors that now seem to await us?

Discovering Arcadia...and Destroying It

Before we arrive at Eldertown, there may be misadventures
along the way, some of them born of the best intentions. Healthy
Americans over the age of 60 are among the most mobile elements in our population. Almost universally, when they pull up
stakes and begin their later-life migration, they insist it is to find
a better quality of life, away from the congestion, the traffic, the
breakneck pace, the crimes of urban living. Ever since retirement became a realistic expectation, it has been associated with
peace and quiet, a healthy climate, and natural beauty: everything the city is not. The locations retirees currently favor are
mainly in the *New West* as it has been called, in a few select cities or in the picturesque towns of Nevada, Arizona, New Mexico, Idaho, Colorado, and Utah. Maricopa County, Arizona,
and St. George, Utah, have replaced Florida as the nation's retirement capitals. Nevada has the fastest growing over-age-65
population in the nation; during the 1990s it increased by

72%, most of it concentrated in water-and-power-guzzling Las Vegas, which, one gathers, is meant to provide amusement in the midst of natural splendor. *Gateway* communities that provide access to national parks and monuments are also prominent destinations where retirees come looking for a charming little cabin with fresh air and a great view. Choices like these are based on an admirable appreciation of a nonurban lifestyle, a desire to enjoy a modest and tranquil *second journey* beyond the big-city rat race. Unfortunately, it can take a great deal of exploratory touring to find such Arcadian tranquility, which can sometimes take the more affluent far afield: to the French Midi, Tuscany, the Spanish Riviera. Some seniors make the hunt for a retirement home a major project that they pursue through years of touring. Older Americans are enthusiastic travelers and, where that involves air travel, they are contributing to one of the worst sources of carbon emissions and the consumption of fossil fuel. This is hardly their fault. Air travel is the most underdiscussed issue in environmental politics, mainly because it has become all but untouchable. Around the world more and more people now treat air travel as a benign entitlement, and more can afford the no-frills service that is now being offered. Travel, once the prerogative of jet-setting celebrities and CEOs, has a sense of luxury and freedom about it. Even environmental leaders are ready to jump on a plane at the least excuse, especially to get to still another conference on global warming. Indeed, the more educated middle-class public at which environmentalists mainly direct their appeals would be outraged if anybody dared to challenge their right to travel. For isn't seeing the world one of those unquestionable virtues, driven by a desire to broaden one's experience, see great art, sample gourmet foods, and meet fascinating new people? And so the airports of the world are mercilessly extended and the number of cheap flights multiplies, not only in the western world but in China, India, and throughout Asia. Whatever we may be gaining by the use of fuel-efficient cars we are losing in the carbon footprints of high-flying tourists.

And what happens when still-healthy and active retirees seeking the beauties of unsullied nature finally arrive at the venue they have had in mind for years? They find the place has already been occupied by thousands of others or will be soon and is well on its way to being *Aspenized* into a tourist attraction, second-home site, and active-retirement community — just for people like them. Highways, airports, and franchised amenities follow, and soon quiet, out-of-the-way Arcadia has become part of the nation's suburban sprawl. Older migrants who have bought into the place have to settle for whatever satisfaction they can find in boasting that "we were among the first to get here." Worst of all, many of these chosen retirement locations are in the mountainous west and arid southwest where water is already scarce. The New West belongs to the great southwestern *Cadillac desert*, where water has been at a premium for two generations. Add on the need for more electrical power, and these once-gorgeous areas are surely doomed — at which point amenity-seeking retirees who can afford to sell out and move on begin hunting for another distant paradise.[5]

Will boomers follow in the footsteps of previous senior migrants? With their greater environmental awareness, they may have a more clear-sighted view of the damage such a wistful infatuation with an Arcadian retirement brings with it. Discovery has become a profession. These days everything secret and small and out of the way gets written up for all the world to know about. The perfect place to retire in peace soon becomes a traffic jam. Getting there ahead of the crowd only means you will be first to be trampled. The planet simply cannot make accessible wilderness and comfortable isolation available to so many millions. What, then, is the alternative? One promising possibility is *aging in place* — and turning that place into an environmentally healthy, life-enhancing community. Staying put is already the primary choice of the older, less mobile sector of the elder population. If they lack the money or physical agility to go searching for a retirement paradise, older people stay where they are. That can be a melancholy fate, even a dangerous one. In July 1995, most of the residents of Chicago who died in a killer heat wave were isolated and immobilized seniors. In 2003 as many as 10,000 citizens died in the deadly heat wave that swept through France, and another 4,000 in Italy — almost all of them older adults.

But, of course, things do not have to turn out like that. With proper preparation and in an economy animated by compassion, cities can be made as livable as rural villages, if not more so, given the access to medical facilities. But a price must be paid to create a place-specific, social ecology that meets the year-round, everyday needs of elders — especially of the oldest old among us. They cannot be left to live in stuffy, dismal, single-room public housing or in a backwater of abandoned buildings, crime, and commercial devastation. They need the amenities of modern life where they are, not in some wishfully well-tended Rocky Mountain retreat. They must be provided with transportation, a decent indoor climate in summer and winter, medical care, and companionship. Some of what elders require can be achieved through casual, private contact: a simple understanding between friends that escapes public visibility. Increasingly the basic units for elder care, as well as the care of the homebound sick, are the apartment complexes and condos where people find themselves living as age and illness descend upon them. With a few modest arrangements — an entry attendant to carry groceries, a visiting nurse, some taxi service, a few neighborhood children to run errands — people often prefer to age in place. One federally funded effort called Gatekeepers enlists mail carriers and delivery drivers to learn about the neighborhoods they regularly visit, especially the shut-ins and the elderly who may need their help. They become part of a watchful mobile network of caregivers. Another rough measure: The National Federation of Interfaith Volunteer Caregivers, which trains and supports those who reach out to neighbors, has grown since the mid-1980s from 25 local chapters to over 600. An important part of that increase has to do with the AIDS crisis in the gay community, with neighbors taking on the role of traditional families for one another. That example has been appropriated for other forms of care, including elder care. The National Alliance for Caregiving estimates that over 22 million households are now caring for neighbors as well as relatives in this way. Needless to add, an assignment like this would give a national Caregiver Corps a chance to prove its lifesaving value.

Where measures like this have been taken, many older adults will choose to remain in familiar neighborhoods, in the house they know best, among neighbors and friends who can be called on for help and to whom they can offer help. Gerontologists have begun to register that preference as a *NORC*: a naturally occurring retirement community. Even those with serious disabilities may be able to hold out in their own homes and apartments if enough support is at hand.[6] Were NORCs to become a prevailing choice among seniors, population pressure on rural land and wilderness would diminish and Eldertown would have a chance to flourish in the midst of the city.

Straws in the Wind

The media continue to give avid attention to every shift and nuance of the young demographic. Fashions, hairstyles, movies, musical tastes, gadgetry, celebrity favorites, Internet innovations, sexual predilections — the cool-hunters are still on the prowl tracking permutations that are as ephemeral as they are titillating. Recently I came across a lengthy article about a new movie based on a popular line of dress-up dolls that are meant to replace Barbie. The target market was girls eight to fourteen. The producers were taking endless pains to run focus groups and process questionnaires to make sure they were *positioning* their film exactly right — somewhere between permissibly raunchy and blushingly innocent. Over the course of the last few years I could have filled several files with bubbling reports on MySpace, YouTube, FaceBook, and similar online fascinations that are usually announced with drum-and-trumpet fanfare as the next hot thing — and always assumed to be a potential gold mine, which sometimes they are, at least as they get traded among ever-watchful digital entrepreneurs. We are still a society that wagers billions on what marketing experts believe teens and 20-somethings will spend two or three hours of their day doing — mainly gazing at a torrent of electronic imagery into which eye-popping commercials might be intruded.

Meanwhile, less commercially attractive, but also less ephemeral, are the things elders are pursuing as they work out better possibilities for their fourth age. Most striking among these social inventions are the efforts that give us a view of what Eldertown may become, developments that will touch the lives of millions in ways that transcend mere fashion and which have little to do with the marketplace. There are now fascinating new designs for living circulating among elders, experiments that seek to integrate health care, spirituality, and environmental sustainability. Among the models for this choice is the cohousing community, a concept that is now well-developed in Denmark as a matter of public policy for accommodating an aging population. This may become the most attractive alternative to the isolated home care and semi-adequate nursing homes that were the only options elders once had. *Aging in community* is an eminently practical proposal grounded in the realities of the real-estate market and nonprofit financing. It is a variation on condominium living, but with design, control, and services determined on a not-for-profit basis by residents with special needs. Most significantly, it is the foundation for a way of life that gives depth and dignity to the elder years. As Neshama Abraham and Kate de LaGrange described it in their 2006 survey of elder cohousing, "'Spiritual eldering' is a term which means the process of conscious aging fostered by elders living in close proximity to one another in a self managed and empowering environment. This setting is conducive for contemplation, and deep inner work, civic participation, social activism, mentoring children and adults, and pursuing one's personal spiritual path enhanced and supported by the company of others."

And they noted, "Environmental consciousness often goes hand in hand with the increased social sustainability of living in cohousing. Cohousing is a return to a sustainable model of living where neighbors typically participate together in recycling, composting, sharing and consuming fewer resources, growing and eating organic produce at community meals, living in smaller than normal clustered energy-efficient homes, obtaining passes for and using public transportation, consuming less water and electricity, exercising together and enjoying the benefit of group wellness practices such as yoga, Tai Chi, Qigong, and so on in the common."[7]

Can we imagine a generation that has the wit and the resourcefulness to create so mature a solution to its needs? The realism of that choice becomes apparent as soon as one considers the alternatives. Those who find it hard to believe any great number of Americans turning to NORCs or elder cohousing might ask if it is easier to imagine 70 million boomers passively following in the footsteps of their parents and grandparents, flocking to the beaches of Florida (if they can afford it) or waiting until their last penurious years before providing for their ever-more- expensive health-care needs, and at last resigning themselves to nursing homes that employ minimum-wage help to provide minimal services. And if they were to choose the latter, who would pay for nursing-home care that already runs to $50,000 a year or more? Or should we expect elder parents to be taken in by their children who are having a harder and harder time affording modest homes of their own? It was, after all, post-boomer families who were among the worst casualties of the great sub-prime mortgage debacle of 2007. They had bought homes on risky, unpredictable mortgages, the only means they had of getting into a home — and finished by losing their homes and their credit ratings. Many boomer children may never own homes of their own, let alone have enough room and resources to shelter elderly parents.

As an ideal, elder cohousing belongs to the tradition of intentional communities, a way of life that reaches back to the monasteries of the middle ages — which once housed more than a third of the European population. Communities that have had a religious connection to a church or a common faith have managed to endure the longest. Otherwise, in modern times as urbanization became the dominant theme, they have usually been seen as quaintly outdated, a marginal choice for the idealistic few. But we should remember that flocking to big cities and their sprawling suburbs to pursue an often isolated and precarious life was the style of the early industrial period when earning a living laid the lash of necessity upon the young and middle-aged. It was a social pattern based on the demands of technology and the marketplace and on the availability of cheap fossil fuels. That era is now fading into the past with alarming speed as the longevity revolution places the momentum of a major and unprecedented demographic shift behind the needs of elders. In this new social reality, elder cohousing may well be an idea whose time has come, at least as one significant choice in building Eldertown.

There is another option, a sort of hybrid of the NORC and elder cohousing. This is the *senior village*, a promising new experiment in aging in place. Emerging in the Beacon Hill neighborhood of Boston in the early 2000s, the senior village is a grass-roots effort to find a more affordable and communitarian alternative to nursing homes and assisted-living facilities. The village in this case is virtual, a network of households perhaps as large as a medium-sized town. Sizes now range up to 400 homes. Seniors who join the village pay a modest yearly fee (usually well under $1000 a year) to hire an administrator who, with the help of volunteers, assembles a list of all the kinds of help and support members may need, from yard work to nursing care. The ideal is for everything members may need to be available from one phone number and at a negotiated cut rate. While services like transportation and home maintenance are a significant feature of every village, the spirit of community and the companionship that comes with membership are valued quite as much. Once Beacon Hill proved the idea was practical, villages began to spread, often with help and advice from the original village. As of late 2008, there were some twenty villages in existence or in the planning stage.[8]

The Green and the Gray: An Unexpected Alliance

The environmental movement has done more to make us rethink our most basic values than any political program of modern times. It has dared to suggest that our amazing industrial power has limits that can only be violated at the cost of our survival. But environmentalism is itself a product of the civilization it addresses so challengingly; more specifically, it is an outgrowth of the baby boom, a response to the misguided affluence of that generation. And like all political movements, it is beholden to its history.

In the early days of the movement, environmentalists saw the world from a narrowly American perspective. The baby-boom United States was regarded as the bellwether of the industrial future, the society that was setting the standard — the very bad, wasteful standard — that other nations were expected to adopt. It never occurred to others that the US might one day experience a declining interest in frivolous, resource-depleting consumption as boomers come to devote ever more of their income to health care or decide to save more money for their grandchildren's education. The resistance of the over-50 population to marketing has nothing to do with the superior virtue of the elderly. A slower pace, a thriftier lifestyle, and a greater concern for health, family, and natural beauty are matters of necessity for an older population. That is why senior organizations and gerontologists have begun to pay serious attention to the environmental impact of aging boomers with an eye to enlisting them in the cause. As long ago as 1991, the AARP, in league with the Environmental Protection Agency, set up EASI, the Environmental Alliance for Senior Involvement. EASI now runs as a nonprofit coalition of aging and environmental groups that draws on the expertise of retired volunteers to promote a heightened sense of stewardship, usually with a highly practical local focus: monitoring water quality, tracking endangered species, educating the young, exposing public-health problems in *brownfield* areas (underutilized urban property). Among the largest of these projects is a state-wide Pennsylvania water-quality monitoring effort funded at $200,000.

More recently, the Environmental Protection Agency has adopted a far-sighted view of the longevity revolution. It has undertaken an *Aging Initiative* to survey the many ways in which aging will impact environmental policy. Among other things, it is seeking to encourage new models for environmentally sustainable communities that address questions of healthy aging. This includes transportation, a line of thought that will surely speed us along the road to Eldertown. It has also made the well-being of elders one of its touchstones for policy recommendations regarding health hazards. Its agenda includes finding better ways to keep the air breathable and to help elders survive heat waves. This is a significant development. By including the physical needs of our society's most fragile members among its criteria, EPA is in effect raising the bar for sound environmental policy. It is not difficult to imagine in the near future an alliance between EPA, the Center for Disease Control, and leading senior groups such as the AARP that will improve our standards of environmental health for society as a whole.

At some point environmentalists may come to see that aging is a radical and a fruitful contradiction in the history of industrial society, the one development most likely to apply the brakes to this runaway system, but such a change of mind may not come easily. Environmental activists are apt to see that possibility as a philosophical concession they feel they cannot allow themselves to make. That is because all the benign changes suggested here come on the far side of industrial development and indeed are the result of the industrial process. The elder culture that transforms the way people understand wealth and use their resources stems from the science and technology one can only have in fully modernized societies. Similarly, it is only in modern societies that women have so many choices in life besides childbearing. For some environmentalists, granting that good things may yet come from our troubled industrial adventure may seem like giving aid and comfort to the enemy. I sympathize with their dilemma. When I first began to write about environmental issues, I assumed that industrialism, with its Promethean obsessions, was inherently hostile to ecological intelligence; the two could not coexist. But I have since come to see there is another way to view the matter. If Eldertown looks like a goal worth pursuing, then the opportunity to build that sustainable future waits for us at the culmination of modern history, where the industrial revolution segues into the longevity revolution. When Lewis Mumford raised his highest hopes for the future of the city, he did not have the elder culture in mind, but his words could not have been better suited to the prospect that the longevity revolution has opened before us. More than a new urban form, his vision required a new population, one that took the search for life's meaning seriously.

The city, Mumford observed,

> …has undergone many changes during the last five thousand years; and further changes are doubtless in store. But the innovations that beckon urgently are not the extension and perfection of physical equipment, still less multiplying automatic electronic devices for dispersing into formless suburban dust the remaining organs of culture. Just the contrary: Significant improvements will come only through applying art and thought to the city's central human concerns, with a fresh dedication to the cosmic and ecological processes that enfold all being.… For the city should be an organ of love; and the best economy of cities is the care and culture of men.[9]

CHAPTER 12

Something Eternal

Tolstoy's short story, *The Death of Ivan Ilych*, is a work that I used to assign in a great books course I taught, always hoping my students would gain as much from it as I have. It has certainly proved to be the most powerful reading experience I have known, a work of literature that captures the pulse beat of life more convincingly than one would believe possible for words on a page. Certainly nobody who ever lived to tell about it has done a more persuasive job of presenting the approach of death than Tolstoy achieved in this work. The final moments of Ivan's life leave you convinced that Tolstoy has been through the ordeal and come back to tell about it. While the assignment is frequently lost upon younger students, who tell me they find the story demanding or morbid, its impact upon more mature students has invariably been enormous. They have no trouble seeing themselves as Ivan and learning from his experience.

If I could, I would at this point make that same assignment to those of you who are about to finish this book. Find the story. Read it. Think it through. Instead, I will offer a brief, and of course inadequate, summary of Tolstoy's tale.

Ivan Ilych is a minor government functionary in czarist Russia, one of thousands of "superfluous men" of that era. As remote as that period in Russian history may seem in every other respect, Tolstoy brilliantly develops Ivan as a modern Everyman, one who has spent his life building a tidy career of little more than personal importance, seeking to make himself moderately successful in one of his society's many bureaucratic niches. One day, while hanging drapes in his home, he injures himself. A doctor is called. The doctor discovers that there is a serious condition, which is never clearly defined in the story. It is death approaching. That is all that matters. The doctors cannot heal what ails Ivan; he becomes sicker and finally realizes he is doomed, though nobody will confirm his fears. The story traces his last days, hours, minutes of bewilderment, anger, self-pity, resignation, and at last triumph. "Death is finished," he said to himself. "It is no more!" That moment — his last — becomes the only moment he has truly *lived*. The story builds until we reach that terrifying climax; it leaps from the page and takes you by the shoulders and shakes you. *Wake up!* it says. *This man is you.*

As a teacher, I have valued Tolstoy's story over the years because it uses death so powerfully to teach the magnificence of life. Yet as universal as Ivan's experience is, the very fact that his plight deals with illness and doctors and patients now limits it to a certain historical period. Tolstoy takes Ivan as far as imagination can reach to bring him to the other side. But a century later, the tale may need to be rewritten to capture the defining life-and-death experience of our time. For us, *the other side* is now the life we gain on the far side of medical crisis, the 20 or more years we get after we have passed through the shadow. What we need in order to make Ivan's story relevant to our era is a *death* that does not happen — not yet. We need the story of an Ivan who comes just that close to dying — but then *survives*. Death pauses at the bedside; death waits, longer for us than for any previous generation. That is becoming more and more the special experience of our time. By the thousands, people now undergo medical miracles that rescue them from diseases and disabilities that would have killed them a generation ago. They pass through the shadow — and are then sent back into the world to start their lives again. As one member of a cardiac support group described his experience, "It was as if the angel of death drove by my house and waved. 'I'm busy now,' he said, 'but I have your address. I'll be back.'" That experience is becoming as commonplace as marriage or divorce, a routine part of the modern world.

Today Ivan Ilych would be likely to confront a greater trial. Life. He would return to take up his career, his family life, his ambitions. But how would life look to someone who has been on such close terms with death? What would it then mean to *wake up*? Tolstoy would have to deal with an Ivan who might not be willing to continue being a bureaucratic zombie, but who insisted on making his life mean something.

I have referred to the modern medical crisis as a rite of passage, a door through which more and more of us enter our elder years. I discovered that experience at the age of 55 when I underwent surgery for a life-threatening condition. At the time, I was not expecting to be long-lived. My father died at 47, his father at 52. But I did survive, and here I am writing another book on countercultural values, hoping to see them reemerge in the later years of the boomer generation.

Soon after I left the hospital I wrote the letter that follows to my daughter, then in her twenties. I have no idea if she learned anything from it, but it was an instructive moment for me. Here I was trying to find words that would tell my child what life was all about. Having brought her into a troubled world filled with so many follies and illusions, what consoling wisdom did I have to pass along that might help her make her way in life? Was there anything at all? Certainly the shape of my life as a whole counted for more than words. But words matter too — at least to me, perhaps because I am a writer. In any event, this is what I came up with, advice that had nothing to do with fame or fortune. I place it here as a recollection of the moment when I realized it was time to become an elder.

The View from the Hospital Bed

It is so very hard to be wise…

And so very easy.

The unexamined life may not be worth living, but there are ways of examining oneself that are plain brutal, ways that are wounding, paralyzing…a sort of philosophical masochism. There are those I once admired — the Nietzschean spirits — who championed the nobility of self-transcendence. I used to believe this was admirable — to want a quality of life that was strenuous, soaring, supermanly.

No longer.

There are conditions of experience that reveal this teaching to be a luxury, perhaps an affectation. One such is the view from the hospital bed — especially if that bed is in the intensive care ward, and you are in that bed uncertain you will ever leave it alive.

Then, if you have enough stamina and presence of mind, you find yourself saying "If I ever get out of here, I'm going to re-member every moment of this like a catechism lesson. Some-thing so simple that everybody ought to know it, might even claim to know it. But they don't. *If you're alive, if you're on your own feet, if you're out of pain…be thankful!* For every little thing. Because none of the 'little' things are really little. Having a meal, looking out the window, feeding Gregory the blue jay his daily peanut, giving Henry the cat a friendly rub, taking a walk, read-ing a good book…Above all, just being with people you love, if only to make small talk, if only to feel their caring nearness and know you exist in somebody's respectful awareness. Remember how these things looked from the hospital bed, when you felt broken into a hundred scattered, irreparable pieces, when there was a good chance it might all be taken away from you once and for all. Remember how rare, special, marvelous — how suf-ficient."

Does that mean you've agreed to settle for very little, lower your expectations, live on short rations? No. It means you learn to fix your expectations on the things that matter. And to despise the things that don't. Such as? *Making it* in the so-called *world* — which isn't the world but a composite of collective illusions. Achieving, winning, beating out the competition, making a name, making big bucks.

I imagine that in Los Angeles, in New York, in all the cultural capitals of the world, if you open your window at two in the morning, you will hear ten thousand voices wailing, wailing across the night, bemoaning the fact that they aren't *number one*. And half of what you hear will be the voices of those who were number one last year. There's not a single person up and about, struggling and suffering with these delusions of grandeur, who won't see it the way you do if they wind up in the hospital bed. It's a persuasive perspective.

And once you've experienced it, you discover that the *little* things can hide very big truths. For me, these sometimes happen when I'm writing — a word, a phrase, just the intonation of a word, just the shape of a phrase might catch something — and you might just recognize it if you aren't blinded by the delusions. All very private. Nobody else may ever know. So what? If you let it, the moment justifies itself. You know you've had the chance to learn something more of what matters. Nothing that has to be put into words, actually. You simply have to know it's there — the Presence.

I find myself living between these two magnitudes: the modestly small and ordinary for which I must always be grateful, and the vastly strange before which I feel humbled, but privileged. The two go together now, the big within the small, the small within the big. Perhaps this is what the Zen teachers had in mind. Take the ordinary into your life, go deeply into it, savor it, take joy in it. "Drawing water, hewing wood…" And through the commonplace, something greater, which need not be named, will catch at the corner of the mind, reminding.

One of my visitors brought me a reproduction of a Chinese scroll painting and pinned it on the wall across from my bed. I spent a good deal of time imaginatively immersed in the quiet wisdom of that painting. Tiny human figures all but lost in the vast but mothering landscape, going about simple things. Taking tea, sitting up late with a friend, reading poems, enjoying the silence. Never a moment lost, sacrificed to some *greater* distant goal. Even the benightedness of the frenzied many can be a source of gentle amusement and useful instruction. "What fools these mortals be!" And yourself among them.

I try to remember this, to be loyal to it. But I slip back often, worrying about money, success, recognition, letting my feelings get hurt, letting my ego get bruised. I should know better. I hope I really do.

Saints and Poets

In *The Death of Ivan Ilych*, Tolstoy leads us to the threshold of death in his effort to teach us the value of life. There is another work that takes us beyond that border in search of the same goal. The final act of Thornton Wilder's *Our Town* is played out among the dead. It is staged in the graveyard that stands on the hill above the town of Grover's Corners. There, at the play's end, the dead souls of the townsfolk offer counsel to the newly arrived Emily, the young heroine of the play who has died in childbirth. An imaginary glimpse of the undiscovered country we can never know, the scene has always held an uncanny validity for me. *Our Town* has become a favorite choice for high-school drama classes in the United States. No doubt the simplicity of the staging (no sets, only a few tables, chairs, ladders and the rest left to the imagination) and the down-home characters (small-town mothers, fathers, children) has convinced teachers that it makes for an economical production well within the range of teenagers. But how many teenagers can be expected to understand what Wilder has to say in that final act? When I was in my senior year in high school, I was cast as the all-knowing stage manager in a production of Wilder's play. Since I had grown up in the big cities of America — Chicago, New York, Los Angeles — I remember feeling a certain condescension for the hicks we were portraying in the play. At that age, it took me a few readings to appreciate that unrelenting ordinariness, even mediocrity, was precisely what Wilder was after. For two acts we are loaded down with nothing special, the most nondescript people in the world going about their uneventful daily business, making small talk, gossiping, passing the time. More effectively than Samuel Beckett, Wilder gives us a play in which nothing happens. Maybe we get a bit bored with these people, who talk in platitudes about nothing very important. *And then comes that third act.*

When I played the stage manager, like all my high school classmates, I was too young to understand Wilder's act three with any great sensitivity. What was most on my mind then was the cast party that would follow the play, a chance to cut loose and goof off. But for some reason that final scene — every line of it — has stuck with me through the years as only great literature can, waiting for me to find its depths. "There's something eternal in every human being," the stage manager tells us. And then the characters play out that truth. Emily, granted a chance to return to watch herself live out one thoroughly ordinary day in her life, realizes as she watches herself, her friends, and parents that nobody knew how precious that uneventful day was when they were alive and together. Not once did they look at one another knowing that time was passing, that this hour would never come again. Not once did they show any awareness of their mortality.

"Do any human beings ever realize life while they live it — every, every minute?" Emily asks at last, as she turns back to her grave where she must wait for her mortal parts to burn away.

"No," says the stage manager. "Saints and poets, maybe they do some."

Now those lines I remember from decades ago return to mark the yawning gap between youth and age, the distance that only years of experience can bridge. For how could anybody in their teens, with all the promise of life opening before them, understand those words? It takes many years and perhaps a few brushes with death to illuminate that commonplace truth.

> Ruskin: "No wealth but life."
> Tolstoy: "Death is finished."
> Wilder: "There's something eternal in every human being."

Wise words from wise minds. To live in the light of such teachings changes everything, every relationship, every value, every goal. It alters consciousness right down to our marrow more effectively than any chemical ever will. We will never have a good society until those who hold power are gifted with that awareness. And if we cannot expect that awareness from our elders, where will we find it?

From Counter Culture to Elder Culture

Issues and Insights for Discussion

Theodore Roszak has called the young people of the 1960s *America's most audacious generation.* Audacious in what sense? It was a generation that was willing to challenge the assumptions and the values of parents and political leaders. That troubled some, inspired many, and probably bewildered most of those who lived through it. That's why the era needs to be revisited. If you're a boomer, you were part of it. It was the world you grew up in. Think back: Did you take part in campus protests, anti-war demonstrations, political action, rock concerts, alternative lifestyles during that period? Do you recall these activities with pride, regret, or wistful fondness? If you were more a witness than a participant (as most of the boomer generation was), how do you think of these distinctive features of your younger days now?

The Making of an Elder Culture seeks to build a bridge between the person you were in the 1960s and the person you are today. In ways you may only recognize now by looking back, the 60s shaped your values and your hopes. It left you with expectations that may linger on — ideas about love, freedom, responsibility, democracy, success, and personal worth. The author believes those expectations are still relevant to our society. That's what *practical nostalgia* (p. 12) means. As you read, see if you agree with the links the author fashions between your youth and your elderhood. "In creating an elder culture, [boomers] have no better place to start then with the unfinished business of their youth" (p. 45).

Chapter 1: Maturity Rules and Chapter 2: Boomers — Act Two

1. The opening chapters of *The Making of an Elder Culture* give a number of statistics that illustrate the steady and accelerated aging of the American, European, and Japanese populations. More

people are living longer...and longer, even in the emerging economies. But statistics are abstract. Try to make those numbers come
alive. Think back in your own family history. Compare your life
expectancy with your parents, grandparents, and great-grandpar-
ents. Of course, you may come from a long-lived family, but most
people don't. Does your life differ from the life of your parents and
grandparents simply because you expect to have more years to live
after you retire and after you have raised your children?

2. As you look around you, do you notice the growing prominence
of elders in everyday life — for example, in the media? Or in advertising? Or in public affairs? Do you welcome this — or does it
seem somehow unnatural?

3. The author also mentioned the role of biotechnology in seeking
to extend life expectancy by decades. Reversing the aging process
at the cellular level has become a serious scientific project. (For
example, Google *Methuselah Mouse* to learn how this project is
progressing.) Boomers will be the first generation that has to face
the issues raised by a rapidly extended life span. Can you imagine
a world in which people live to 150 or longer? Would you choose
to live in such a world?

4. "Every new generation born from here on out will be a smaller
part of the total population, but every child born is apt to enjoy a
longer, healthier life. Put those two facts together and the demographic logic is undeniable. Every society in the world, and especially those that join the global economy, is destined to tilt in the
direction of age" (p. 47). What are the forces that make increasing
longevity inevitable?

5. The author observed that "When the Summer of Love was happening in San Francisco in 1967, there were 90 million people
below the age of 25 in the United States — nearly half the population. Youth seemed in a permanent ascendancy" (p. 3). If aging is
the dominant trend in modern life, what persuaded Americans
of the post–World War II period to believe the world was getting
younger? What accounts for the cult of youth during the baby
boom era? What did Thomas Frank mean by *the conquest of the
cool* (pp. 5–6)?

6. In 1937 the American philosopher John Dewey warned that
America should get ready for a larger and larger senior population (p. 4). Why did his words go unheeded?

7. The author believes that elders have important sources of political power (pp. 14–16). What are they? How do you think they can best be used? How can boomers avoid becoming a selfish interest group?

8. Allan Bloom, a prominent conservative looking back from 1987, found a great many negative things to say about the counter culture. In fact, he dismissed it as an *unmitigated disaster* (pp. 27–28). What do you think of what he said, especially about multiculturalism and feminism? To sample the flavor of anti-boomer opinion, you might want to include Bloom's book *The Closing of the American Mind* among your readings.

9. A Gray Panther leader once said "being retired is like being back on the campus" (p. 31). Would you agree?

Chapter 3: You Say You Want a Revolution

1. The chapter begins with a quotation from *The Port Huron Statement*, a student manifesto written in 1962. This is a good example of 1960s idealism. How relevant do these words seem today?

2. The author believes the industrial revolution was really the beginning of something much bigger and more important: the longevity revolution. What is the connection between these two revolutions (pp. 44–48)? What role did children play in launching the longevity revolution (pp. 43–44)?

3. In the 1980s, elders were often condemned as *greedy geezers* (pp. 55–56). Where did this stereotype come from? How was it used politically?

4. In the section called *Boomers, Know Your Enemy*, (pp. 57–63) the author reviewed the forces that are determined to eliminate entitlements. Who are these enemies, and what is the basis of their hostility? What role does the philosophy of Social Darwinism play in that hostility (pp. 10, 72, 130–132, 197)?

5. Who was Dr. Francis Townsend (pp. 59–61)? Before reading *The Making of an Elder Culture* were you familiar with this social hero?

6. "As anti-entitlements critics would have it, the old are a curse in every respect. They are too numerous, they insist on living too long, but worst of all, they are just plain *bad*, a failed generation of weak, self-indulgent freeloaders" (pp. 67–68). How would you reply to these critics? What arguments do anti-entitlements critics use to discredit Social Security and Medicare (pp. 63–65)?

Chapter 4: Elder Insurgency

1. Who was Maggie Kuhn (pp. 71–74)? What contribution did she make to the political thought of the 1960s? You may want to read her life story and discuss it. Her autobiography is: Maggie Kuhn. *No Stone Unturned: The Life and Times of Maggie Kuhn.* Ballantine, 1991.

2. "By the time health care begins to consume 40 or 50% of US GDP, we will have learned to see the benefits of such an investment.... We will wake up to the fact that health and longevity are, at last, the highest stage of industrial development" (p. 84). This is one of the most controversial points in the book. Do you agree? Why is health care seen by so many others — including economists and political leaders - as a frightening and unaffordable liability?

3. The author introduces a woman named Mamie as a savvy commentator on health care (pp. 85–87). What does her example tell us about the health-care economy?

4. What does the author mean by *the compassionate sector* (p. 90)? Why does he believe elders will play an important role in this new economic form?

5. "[T]he rise of the elder culture will take place against stubborn conservative resistance" (p. 94). *The Making of an Elder Culture* speaks of this as *the crunch* (p. 94). Why does the author believe elders will prevail in this confrontation?

6. What central and decisive role will boomer daughters play in that crunch (pp. 98–103)? Have you experienced the *sandwiched* life of many boomer daughters (p. 100)? How would you like to see long-term home care handled in our society?

Chapter 5: Entitlements for Everyone

1. Most Americans — even elders and boomer-elders-to-be — seem to have, at best, a vague idea about how entitlements (Social Security and Medicare) work. Do you know how the nation pays for Social Security and Medicare? How sustainable are they? How fair are they? Is the author realistic in believing we can have *entitlements for everyone*?

   You can find a great deal of helpful information about Social Security on the Social Security Administration website (ssa.gov), including a history of the program. You may want to schedule time to get these facts under control. The AARP has drawn up a list of ways to keep Social Security solvent for the next hundred years. It appeared in the May 2007 edition of the *AARP Bulletin*. If you can get a back issue of that edition, review the eight ways we can save Social Security. Which would you choose? Another good source of information on the funding of Social Security is: Mark Weisbrot and Dean Baker. *Social Security: The Phony Crisis*. University of Chicago, 2000.

2. Anti-entitlements critics often merge Social Security and Medicare in their critiques. Why is this misleading (p. 66)?

3. Another frequent argument against Social Security cites the ratio of workers to retirees. Critics claim there aren't enough workers to support the system (pp. 117–120). Why did the author dismiss this argument as irrelevant and deceptive ("Social Security has never been based on that ratio. No sensible retirement plan could be" (pp. 118–119)? If the ratio of workers to retirees doesn't determine how sustainable Social Security is, what does?

4. Retirees are part of every society's *dependency ratio* (p. 121). What other groups belong in that ratio? What determines how large a dependency load a society can afford?

5. What is *generational accounting*, and how does it work to undermine Social Security and Medicare (pp. 112–117)? What do the generational accountants overlook in their narrowly economic analysis of entitlements? How would you respond to their accusation that Social Security and Medicare amount to *fiscal child abuse* (p. 78)?

6. Lester Thurow stated that "in the years ahead, class warfare is apt to be redefined as the young against the old" (p. 56). Some conservative thinkers agree, predicting that the longevity revolution will lead to serious conflict between young and old. But *The Making of an Elder Culture* claimed "The longevity revolution is hardly a geriatric conspiracy. It is the result of intergenerational choice.... Young and old, we are all in this together" (p. 243). What choices have young Americans made that define the longevity revolution as an intergenerational development?

7. What does the author mean by *the ethics of affordability* (pp. 120–121)? How do the ethics of affordability affect the future of entitlements?

8. Would you agree that the National Life Expectancy is the most important economic indicator (p. 122)?

9. *The Making of an Elder Culture* characterizes elders as *odd political animals* (p. 132). Speaking generally, would you say the older population is liberal, radical, conservative, populist? Or do we need a new category for the elder population? If you were running for office, how would you deal with older voters, especially with respect to the entitlements?

Chapter 6: Utopia Revisited — An Exercise in Cultural Archaeology

1. "Utopianism was among the features that most distinguished the radicalism of the 1960s from earlier eras of protest" (p. 139). Were you a member of a commune, a collective, a utopian experiment of any kind during the 1960s? How do you feel now about that episode in your life?

2. The author believes the communitarian experiments of the counter culture "found their way back to the root meaning of Utopia" (p. 143). What is that *root meaning*?

3. Chapter 6 reviewed the work of three prominent social thinkers of the 1960s: Paul Goodman, Kenneth Galbraith, and Robert Theobald. What assumptions and values do all three share? Do you believe their ideas have any relevance to our society today?

4. Conservatives like Milton Friedman preferred to share the wealth of the society by way of a negative income tax (p. 159). In making this proposal, what common ground did Friedman share with Goodman, Galbraith, and Theobald?

5. What did conservative thinkers and political leaders of the 1960s and 1970s fear most about ideas like the guaranteed annual income (pp. 163–164)?

Chapter 7: The Doors of Perception

1. Did you ever take a serious interest in achieving an altered state of consciousness by the use of drugs? What substances did you try? What was the result?

2. "For all the zaniness that surrounded the drug culture of the time, dope was part of a new political agenda" (p. 168). What was that agenda and how did consciousness transformation relate to it?

3. The author believes that "nothing changes consciousness more effectively than growing older, especially when we reach the last few decades of life" (p. 175). Do you agree? How has growing

older changed your view of such things as family, career, love, sex, wealth, patriotism?

4. What objection does the author have to the consciousness transformation achieved by some evangelical and born-again Christian churches (pp. 174–175)?

5. How has *help* become the *dirtiest four-letter word* in our language (pp. 177–178)? Do you agree that *self-reliance is a lie* (p. 191)? Comment on the author's Declaration of Interdependence. (pp. 191–192). Do you find it a persuasive rejection of self-reliance?

6. What role does the near-death, return to life experience play in the future of the elder culture (pp. 179–181)?

7. Have you been through a medical crisis that significantly altered your view of life?

8. Do you believe there is another stage of life — a *fourth age* — on the far side of old age (p. 187)?

Chapter 8: Aging and the Alpha Male

1. "If there is one style of consciousness that will surely have to change radically in the elder culture, it is that of the alpha male." (p. 195) In what ways is our standard of masculinity at odds with the values of an elder culture?

2. Why does the author believe alpha males are *false elders* (p. 198)?

3. The author believes the counter culture of the 1960s was deeply conflicted about issues of gender (pp. 205–206). Do you remember any experiences you had of man-woman relations during that period that confirm that conclusion?

Chapter 9: Love, Loyalty, and the End of Sex

1. "From the invention of the contraceptive pill in the early 1950s to the outbreak of AIDS in the mid-1980s, boomers enjoyed an unprecedented sexual freedom, a window of erotic opportunity the world may never see again. They are the only generation in history to have known risk-free, care-free, responsibility-free sexuality" (p. 214). If you lived through that period, do you remember it fondly, regretfully, resentfully? Was sexual liberation all it was advertised to be? Did it have a down side?

2. Do you agree that in the elder culture loyalty may become more important than love in our homes and families? What special

virtues does the author find in loyalty as a basis for enduring relationships?

3. "[T]he goal toward which sexual partnering leads (if we are lucky) is not some kind of score in a hard-fought game. It is loyalty, the willingness to be there for one another when little remains of the beauty, vitality, or excitement of our youthful encounters" (p. 220). What place does this leave for sexual passion in the later years?

Chapter 10: Ecology and Longevity

1. The final chapters of *The Making of an Elder Culture* deal with the ecological consequences of the longevity revolution. The most controversial idea presented suggests that aging is the solution to the problems of overpopulation and overconsumption. "Fertility and life expectancy may be linked in ways that make it biologically and sociologically impossible to expect a baby boom from long-lived societies. If that is so, then the longevity revolution has brought us a new law of population" (p. 241). Do you find this line of thought convincing?

2. Comment on how aging has changed your consumption habits.

3. In what ways was Thomas Malthus wrong in his predictions about overpopulation and starvation (pp. 230–231)? How has women's liberation impacted Malthusian ideas about overpopulation (pp. 242–243)?

4. How have changing habits of reproduction among women altered our demographic future (pp. 247–249)?

Chapter 11: Welcome to Eldertown

1. Has aging changed your choices about where to live and how to live? Do you find suburban housing developments attractive?

2. How has aging affected your attitude toward driving? Would you ever support a campaign to delicense over-age drivers?

3. Imagine an ideal Eldertown that can accommodate residents of all ages and yet be environmentally sustainable. What sort of homes, shops, workplaces, parks, and cultural facilities would you include in your design?

4. Would you agree that "aging is a radical and a fruitful contradiction in the history of industrial society, the one development most likely to apply the brakes to this runaway system" (p. 276)?

Endnotes

Chapter 1: Maturity Rules

1. John Dewey. "Introduction." in E. V. Cowdry, ed. *Problems of Aging: Biological and Medical Aspects*. Williams and Watkins, 1942, pp. xxvi, xxii.
2. Thomas Frank. *The Conquest of Cool: Business Culture, Counterculture, and the Rise of Hip Consumerism*. University of Chicago, 1997, pp. 5, 26.

Chapter 2: Boomers — Act Two

1. Norman Mailer. "The White Negro" in *The American Experience*, Harold Jaffe and John Tyrell, eds., Harper & Row, 1970, pp. 11, 13.
2. Allan Bloom. *The Closing of the American Mind*. Simon and Schuster, 1987, p. 234.

Chapter 3: You Say You Want a Revolution

1. The phrases come from an anti-entitlements publication that reveals how vitriolic the issue can become: Mike Males. *Scapegoat Generation: America's War on Adolescents*. Common Courage, 1996.
2. William H. Frey and Ross C. DeVol. *Amerca's Demography in the New Century: Aging Baby Boomers and New Immigrants as Major Players*. Milken Institute Policy Brief #9, March 8, 2000. [cited March 31, 2009] milkeninstitute.org/pdf/frey.pdf.
3. Lester Thurow. "The Birth of a RevolutionaryClass." *New York Times Magazine*, May 19, 1996, pp. 46–47.
4. Roy Lubove. *The Struggle for Social Security, 1900–1935*. Harvard, 1968, p. 39.
5. Lubove, p. 117.
6. Edward D. Berkowitz. *America's Welfare State From Roosevelt to Reagan*. Johns Hopkins, 1991, p. 19.
7. Stuart Butler and Peter Germanis. "Achieving Social Security

Reform: A 'Leninist' Strategy." *Cato Journal*, Vol. 3#2 (Fall 1983), pp. 547–556.

8. Peter G. Peterson. *Will America Grow up Before It Grows Old?: How the Coming Social Security Crisis Threatens, You, Your Family, and Your Country.* Random House, 1996, and Peter G. Peterson. *Gray Dawn: How the Coming Age Wave Will Transform America — and the World.* Crown, 1999. For a pro-entitlements review of Peterson, see Dean Baker. "Granny Bashing." *In These Times*, December 23, 1996, pp. 32–35. As Baker, the Social Security analyst at the Economic Policy Institute, has put it, "If there are any claims in Peterson's book that are not outright false or seriously misleading, I was unable to find them."

Chapter 4: Elder Insurgency

1. Robert H. Binstock and James H. Schultz. *Aging Nation: The Economics and Politics of Growing Old in America.* Praeger, 2006. On Maggie Kuhn, see Dieter Hessel and Maggie Kuhn, *Maggie Kuhn on Aging.* Westminster , 1977, and Maggie Kuhn, *No Stone Unturned: The Life and Times of Maggie Kuhn.* Ballantine, 1991.

2. Noriyuki Takayama quoted in Robert Stowe. "The Fiscal Challenge of an Aging Industrial World: A White Paper on Demographics and Medical Technology." Center for Strategic and International Studies, Washington, DC, January 12, 2001.

3. Laurence J. Kotlikoff and Scott Burns. *The Coming Generational Storm: What You Need to Know about America's Economic Future.* MIT, 2004. Also see Theodore Roszak. "Accounting for What Matters: Are More Elders the Problem?" *Aging Today*, Vol. 26#4 (July-August, 2005), p. 3.

4. Phillip Longman. *The Empty Cradle: How Falling Birthrates Threaten World Prosperity and What to Do About It.* New American Books, 2004, p. 5.

5. Charles Morris. *The AARP: America's Most Powerful Lobby and the Clash of Generations.* Crown, 1996, pp. 165–169.

6. David Lazarus. "Betting on a Sick Boom." *San Francisco Chronicle*, July 28, 2006, p. D1.

Chapter 5: Entitlements for Everyone

1. Kevin Phillips. *Wealth and Democracy: A Political History of the American Rich.* Broadway, 2002, p. 419.

2. See Laurence J. Kotlikoff. *Generational Accounting: Knowing Who Pays, and When, for What We Spend*. Free Press, 1993. Also see Rob Norton. "Cheating Tomorrow's Children." *Fortune*, July 10, 1995.

3. Laurence J. Kotlikoff and Scott Burns. *The Coming Generational Storm: What You Need to Know about America's Economic Future*. MIT Press, 2004.

4. See the AARP Bulletin, May 2007, p. 11.

5. The calculations are from Allan Sloan. "The Big Value of Small Increases." *Newsweek*, November 6, 2006, p. 17.

6. These figures come from the Giving USA Foundation, as reported on June 25, 2007, by the Associated Press.

Chapter 6: Utopia Revisited: — An Exercise in Cultural Archaeology

1. Timothy Miller. "The Sixties-Era Communes" in Peter Braunstein and Michael William Doyle, eds. *Imagine Nation: The American Counter Culture of the 1960s and 70s*. Routledge, 2001, pp. 327–353.

2. Paul and Percival Goodman. *Communitas: Means of Livelihood and Ways of Life*, 2nd rev. ed. Vintage, 1960, p. 192.

3. The Chamber of Commerce of the United States. *The National Symposium on Guaranteed Income*. Washington, DC, 1966.

4. J. Philip Wogaman. *Guaranteed Annual Income: The Moral Issues*. Abingdon, 1968.

5. Milton Friedman. "The Case for the Negative Income Tax." *National Review*, March 7, 1967, p. 239.

6. See the report "Guaranteed Annual Income: A Hope and a Question Mark" in *America*, December 11, 1971, p. 263.

7. Christopher Green. *Negative Taxes and the Poverty Problem*. Brookings Institute, 1967.

8. Herman Kahn and Anthony Wiener. *The Year 2000: A Framework for Speculation on the Next Thirty-Three Years*. Macmillan, 1967.

Chapter 8: Aging and the Alpha Male

1. Betty Friedan. *Fountain of Age*. Simon and Schuster, 1993, p. 165.

2. David Gutmann. *Reclaimed Powers: Toward a New Psychology of Men and Women in Later Life*. Basic, 1987, p. 236.

3. Jean Baker Miller et al. *Women's Growth in Connection: Writings*

from the Stone Center. Guilford, 1991, pp. 25–26. Also see Catherine Keller. *From a Broken Web: Separation, Sexism, and Self.* Beacon, 1986.

4. Paul Shepard. *Nature and Madness.* Sierra Club, 1982, pp. 15, 126.
5. Royda Crose. *Why Women Live Longer Than Men, and What Men Can Learn from Them.* Wiley, 1997, p. 74.
6. Erik Erikson. "Identity and the Life Cycle." *Psychological Issues,* Monograph #1. International Universities, 1959, p. 41.
7. Daniel Levinson, *The Seasons of a Man's Life.* Alfred A. Knopf, 1978, pp. 98–99.
8. Robert Bly. *The Sibling Society.* Addison-Wesley, 1996, pp. 44–45, 180.
9. Beth Bailey. "Sex as a Weapon" in Peter Braunstein and Michael William Doyle, eds. *Imagine Nation: The American Counter Culture of the 1960s and 70s.* Routledge, 2001, p. 308.
10. Robin Morgan. "Good-bye to All That" in Betty and Theodore Roszak, eds., *Masculine/Feminine: Readings in Sexual Mythology and the Liberation of Women.* Harper, 1969, pp. 242–243.

Chapter 9: Love, Loyalty, and the End of Sex
1. Robert Butler and Myrna Lewis. *The New Love and Sex After 60.* Ballantine, 2002.

Chapter 10: Ecology and Longevity
1. Gary Snyder. *Journal for the Protection of All Beings #1.* City Lights, 1961, p. 11.
2. Anne and Paul Ehrlich. "Growing Beyond Our Limits," in *Triumph of Discovery.* Published by *Scientific American,* 1995, p. 182.
3. Fred Pearce. "Population Bombshell." *New Scientist* #2142, July 11, 1998.
4. Wattenberg, quoted in "Population Crowding Edges of Age Spectrum." *San Francisco Examiner,* October 2, 1999.
5. James Kingsland. "Golden Oldie." *New Scientist,* June 12, 1999, p. 46. On the disposable soma theory, see also Tom Kirkwood, *Time of Our Lives: The Science of Human Aging.* Weidenfeld and Nicholson, 1999.
6. Rudi Westendorp and Thomas Kirkland. "Human Longevity at the Cost of Reproductive Success." *Nature* #396, December 24, 2998, pp. 743–746.

7. T. T. Perls, L. Alpert, and R. C. Fretts. "Middle-aged Mothers Live Longer." *Nature* #389, September 11, 1997, p. 133.

8. Gail Vines. "Some of Our Sperm Are Missing." *New Scientist* #1992, August 26, 1995, pp. 22–25. Also see Theo Colborn et al. *Our Stolen Future: Are We Threatening Our Fertility, Intelligence, and Survival? — A Scientific Detective Story.* Dutton/Signet, 1996, and Lawrence Wright. "Silent Sperm." *New Yorker*, January 15, 1996, p. 42.

9. On the marriage and childbearing patterns of boomers, I am grateful to have the research of Suzanne Reynolds-Scanlon of the Florida Policy Exchange on Aging at the University of South Florida.

10. Pew Research Center survey as reported by David Crary. *Key to a Good Marriage? Share Housework.* Associated Press, July 1, 2007.

Chapter 11: Welcome to Eldertown

1. As an example of city planning with an aging population in mind, see B. Kweon, et al., "Green Common Spaces and the Social Integration of Inner-City Older Adults," *Environment and Behavior*, Vol. 30 (November 1998), pp. 832–858. Also see the periodical *Sustainable Communities Review*, published by the Center for Public Service at the University of North Texas in Denton, Texas.

2. On the underground food collective, see Sandor Ellix Katz. *The Revolution Will Not Be Microwaved: Inside America's Underground Food Movements.* Chelsea Green, 2006, and Heather Flores. *Food Not Lawns: How to Turn Your Yard into a Garden and Your Neighborhood into a Community.* Chelsea Green, 2006. Also see Patricia Klindienst. *The Earth Knows My Name: Food, Culture, and Sustainability in the Gardens of Ethnic America.* Beacon, 2006.

3. Michael Corbett. *A Better Place to Live: New Designs for Tomorrow's Communities.* Rodale, 1981.

4. Richard Register. "EcoCities: Making Cities Sustainable is a Crucial Challenge." *In Context* #8 (Winter 1984), p. 31.

5. For a thorough critique of senior migration, see Scott D. Wright, "Gray and Green?: Aging Baby Boomers — A Profile of Environmental Impact and Environmental Risk," a paper prepared for the National Council on Aging in 2004. Contact scott.wright@nurs .utah.edu.

6. J. A. Krout and E. Wethington. *Residential Choices and Experiences of Older Adults: Pathways to Life Quality.* Springer, 2003. Also see David Tilson, ed. *Aging in Place: Supporting the Frail Elderly in Residential Environments.* Scott, Foresman, 1989, and David France. "The New Compassion." *Modern Maturity*, May-June 1997, pp. 33–41.

7. Neshama Abraham and Kate de LaGrange. "Elder Cohousing – An Idea Whose Time Has Come." *Communities Magazine*, Vol. #132 (Fall 2006). The article lists a number of cohousing projects in the United States and offers helpful resources for research. Also see Charles Durrett. *Senior Cohousing: A Community Approach to Independent Living.* Ten Speed, 2005, and Charles Durrett, *The Senior Cohousing Handbook*, New Society Publishers, 2009.

8. Beacon Hill Village can be contacted at bhvillage@aol.com. Avenidas Village, a well-developed west-coast community in Palo Alto California, can be reached at avenidas.org.

9. Lewis Mumford. *The City in History.* Harcourt, Brace & World, 1961, p. 575.

Index

About the Author

In 1969, author Theodore Roszak took his first look at the boomer generation with his award-winning social commentary, *The Making of a Counter Culture*. Now — 40 years later — with *The Making of an Elder Culture*, he returns to the subject, examining the way in which the past countercultural values of this *audacious generation* can be made relevant to an elder-dominated society.

Photo © Gilles Mangasson

Theodore Roszak is the author of 15 works of nonfiction and five novels. He was educated at UCLA and Princeton and has taught at Stanford, the University of British Columbia, San Francisco State University, and the State University of California — East Bay. He and his wife and occasional coauthor, Betty, live in Berkeley, California.

If you have enjoyed *The Making of an Elder Culture*,
you might also enjoy other

Books to Build a New Society

Our books provide positive solutions for people who
want to make a difference. We specialize in:

Sustainable Living ✦ Ecological Design and Planning

Natural Building & Appropriate Technology ✦ New Forestry

Environment and Justice ✦ Conscientious Commerce

Progressive Leadership ✦ Resistance and Community

Nonviolence ✦ Educational and Parenting Resources

New Society Publishers

ENVIRONMENTAL BENEFITS STATEMENT

New Society Publishers has chosen to produce this book on recycled paper
made with 100% post consumer waste, processed chlorine free,
and old growth free.

For every 5,000 books printed, New Society saves the following
resources:[1]

28	Trees
2,495	Pounds of Solid Waste
2,745	Gallons of Water
3,580	Kilowatt Hours of Electricity
4,535	Pounds of Greenhouse Gases
20	Pounds of HAPs, VOCs, and AOX Combined
7	Cubic Yards of Landfill Space

[1]Environmental benefits are calculated based on research done by the
Environmental Defense Fund and other members of the Paper Task Force who study
the environmental impacts of the paper industry.

For a full list of NSP's titles, please call 1-800-567-6772 or check out our web site at:

www.newsociety.com

NEW SOCIETY PUBLISHERS